THE
PLACE OF
REALITY
in Psychoanalytic Theory and Technique

CURRENTS IN THE QUARTERLY

A Book Series
edited by Sander M. Abend, M.D.

Published continuously since 1932, *The Psychoanalytic Quarterly* is one of the oldest psychoanalytic publications in the United States. Free of ties to any school, institute, or organization, the editors have, over the years, maintained an independent spirit that has allowed for the publication of thoughtful, insightful, and often controversial papers from a wide range of psychoanalytic perspectives. Now in this series, *Currents in the Quarterly*, a group of its most distinguished editors bring together classic and new papers devoted to topics that continue to spark interest and debate in the field today.

THE PLACE OF REALITY

in Psychoanalytic Theory and Technique

Sander Abend,
Jacob Arlow,
Dale Boesky, and
Owen Renik, Editors

JASON ARONSON INC.
Northvale, New Jersey
London

Director of Editorial Production: Robert D. Hack

This book was bound by Book-mart Press of North Bergen, New Jersey.

Library of Congress Cataloging-in-Publication Data

The place of reality in psychoanalytic theory and technique / edited by
    Sander Abend . . . [et al.].
        p.   cm.
    Papers originally published over the last 50 years in The
Psychoanalytic quarterly.
    Includes bibliographical references and index.
    ISBN 1–56821–866–4
    1. Reality—Psychological aspects.   2. Psychoanalysis.
I. Abend, Sander M., 1932–
BF175.5.R4P53   1996
150.19´5—dc20   96-33864

Manufactured in the United States of America. Jason Aronson Inc. offers books and cassettes. For information and catalog write to Jason Aronson Inc., 230 Livingston Street, Northvale, New Jersey 07647.

CONTENTS

INTRODUCTION

Lawrence Friedman, M.D.

If we were asked why *Studies on Hysteria* was not psycho-analysis proper, we might answer that the procedure was not psychoanalysis until it became the study of personal reality. To be worthy of the name, psychoanalysis had to give up hunting for traumas and examine the way a person pictures his world. Psychoanalysis earned its title only when it became less obsessed with (individual) features of reality and more obsessed with the nature of reality (for individuals).

For that reason people frequently say that analysts are concerned only with psychic reality. But that way of putting it is at once too inclusive and too restrictive. It is too inclusive because most analysts sort psychic reality into parts that are more accurate and parts that are less so. And it is too restrictive because psychic reality sometimes seems co–extensive with the whole of human reality (or social reality), leading some analysts to become philosophers and take up the problem of reality *tout court*. The basic topic of psychoanalysis—how people configure their world—has encouraged psychoanalysts to poach on philosophy and question whether there can be any aspect of reality that is not configured by mind.

But psychoanalysis is a practical, not a speculative, investigation of reality. The big question may be what it means for an individual to construct reality, but the urgency of practice leaves scant leisure for such large deliberations. The literature is sensibly devoted to the particular shapes of reality that we meet in practice. Although analysts always think and frequently write about their patients' fantasies, we do not so often read about what fantasy *is*. And the same is true about what in general makes reality feel real, and what makes features appear or disappear from it. We have to hunt through shelves of journals to find a sprinkling of comment about such fundamental problems.

That is precisely what the editors of the *Psychoanalytic Quarterly* have done for us in this volume. They have scanned more than fifty years of the journal for landmark contributions to the psychoanalytic study of reality. Drawn together they reveal the overlapping facets that make the issue so slippery. We see how *views* of reality may be warped by efforts to maintain a threatened social bond (Deutsch). We are told that parts of reality may be excised from experience because they are too frightening (Lewin). As to the *quality* of reality, the feeling that the world is real or unreal may reflect the lure and danger of libidinal interests (Greenacre). Then there is the other half of the problem: one's *inner reality* can be obscured by having it consistently misread early in life; a person may be completely unable to reach feelings that were ignored by selfish caretakers to whom a child must adapt, and the vacuum may be filled with fake feelings (Ogden, Shengold, Modell). Then there is the *function* of judging reality. It has sometimes been taught that reality–testing is a faculty with its own resources, of which people are blessed with more or less. But in these pages we find some clinical evidence that bad and good reality–testing are simply the way the mind works under the influence of more and less conflict (Abend).

Shadowing the problem of judging reality is the tormenting question of whether all human reality isn't, after all, a compound of fact and value. At one extreme, the reader of this book will be startled to find an argument by Zilboorg that the illusions of civilization comprise not just myths and religion, but also metapsychology and ego psychology (and sophisticated concepts in general!)—all of them simply comforting ways of dressing up libidinal truths in animistic dignity. Zilboorg would have us believe that social psychology and elaborate, intrapsychic theory, no less than superstition, interfere with the scientific understanding of unadorned, "concrete," empirical fact. Thirty-eight years later, that theme is picked up more tolerantly (by Lacan) in the argument that significant reality always falls short of the (symbolic) meaning it carries: fathers are never really the fathers we suppose; no person is the figure he sees in the mirror. We are moved to wonder: Does thinking actually distort reality, or is reality partly made up by our thinking (Modell)? Are life–historical accounts merely conveniences, bearing little relationship to actual history (Spence)? Has reality no particular definition outside of the ways that we grasp it? Or do some of these perplexities spring needlessly from a misunderstanding of modern philosophy? (This volume includes one of the few available critiques of the critics of reality [Leary].) These issues are debated here.

Fantasy is what usually brings airy questions about reality down to the practitioner's work bench. I would be surprised if the reader doesn't close this book with a yearning to fathom the profound riddles of fantasy's relationship to reality. A good starting point is Arlow's celebrated discussions of the interrelationship of unconscious fantasy, conscious fantasy, bits of fantasy *cum* reality, and the multiplication and overlap of versions of the few core fantasies that surround basic libidinal issues.

Let us follow that line of thought in general terms. Since its inception, psychoanalysis has worked on the assumption that people label and connect events in humanly meaningful ways, sometimes without realizing it. Some of these vignettes take narrative form. The earliest meanings and scripts may continue to find parallels in later experience, accomplishing the same personal aims as they did in childhood. Some of the meanings and connections "grow up" and some don't. (For example, every thought that begins, "I always wanted to . . ." explicitly proclaims its origin in early fantasy, and yet such thoughts generate many a "grown-up" accomplishment.) By the "growing up" of a fantasy, we mean to say that the connections and narratives that underlie it are adjusted to reality (sublimation).

Thus, analysts have distinguished two pairs of contrasts among human patterning. One contrast is between those meanings and meaningful connections that people allow themselves to think in words or pictures (conscious fantasy) and those that are only implicit and unconscious (though mixtures of both are thought to predominate). The other contrast is between patterns of connectedness that are relevant to child state and childhood world, on the one hand, and patterns that are adjusted to the person's grown–up being and contemporary world (again, with mixtures predominating).

The first distinction—between conscious and unconscious meanings and connections—raises the question of the form in which unspoken and unvisualized meanings and connections exist in the mind, their relationship to each other and to conscious thought (e.g., Arlow's metaphorical relationship). Is it possible to confirm our deductions of the earliest, unmodified fantasies from which modified and blended varieties are derived? That is the question raised by factional disagreements among psychoanalysts. Are these meanings always either worded or pictured, or do they also include dramatic behavior patterns, sets of wordless expectations, an arsenal of coping styles, a range of hopefulnesses? (Any fantasy that is non-articulated would seem to tolerate a wide range of verbal translations, which would imply that competing schools of interpretation might be equally apt.)

The second distinction—between unrealistic and realistic meanings—poses and even harder problem, because the most

realistic of human realities is already composed of meanings
and meaningful patterns. Presumably, what we want to say is
that a sublimated fantasy (e.g., an ambitious but practical day
dream) is realistic because it finds its significance less in the
meanings attributed to a remembered infantile situation than
in the world of today's meanings. The distinction between
childhood dramas and adult dramas works well enough in
day–to–day treatment, but it is not a sharp enough contrast for
theoretical understanding. We find it a convincing principle
for separating realistic from unrealistic fantasy, only because it
calls up a contrast between our tiny, helpless beginnings and
our "realistic" adulthood, grown and strong. The dodge does-
n't work for two reasons: first, analysts want to examine desires
as well as fears, and if desires are still present, they are still present, big or little. And, second, the reality to which adult fantasies must be sublimated is largely symbolic (social), not physical, and so physical growth may not change things all that
much. It is easy to compare a person's imagined smallness with
his or her adult weight, and his realistic ability to protect his
penis may change accordingly, but it is not so easy to say which
meanings are and are not "really" latent in other meanings
(e.g., whether castration is or is not a realistic readout of public humiliation). "Realistic" fantasy (and even unrealistic fantasy) is nothing else but the way that the individual makes
social meaning individually useful. It capitalizes on the "realistic" narratives and "realistic" opportunities that society makes
available. What can realistic and unrealistic possibly mean in
this context?

One answer is Zilboorg's. He seems to think that only libidinal urges are real, and everything else (including normal,
human living) is a conscious or unconscious, mythic, "dereistic" embellishment. For Zilboorg, reality is bravely faced only
by "concrete," empirical science, which, one suspects, ends for
him with biology. Zilboorg's factional special pleading should
not distract us from his modernity. He was ahead of his time in

characterizing at least some psychoanalytic theory as a mythic story. After all, we may well ask, are there any areas of experience untouched by fantasy? What is the relationship between specific fantasies, as a psychoanalyst would call them, and the tincture of meaningfulness that bathes everything in life? And yet even Zilboorg would have wanted to distinguish between more or less realistic living. For instance, he is implicitly urging psychoanalysts to *conduct* themselves realistically with their patients, and conduct always has a human (dramatic) dimension.

The diametrically opposite approach is hinted at in different ways by Spence and Modell (and some of the authors discussed by Leary): Instead of the human twist being a disguise for brute reality, one can see individual, meaningful constructions as the very substance of (human) reality. But that answer leaves us in the same quandary. It would be just as hard to distinguish between realisticness and unrealisticness if reality is always fantasy as it would be if fantasy is never reality. In short, what we need is an account of what human reality is *as an objective reality,* and how—sometimes accurately and sometimes inaccurately—it is apprehended *in* individuals' fantasies. We know a lot about the "why" of unrealisticness, as witness this volume, with its many accounts of the motives that incline a person to form unrealistic meanings. Indeed, that is all the answer we need when we are looking at the sort of delusional thinking that distorts physical reality. But when it comes to the more common misconstruing of social realities, we have yet to fill in the generic "what" of the misconstruction, i.e., in what way the alleged distortion isn't just a different perspective. This book launches us on that voyage. (And not a moment too soon, since the new challenge of constructivism in psychoanalysis is about to force the issue.) The papers of Modell and Ogden are contributions to this project.

We might even hope that some other "what" answers will emerge from an inquiry into human reality, such as what the feeling of reality amounts to, and what is the normal procedure for checking out one's perceptions. (Modell's paper shows how the "what" of the feeling of reality can be used to explore the "what" of reality–testing.) Some would say that the postmodern critique of reality that creeps into the later issues of the *Quarterly* may settle questions about the "what" of reality itself, both physical and social.

Would it be too much to hope that the same inquiry might illuminate the other mystery, the "what" of inner reality? In this volume, we read of feelings that are unknown to the subject (Shengold, Ogden, Modell). These are not unconscious attitudes in the usual sense. They are more like an untapped potential for conscious feeling. That sort of reality needs further elucidation, especially since the final paper in our collection suggests that even the analyst cannot know the reality of his own feelings until he sees himself in interaction (Renik).

Psychoanalysts disagree about many things: how to model the mind, what causal chains to feature, how treatment works, and so on. But on a practical level their disagreements are likely to be about how a given patient organizes reality. The challenges that cluster around this question are neatly set before us in this primer of psychoanalytic theory of reality.

1

FANTASY, MEMORY, AND REALITY TESTING

FANTASY, MEMORY, AND REALITY TESTING

BY JACOB A. ARLOW, M.D. (NEW YORK)

Reality testing, one of the most important of the functions of the ego, is relatively easy to define but quite difficult to comprehend. It is part of a conglomerate of ego functions which include such activities as perception, memory, object relations, sense of reality, superego, and the more recently discussed concept of reality constancy (*19*).

As used in psychoanalysis, reality testing refers to the ability to distinguish between perceptions and ideas. It is quite different from the philosopher's concept of the nature of reality. As defined in analytic terms, emphasis is placed upon the differentiation between representations of what is external—of the object world—from representations of what is internal—of the self or of mental life. The feeling of reality is not necessarily a part of perceptual experience. It does not have the sense of immediacy that characterizes consciousness. There is nothing in the quality of the perceptual experience which makes it apparent at once whether a mental representation is external or internal, real or unreal. An additional mental function, perhaps a set of mental functions, have to be called upon in order to make this decision. This operation has to be applied to all data registered at that station of mental experience that we call awareness.

A great deal has already been learned concerning how the function of reality testing develops but much still remains to be understood. Reality testing develops gradually. The early stages of this process are particularly difficult to study. In addition to the maturation of the essential ego apparatuses, the vicissitudes of development are very important. All workers in

John B. Turner Lecture presented at the New York Academy of Medicine under the auspices of the Columbia University Psychoanalytic Clinic for Training and Research, March 1, 1968.

the field see the development of reality testing as a gradual evolution in the child from an attitude toward the world which is self-centered, pleasure seeking, animistic, and magical, to a later capacity to differentiate between inner fantasy and objective reality *(9, 12, 29)*.

There is yet another dimension to reality testing. According to Hartmann *(20)* it consists of the ability to discern subjective and objective elements in our judgment of reality. Learning to do this is an unending process. Essentially this is the principal task which the analyst poses to his patient. He helps the patient to delineate in his assessment of and response to reality the contribution made by inner, subjective pressures from the past. In this paper I hope to demonstrate that how reality is experienced depends for the most part on the interaction between the perceptions of the external world and the concomitant effect of unconscious fantasy activity.

The perceptions of reality are sensed against the background of individual experience. Memory, recording conflicts, traumata, vicissitudes of the drives and of development are organized in terms of the pleasure-unpleasure principle into groups of schemata centering around childhood wishes. These make up the contents of a continuous stream of fantasy thinking, which is a persistent concomitant of all mental activity and which exerts an unending influence on how reality is perceived and responded to.

How can one describe in functional terms the interplay of these forces? It is as if the perceptual apparatus of the ego were operating at the same time in two different directions. One part of it looks outward, responding to the sensory stimuli of the external world of objects. The other part looks inward, reacting to a constant stream of inner stimulation. The organized mental representations of this stream of inner stimulation is what I call fantasy thinking. It includes fantasies and the memory schemata related to the significant conflicts and traumatic events of the individual's life. Fantasy thinking may be conscious or unconscious. It is a constant feature of mental life. It persists all the time that we are awake and most of the time we are asleep.

The data or contents of our fantasy thinking become known to us through the process of introspection. There is no direct antonym to the word introspection which we could conveniently juxtapose to it and then apply to the process of perception of stimuli from the external world. Etymologically exterospection would be correct but it seems an awkward term. Traditional usage refers metaphorically to the functional separation of these two concomitant orientations of perception in terms of the inner eye and the outer eye.

How does the external perceptual apparatus of the mind function? According to Freud *(16)* so long as there is consciousness all external sensory stimuli are passively and indiscriminately received. He states: '. . . cathectic innervations are sent out and withdrawn in rapid periodic impulses from within into the completely pervious system *Pcpt.-Cs.* So long as that system is cathected in this manner, it receives perceptions (which are accompanied by consciousness) and passes the excitation on to the unconscious mnemic systems; but as soon as the cathexis is withdrawn, consciousness is extinguished and the functioning of the system comes to a standstill. It is as though the unconscious stretches out feelers, through the medium of the system *Pcpt.-Cs.,* towards the external world and hastily withdraws them as soon as they have sampled the excitations coming from it' (p. 231).[1]

The data of perception are not experienced in isolation. They are experienced against the background of the individ-

---

[1] In another publication written in the same year as the one just quoted, Freud *(17)* returns to the subject but this time he states that the cathectic energy innervating the perceptual system originates in the ego. From the context of the two different quotations it would appear that in the former he was concerned with the utilization of the perceptual apparatus in the service of the pleasure-dominated unconscious wishes; in the latter he was concerned with the ego function of judgment achieving mastery over repression and at the same time achieving independence from the rule of the pleasure principle.

ual's past development and are checked against earlier perceptions and the memory traces which they have left. Stimuli are
selectively perceived in terms of the mental set operative in the
individual at the time. The mental set is determined both consciously and unconsciously, consciously by the nature of the
task before the individual, unconsciously by the cathectic level
of the dominant unconscious fantasy system. Percepts become
meaningful almost immediately as they are perceived because
they are compared with other data and integrated into memory schemata.

Certain aspects of the development of this process were carefully studied by Freud (17). He wrote that at the beginning
the essential task of judgment, as far as reality testing is concerned, is to determine whether something which is present in
the ego as an image can be rediscovered in perception (reality)
as well. The process of reality testing develops this way, he
says, because 'all presentations originate from perceptions and
are repetitions of them. Thus originally the mere existence of
a presentation was a guarantee of the reality of what was presented. The antithesis between subjective and objective does
not exist from the first. It only comes into being from the fact
that thinking possesses the capacity to bring before the mind
once more something that has once been perceived, by repro-
ducing it as a presentation without the external object having
still to be there. The first and immediate aim, therefore, of reality testing is, not to *find* an object in real perception which
corresponds to the one presented, but to *refind* such an object,
to convince oneself that it is still there' (pp. 237-238).

It would seem that this would be a simple enough task for the
mind; but this is far from the fact. As Freud noted, the re-
production of a perception as an image—in other words, how
we recall parts of our experience—is not always a faithful one;
it can be modified by omissions or by the fusion of a number of
elements. The process of testing a thing's reality must then investigate the extent of these distortions. If one cannot be sure
that the image (or set of images) that he is trying to rediscover

in the form of a perception (of reality) actually corresponds to the earlier perceptions which the image supposedly reflects, reality testing becomes difficult indeed.

The most powerful influence distorting the image of the past and contributing to the misperception of the present is the intrusion of unconscious fantasy thinking. During our busy wakeful life, dominated by the reality principle, we are only intermittently aware of the persistent intrusion into our conscious experience of elements of fantasy thinking. Nevertheless the stream of perceptual data from the external world which passes before the outer eye is paralleled by a stream of perceptual data from the inner world which passes before the inner eye. Although Freud wrote often about the process of exteroception *(Pctp.Cs.)* he said little about the so-called endopsychic observer. Perhaps he took it for granted that psychoanalysts, so fully involved in their own and in their patients' introspection, required little instruction in this area. His description of the process of free association as given in the Introductory Lectures is probably his most definitive statement on the subject. What the patient does while associating freely on the couch is compared to a train traveler looking out of the window and reporting as much as he is able to of the scenes flashing by his view. There is much more that he notices than he reports but he does the best he can. Free association in the analytic situation, it should be emphasized, corresponds to the reporting aspect of the experience. The really significant part of the analytic situation is the concentration of attention on the process of introspection, that is, the creation of a set of conditions that minimize the contribution of the external world and enhance the emergence of derivatives of the inner world— the world of fantasy thinking *(3, 8).*

Because dreams are perhaps the richest and clearest expression of fantasy thinking and because dreams are part of the experience of sleep, several authors have linked the emergence of daydreams, fantasies, and other regressive, visually experienced phenomena with alterations in the state of consciousness resembling sleep. Lewin (27) says: 'Psychoanalysts are now aware that subtle signs of the sleeping state may be intermingled with thinking, particularly in free association, but in general and in "nature" also, so as to say, even when there is no conscious somnolence'. He supports his statement with a quotation from Kubie (24): 'We are never really totally awake or totally asleep. These are relative and not absolute terms. Parts of us are asleep in our waking moments and parts of us are awake in our sleeping moments, and in between lie all the gradations of states of activity and inactivity.'

One can hardly take issue with Kubie's statement; however, Lewin's formulation seems to beg the question, inasmuch as from the outset his statement defines sleep in terms of dreaming. It does not follow that because when we are asleep, we dream, that when we dream (or daydream or have other similar, related experiences), we are asleep. I emphasize this point because clinical experience demonstrates how daydreaming may intrude upon the conscious experience of the individual at all levels of wakefulness and somnolence. In a previous contribution (5) I dealt with the ubiquitous intrusion of daydreaming activity into conscious experience, under circumstances which Lewin would say corresponded to the state of 'nature'. Several clinical experiences were cited from the daily lives of patients. In some of these experiences while the patients were alert and vigorously involved in reality oriented activity, their judgment of reality and their response to it was completely distorted by the intrusion of an unconscious fantasy. Actually this kind of distortion is one of the essential features of the neurotic process and of the transference. Aphoristically we may describe the state of mind in such patients by stating that while the outer eye was perceiving quite accurately the sensory stimuli from reality, the inner eye was focused on a fantasy. The response of the patient was appropriate enough, not in terms of reality, but in terms of the inner, unconscious fantasy.

This is the approach we use all the time in connection with neurotic symptoms. We understand our patients' anxiety not in terms of the realistic situation, but as a misperception of reality in terms which are appropriate for the contents of the unconscious fantasy. It would seem difficult to maintain that every time a neurotic patient experiences a symptom he is undergoing an alteration in the state of consciousness. In some instances alterations in the state of consciousness do occur, but they represent the effect of and not the cause for the emergence of an unconscious fantasy. I have presented material previously describing how in certain distortions of the sense of time *(1)*, in the *déjà vu* experience *(2)*, and in states of depersonalization *(6)*, the state of consciousness and/or the experiencing of reality were altered in consequence of the defensive needs of the ego resulting from the pressure of an emerging fantasy. To return to Lewin's statement, it would seem that it is not the subtle signs of sleep that we perceive intermingled in our thinking, but the subtle evidence of the intrusion of fantasy thinking.

These considerations are pertinent to the initiation of the anxiety signal. When the ego becomes aware of the threatening development of the danger situation associated with the emergence of an instinctual demand, it institutes the signal of anxiety to stimulate the function of defense. How does the ego become aware of the threatening danger? What data does it use to reach such a conclusion? My answer would be: from the data of introspection, from the perception, mostly outside of consciousness, of the contents of the stream of fantasy thinking. Introspection of fantasy thinking provides the data leading to the conclusion that a danger may develop and the individual then begins to feel anxious. In this last instance, the endopsychic observer (Descarte's *res cogitans* which Lewin [26] has so brilliantly and wittily elucidated for us) acts like an internal psychoanalyst, observing the stream of fantasy thinking and making an interpretation for himself before the disturbing material appears in undisguised, panic-provoking form. The interrelation of the successive contents in the stream of unconscious fantasies under those circumstances would resemble that of certain sequences of dreams with which we are familiar. I refer to those series of dreams where each one conveys the same instinctual wish, one dream following another, the manifest content of each dream progressively less disguised and less distorted than the previous one, until the final dream appears—a dream with manifest content so distressingly close to the dangerous unconscious wish that panic develops, sleep is broken off, and the patient awakens as from a nightmare.

Free association in the psychoanalytic situation represents an artificial method for tapping samples of the constantly flowing stream of fantasy activity. There are however natural, spontaneous sources of information concerning what is contained in fantasy thought. Children daydream frequently, vividly, and often report them openly. Many retain this capacity into adult life. Freud (14) called the primitive, self-centered world of daydreams the individual's secret rebellion against reality and against the need to renounce pleasurable instinctual gratification. Masturbation fantasies are a particularly striking example of vividly experienced daydreaming associated with instinctual gratification. Creative people are particularly perceptive of their fantasy thinking. Many retain a capacity for vivid visual daydreaming to a remarkable degree.

Young children regularly intermingle their perceptions of reality with wishful fantasy thinking and sometimes find it hard to distinguish in recollection between what was real and what was imagined—between what constituted fantasy and what constituted accurate memory. The intensely visual nature of children's fantasies endows them with a quality of verisimilitude. As the individual grows older and reality increases its domain at the expense of the pleasure principle, visual daydreams and visual memories become fewer. There are notable exceptions, some of which have been referred to above.

Most adults probably have explicit, conscious fantasies many times during the day only to forget them as promptly as they do night dreams—and for the same reasons. The experience of being an analysand provides the conditions, the training, and the motivation to take note of the fleeting fantasy thoughts and to hold them fast, long enough to examine them. The constant inner stream of fantasy thinking nevertheless produces many derivatives which present themselves, often unexpectedly, to the inner eye of introspection. In fleeting thoughts, misperceptions, illusions, metaphors of speech and action, the analyst can detect the influence of unconscious fantasy. As I have suggested, the æsthetic effectiveness of metaphor in literature is derived in large measure from the ability of metaphorical expression to stimulate affects associated with widely entertained, communally shared, unconscious fantasies (5). Róheim (31) said that the mythology of a people is an indicator of their dominant psychological conflicts. Mythology thus is a culturally organized, institutional form of communal daydreaming (3). The same is clearly true of many aspects of religious and artistic experience. A person's favorite joke or the kind of humor he generally prefers usually leads directly to the nature of his fantasy thinking inasmuch as every instinctual fixation is represented at some level of mental life in the form of a group of associated unconscious fantasies (cf. Ref. 34).

Evidence of the subtle intermingling of fantasy thinking with the perception of everyday reality may take the most subtle of forms and may be overlooked if one is not alert to its operation. Two examples will illustrate what I mean. In a session during which he was working through certain memories and fantasies connected with the primal scene, a patient mentioned quite in passing—or at least so it seemed—that he had seen a former professor of his, a respected and friendly father-figure. He had wanted to approach this man and greet him but, for reasons which he could not understand, felt extremely inhibited and failed to do so. The patient went on to say: 'Perhaps it was because Professor X was busy at the time putting on his galoshes. It would be an awkward time to disturb him.' Or another patient, a woman, one of a set of identical twins whose fantasy thinking was dominated by impulses of hostility and competition toward her sibling, impulses which were fought

out in the inner vision of her mind on the intrauterine bat-
tlefield. She reported: 'While I was cleaning out the closet and
getting rid of a lot of junk, I remembered a dream I had the
night before'. The patient went on to relate the dream which
concerned an underwater struggle in a diving bell with a shark
which threatened to devour her. In both patients, reality was
metaphorically perceived in terms of fantasy thinking. In other
words, disturbing a man putting on his galoshes was like interfering with a person having intercourse; emptying junk out
of a closet in reality was in fantasy killing a rival in a claustrum.

The adventitious words describing the realistic setting in
which introspective data are perceived exemplify this process
in daily analytic work. Like the comments which a patient
makes about the form or structure of a dream, these adventitious comments may be considered part of the inner fantasy.
Thus if a patient says: 'As I stepped into the elevator, or as I
entered the door of the building, I had the following thought',
the analyst should be alerted to the possible intrusion of some
fantasy about penetration of the body or incorporation into it.
Similarly if the patient introduces some idea with a statement:
'While I was in the bus', he may be introducing thereby a fragment of a fantasy of pregnancy or of being within a claustrum.

This constant intermingling of fantasy and perception helps
make it clear why memory is so unreliable, especially memories
from childhood, because in childhood the process of intermingling perception and fantasy proceeds to a very high degree.
Klein (22) and Joseph (21) in recent contributions have called
attention to the many problems concerning the function of
memory which remain to be solved. What is forgotten and
what is remembered? What can and what cannot be recalled?
Just where in the therapeutic process do we place the recollection or retrieval of the memory of a childhood experience?
How does a patient come to have a sense of conviction, a feeling about the reality of a childhood experience which is re-
constituted by way of reconstruction, reconstruction which
utilizes primarily the data available from screen memories?

Both Klein and Joseph, following Hartmann (20), call attention to the need to redefine some of these problems in terms of the structural theory. Joseph in particular stresses the importance of approaching these problems from the point of view of the defense function of the ego.

In reviewing the early literature of the subject, I was struck by the fact that there were many more references to forgetting than to remembering. Sometimes the only reference to be found under memory was 'See Amnesia'. The juxtaposition of memory to amnesia was of course a major element in the topographic theory based, as it was, on the essential dichotomy of mental contents into what could and could not be remembered. This led to some interesting formulations which, superficially viewed, seem like amusing paradoxes. For example, the hysteric whose problem is amnesia suffers mainly from reminiscences. He cannot recall the important events which shaped his life, yet his recollections are characterized by a 'wonderful freshness of memory'.

The resolution of this paradox is contained, of course, in Freud's early paper on screen memories (13). Like so many of Freud's ideas, the ideas contained in that paper have to be rediscovered periodically. If we review that classic paper in the light of our present knowledge we can understand screen memories as an exquisite example of the mingling of fantasy with perception and memory, the raw material for the construction of the screen memories originating from many periods of the individual's life disguised and rearranged in keeping with the defensive needs of the ego. The same principles we understand today operate in the construction of dreams, fantasies, and in what Kris (23) has called the 'personal myth'. We can thus amend Freud's original statement to read that the recognition of *how the ego operates in the service of defense* tends to diminish the distinction between memory and fantasy. Freud goes on to say: 'It may indeed be questioned whether we have any memories at all *from* our childhood:

memories *relating* to our childhood may be all that we possess. Our childhood memories show us our earliest years not as they were but as they appeared at the later periods when the memories were aroused. In these periods of arousal . . . memories did not . . . *emerge;* they were *formed* at that time. And a number of motives, with no concern for historical accuracy, had a part in forming them, as well as in the selection of the memories themselves' *(13,* p. 322*).*

In the context of intrapsychic conflict, the ego integrates drives, defense, memory, fantasy, and superego in keeping with the principle of multiple function *(33).* What we think was real, or what we think really happened, is a combination or intermingling of fantasy with perception of reality. When memory and perception offer material which is in consonance with fantasy thinking, the data are selectively perceived and the memories are selectively recalled and used as material to serve as a vehicle for the unconscious fantasy. When we are able to undo the defensive distortion which the ego has imposed upon the material, we can see that the fantasy contains the kernel of what really happened. This is not the objective reality which can be observed by outsiders and validated consensually. This is almost impossible to recollect because what the child experiences is at the very moment of experience a complex intermingling of perception and fantasy. This complex intermingling is what 'really' happened as far as the individual is concerned. Only through the process of inference can the analyst sometimes elucidate from the material that part of the individual's recollection which belongs to objective history, as it were, as opposed to the patient's personal 'mythological' past.

I would like to illustrate my point by citing a reconstruction of the past based upon the interpretation of a fantasy. There is nothing particularly unusual or striking about this example. Every experienced analyst will recall many similar instances from his own practice. For purposes of discretion certain details have been changed and displaced, but the essential features of the material, namely, the relationship of the interpretation to the data, has not been altered in any significant way.

This material is taken from the case of a male adult who spent several years of his early childhood, perhaps as many as three, possibly four, in his parents' bedroom. Except for some few peripheral or tangential memories like the sounds of neighbors quarreling, the patient could remember nothing of the events in the bedroom. However, his life story, his character formation, the symptoms which he developed, the nature of the transference, and how he behaved toward his children during their œdipal phase all bore more than ample testimony of how deeply he had been affected by this early experience.

He developed into a pseudo-imbecilic 'detective'. He noticed nothing but knew everything. He was constantly looking but never seeing. What he could not remember, he kept repeating. In all sorts of 'innocent' ways he managed to stumble upon and interfere with couples engaged in private activities. A constant trend which appeared in dreams, fantasies, and sometimes in real life behavior contained the elements of disturbing a performance or a spectacle in which a father image was figuring in a prominent and successful role. His favorite joke was about a famous Shakespearean actor whose successful performance was ruined by absurd and obscene requests originating from some obscure member of the audience sitting in the back stalls of the balcony.

The privacy of the analytic twosome accordingly was highly consonant, one could say congruent, with elements in his fantasy life. As analysts we understand that external, realistic elements which are consonant with fantasy elements are selectively perceived and seem to have the capacity to intensify the cathectic pressure of unconscious fantasy. Under these circumstances the fantasies tend to come to the fore in the sense that they produce more and clearer mental derivatives or propel the individual toward some form of action. In this respect their dynamic thrust resembles the role of the day residue in dream formation. Day residues are selected for inclusion in dreams not so much because of their neutral, inconspicuous nature as for the fact that they are congruent with or reminiscent of certain important fantasies or memory schemata. There is, accordingly, a reciprocal interplay between reality and fantasy, selective perception on one side, cathectic intensification on the other. For our pseudo-imbecilic detective therefore the analytic situation, one could say, was made to order.

During the period when we were working on the problem of œdipal rivalry as it came up in the transference and in connection with his son, the patient reported the following fantasy:

> I had a fantasy that I came for my session and headed toward the couch. You were annoyed with my behavior in the analysis and decided to terminate treatment. I wanted to go to the couch but you waved me to the chair and told me that the treatment was over. I objected violently. I became very angry. I rushed to the couch, laid down and said I would not budge. You decided that if I did not move you would call the police to remove me. Your next patient was around. You told her to wait. You would go on with her as soon as you got rid of me. In the fantasy you were also frightened. You thought that I could get away from the police and come back to get you.

The key to the understanding of the fantasy came in the first associations which dealt with the theme of reversal of roles, the patient taking the analyst's role, the analyst becoming the patient. Other associations concerned the sexualization of the analytic situation, the couch as a bed, the attractive woman patient as an object of our competitive rivalry, three people in a room where only two should be, biding one's time until one gets rid of a rival, how weak and helpless people need the police in situations where their own physical force is insufficient.

By invoking the principle of dream interpretation concerning opposites, the fantasy could be explored as a reversal. With the knowledge of the previous material, of the transference situation, and of the associations, this fantasy could be interpreted first in terms of the transference and then much more meaningfully as a reconstruction concerning the past. At the level of transference the patient is angry and jealous. He wishes to get rid of me but I cling to my possessions. He will use greater force, throw me out, and claim my position, my office, and the attractive woman patient as a special prize. As a reconstruction of the past, the interpretation could be quite precise because of the unusually rich material. The patient in his parents' bedroom had awakened from sleep and tried in various ways, or perhaps many times, to get his father to abandon the bed, hopefully for good. But the father persisted in returning to his bed and there was very little that the weak and small Œdipus could do. If only he could call the police or perhaps some criminals. They are stronger, they would get rid of father, take him away, and the little boy could enjoy mother for himself. Of course father is strong. He could get away. He would be very angry. He could return and punish the little boy. (The patient's childhood neurosis consisted of a fear of criminals who might intrude during the night and kidnap or injure him.) The interpretation was confirmed at the next session in a dream which recapitulated all the events mentioned above and carried the reconstruction further by introducing the element of relations with the mother and giving her a child.

What can we say about this fantasy and the reconstruction built on it? What was real in the sense that it actually happened and what was unreal in the sense that it was only imagined? Distracting the father, calling him from his bed, a temper tantrum, perhaps, and the father returning and persisting in possession of his bed and his mate—these are all events which possibly could have happened and presumably did happen. The calling of the police (or the robbers) assuredly did not happen. The appreciation of the role of police or the significance of kidnaping may even date from a later period. Whether at any time the patient overtly expressed to his mother the classical œdipal wishes is hard to say. Probably he did. Yet in the fantasy, all elements are given equal weight in a well-integrated

story that seems consistent, logical, and realistic, if not probable. The point is that the intermingling of real events, real
perceptions with the elements of fantasy and wishful thinking
must correspond quite closely to what the patient actually experienced as a child at the time. External perception and internal fantasy were intermingled at the time of the experience
and together they formed the reality which to the patient was
the record of his past. It was upon this confused fantasy thinking, which was dynamically effective in influencing so many
aspects of his life, that the inner eye of the patient remained
consistently focused.

This is what I think is the proper understanding of the concept 'psychic reality'. It is not a fantasy that is taken for the
real truth, for an actual event, but the 'real' recollection of a
psychic event with its mixture of fact and fantasy. This becomes the dynamic reality for the patient under the influence
of the traumatic events which live on in his inner fantasy. Subsequent events and perceptions of reality are selectively organized into memory schema consonant with inner fantasy
thinking.

To recapitulate, in keeping with the synthetic function of
the ego and the principle of multiple function, the traumatic
events in the individual's life and the pathogenic conflicts that
grow out of them are worked over defensively by the ego and
incorporated into a scheme of memories and patterns of fantasy. In one part of the mind the inner eye, as it were, remains
focused on an inner stream of fantasy thought in which the
traumatic memories are retained in a disguised form. Freud
conjectured that the delusion owes its convincing power to the
element of historical truth which it contains and which it in-
serts in place of the rejected reality. It would follow, he added,
that what pertains to hysteria would also apply to delusions;
namely, that those who are subject to them are suffering from
their own recollections. What I have tried to demonstrate in
this paper is that this is a general principle of mental life. The

traumatic events of the past become part of fantasy thinking and as such exert a never-ending dynamic effect, occasionally striking, sometimes less so, on our responses to and appreciation of reality.

One of the measures of the involvement of a person in the neurotic process and his traumatic past can be taken from the extent to which his mental functioning is pulled toward concentrating on the inner stream of fantasy thinking in competition with realistic daytime preoccupations. This can be clearly seen in fetishists and in some former fetishists who develop unusual responses to the perception of reality. The fetishist suffers from the memory of a traumatic perception, a confrontation with the sight of the penisless female genital at a time when he was particularly vulnerable to castration anxiety. He seems unable to get over it. Around the traumatic events he weaves a wish-fulfilling, reality-denying fantasy, the illusion of the woman with a phallus. But it does not seem to help. Before his mind's eye, even through the compensating fantasy, he continues to see, however dimly, the original perceptions of the female genital proclaiming the danger of castration. Looking at reality becomes a hazard, for at any moment he fears he may encounter a set of perceptions identical with those that precipitated the original panic.

In some individuals this leads to a peculiar relationship to reality in general (7) because they make an unconscious equation of reality with the female genital (25) and they treat the former the way the fetishist treats the latter. They refuse to face it. They cannot take a really good look at anything. This tendency influences them in the direction of impracticality and propels them into unrealistic behavior in many areas of their lives. During analytic sessions it is hard for them to look at their productions or at the analyst's interpretations. At best they give them only a fleeting glance. In presenting a problem such patients tend to seize upon some insignificant, minor detail, tangential and peripheral to the heart of the matter. Although at one level they clearly perceive the true nature, the real nature of the problem, at another level they persist in 'beating around the bush'. During the analysis they have a set of mannerisms involving their eyes. Either they keep them closed, shield them with their hands, rub them, or blink continually throughout the session. In speaking, they express themselves in the conditional voice, for example—It seems, I suppose, Perhaps, Maybe, Could it be that?, etc. Nothing is definitely asserted. The central reality has to be obscured and denied, but in the manner of the fetishist, these patients have to fasten their attention on some distracting, peripheral, reassuring perception that corresponds to the female phallus as envisaged in their inner fantasy. A variation of these trends may be seen in individuals who are petty liars, who have a compulsive need to embellish, adorn, and obscure reality.

From a study of these unusual character traits one can see how painful events are woven into fantasy thinking and how persistent focusing on these elements in the stream of fantasy thought leads the individual to scan the data of perception of reality to discover reassuring evidence of the validity of the solution which he arrived at in fantasy. Under the pressure of unconscious wishes and in keeping with the need to fend off anxiety, the perceptual apparatus of the ego is oriented and alerted to incorporate, integrate, correlate, deny, or misinterpret the data of perception.

The interplay between unconscious wishes, defense, and perception may serve as a transition to the next point concerning the psychology of moods. Growing as they do out of the vicissitudes of individual experience, the memory schemata of each person are typical and idiosyncratic. The memory patterns which are important in psychoanalytic treatment are grouped together according to the pleasure-unpleasure principle and are reactivated in the context of emerging conflicts over instinctual wishes. I referred earlier to the capacity of external perceptions to intensify the cathectic pressure of fantasy. Thus it is easy to see how moods may be evoked by perceptions of reality in the sense that real experience stimulates the emergence of specific memories and systems of fantasy.

Most often, but not always, the patient is aware of which event it was that precipitated or provoked his mood. For the duration of the mood the thoughts that come to mind are in consonance with the fantasy that gave rise to it. No other thoughts seem to present themselves to awareness. Opposing thoughts are brushed aside and the perceptions of the external world are selectively attended to and interpreted in terms of the mood.

During analytic treatment, we are in a position to correlate the mood with the fantasy whose content is appropriate to the affects, thoughts, and perceptions characteristic of that specific mood. It is the pervasive quality of the fantasy which establishes the nature of the mood and its cathectic potential perpetuates its existence. I have illustrated this point with the material from a patient who was in a depressed mood (5). His realistic perceptions—breakfast, birthday, and oranges—intensified the cathexis of a latent cannibalistic fantasy. The mood, thoughts, and activities and the response to reality were in keeping with the contents of the stream of fantasy thoughts.

But what can we say about moods whose appearance cannot be traced to any specific event or external perception? The evocation of such moods I would suggest might still be related to some perception of external reality, to some sensory stimulus which found registration *outside* of consciousness. Clinical experience and experimental studies offer abundant proof of Freud's idea that while the perceptual system is functioning it is completely pervious to external stimuli. Pötzl (30), Fisher (10, 11), and others have demonstrated conclusively that even stimuli which are subliminal in intensity may find registration outside of consciousness. It seems highly plausible that, like the day residue of a dream, percepts registered outside of awareness may dynamically affect fantasy thinking to the end that a fantasy is cathected, stimulating emergence of the mood.

Finally, another question must be raised. What is the form of fantasy thinking? How highly structured is it? Some authors, for example, have rejected the suggestion that unconscious fantasies may have a complicated organization or contain elements of imagery that are visually representable. My own experience and thinking have led me to the conclusion that for the most part fantasy thinking has a quasi-visual nature. It is easily transformed and transformable into visual representations. At first I thought of this relationship in terms that were uncomfortably static. In connection with an attempt to demonstrate how reality is experienced in terms of inner fantasy needs, I wrote:

> There is a hierarchy in the fantasy life of each individual, a hierarchy which reflects the vicissitudes of individual experience as well as the influence of psychic differentiation and ego development.[2] To use a very static analogy for a highly dynamic state of affairs, we may say that unconscious fantasies have a systematic relation to each other. Fantasies are grouped around certain basic instinctual wishes, and such a group is composed of different versions or different editions of attempts to resolve the intrapsychic conflict over these wishes. Each version corresponds to a different 'psychic moment' in the history of the individual's development. It expresses the forces at play at a particular time in the person's life when the ego integrated the demands of the instinctual wishes in keeping with its growing adaptive and defensive responsibilities. To continue with a static analogy, we may conceive of the interrelationship between unconscious fantasies in terms of a series of superimposed photographic transparencies in which at different times and under different psychic conditions one or more of these organized images may be projected and brought into focus (3, p. 377).

A few years later it occurred to me that the interaction between fantasy thinking and reality could be expressed illustra-

---

[2] The expression 'hierarchy of fantasies' is meant to convey the idea that instinctual derivations operate throughout life in the form of fantasies, usually unconscious. The organization of these fantasies takes shape early in life and persists in this form with only minor variations throughout life. To borrow an analogy from literature, one could say the plot line of the fantasy remains the same although the characters and the situation may vary.

tively through the use of a visual model. I compared this aspect of the operation of the mind to the effect that could be obtained if two motion picture projectors were to flash a continuous series of images simultaneously but from opposite sides onto a translucent screen. Here I have altered the analogy in order to carry it further. There are two centers of perceptual input, introspection and exterospection, supplying data from the inner eye and data from the outer eye. It is the function of a third agency of the ego, however, to integrate, correlate, judge, and discard the competing data of perceptual experience. All of these factors influence the final judgment as to what is real and what is unreal. In addition I have tried to make room in my conceptualization for the infinite complexity of the relationship between the outer world of perception and the inner world of thought.

The predominant role of vision in the totality of human perception can hardly be overstressed. Supposedly eighty percent of learning is affected through vision. There is a vast literature of psychological studies of visual perception. In those areas which are of particular interest to psychoanalysts, namely, the development and alteration of mental functions under the impact of intrapsychic conflict, the study of visual experience has always been considered to be of special importance. Many, perhaps most, of the models of the psychic apparatus which Freud devised to illustrate his concepts of the functioning of the mind were either visually representable or based on analogies either to optical instruments or to contraptions which could somehow record experience in visual form. In most of these models he discussed perception in terms that were primarily, if not exclusively, applicable to visual perception, although it is always clear that he had no intention of treating the two as if they were identical. It is possible that this resulted from the fact that his earlier models were devised to integrate the data derived mostly from the study of the psychology of dreams and of the neuroses. In the case of the former, he was concerned with the problem of why the sleep-time hallucinations which we call dreams are almost exclusively visual in nature. In the case of the neuroses, he was impressed by the etiological significance of memories and fantasies and of the vivid visual form in which they are recalled. According to Freud, the closer a thought or fantasy is to the pleasure-dominated unconscious instinctual tendencies, the greater the possibility that it will be represented mentally in a visual form *(15)*.

The element of visual representability of fantasy thinking has an important bearing on psychoanalytic technique. In his 1966 Nunberg lecture *(27)*, and in a number of as yet unpublished works which I have been privileged to read, Lewin refers to the pictorial nature of the individual's store of memories. In connection with the patient's response to a construction he says: 'It is as if the analysand was trying to match the construction with a picture of his own'. Each analyst has a different capacity for visual memory or fantasy representation. But following Lewin, I think it is correct to say that some form of visual thinking occurs in the analyst's mind as he thinks along with his patient's free associations. The joint search by patient and analyst for the picture of the patent's past is a reciprocal process. In a sense, we dream along with our patients, supplying at first data from our own store of images in order to objectify the patient's memory into some sort of picture. We then furnish this picture to the analysand who responds with further memories, associations, and fantasies; that is, we stimulate him to respond with a picture of his own. In this way the analyst's reconstruction comes to be composed more and more out of the materials presented by the patient until we finally get a picture that is trustworthy and in all essentials complete.

The successfully analyzed patient stands in contrast to the hero of Antonioni's poetic motion picture, Blow Up. The photographer hero has witnessed and recorded a traumatic event, a sadistic conceptualization of the primal scene. His life has been altered thereby but out of the vast storehouse of his (memory) pictures he can no longer retrieve the one that contains the record of the trauma. Not being able to produce the

photograph is the analogue of being unable to recall the traumatic event. Thus the hero in Blow Up becomes a kind of
twentieth century Everyman traumatized in childhood. He
has lost his connection with his past and has, in his hand, only
the fragment of the experience, a fragment out of context,
enlarged to the point of unreality. Is it memory or fantasy?
Without confirmatory evidence he begins to doubt his own
reality. Only through psychoanalysis can the picture be restored and the individual be reintegrated with his past. In this
way he comes to appreciate the connection between fantasy,
memory, and reality.

REFERENCES

1. ARLOW, JACOB A.: *A Contribution to the Psychology of Time.* Unpublished.
2. ———: *The Structure of the Déjà Vu Experience.* J. Amer. Psa. Assn., VII, 1959, pp. 611-631.
3. ———: *Ego Psychology and the Study of Mythology.* J. Amer. Psa. Assn., IX, 1961, pp. 371-393.
4. ———: *Silence and the Theory of Technique.* J. Amer. Psa. Assn., IX, 1961, pp. 44-55.
5. ———: *Unconscious Fantasy and Disturbances of Conscious Experience.* This QUARTERLY, XXXVIII, 1969. pp. 1-27.
6. ———: Depersonalization and Derealization. In: *Psychoanalysis—A General Psychology. Essays in Honor of Heinz Hartmann.* Edited by Rudolph Loewenstein, Lottie M. Newman, Max Schur, and Albert J. Solnit. New York: International Universities Press, Inc., 1966.
7. ———: *Character and Perversion.* Unpublished.
8. ——— and BRENNER, CHARLES: The Psychoanalytic Situation. In: *Psychoanalysis in the Americas: Original Contributions from the First Pan-American Congress for Psychoanalysis.* Edited by Robert E. Litman. New York: International Universities Press, Inc., 1966.
9. BERES, DAVID: Ego Deviation and the Concept of Schizophrenia. In: *The Psychoanalytic Study of the Child, Vol. XI.* New York: International Universities Press, Inc., 1956, pp. 164-235.
10. FISHER, CHARLES: *Dreams and Perception.* J. Amer. Psa. Assn., II, 1954, pp. 389-445.
11. ———: *Dreams, Images, and Perception.* J. Amer. Psa. Assn., IV, 1956, pp. 5-48.
12. FREUD, ANNA: The Mutual Influences in the Development of Ego and Id. In: *The Psychoanalytic Study of the Child, Vol. VII.* New York: International Universities Press, Inc., 1952, pp. 42-50.
13. FREUD: *Screen Memories* (1899). Standard Edition, III.

14. ———: *Creative Writers and Day-Dreaming* (1908). Standard Edition, IX.

15. ———: *The Ego and the Id* (1923). Standard Edition, XIX.

16. ———: *A Note upon the 'Mystic Writing Pad'* (1925 [1924]). Standard Edition, XIX.

17. ———: *Negation* (1925). Standard Edition, XIX.

18. ———: *Constructions in Analysis* (1937). Standard Edition, XXIII.

19. FROSCH, JOHN: A Note on Reality Constancy. In: *Psychoanalysis—A General Psychology. Essays in Honor of Heinz Hartmann.* Edited by Rudolph Loewenstein, Lottie M. Newman, Max Schur, and Albert J. Solnit. New York: International Universities Press, Inc., 1966.

20. HARTMANN, HEINZ: Notes on the Reality Principle. In: *The Psychoanalytic Study of the Child, Vol. XI.* New York: International Universities Press, Inc., 1956., pp. 31-53.

21. JOSEPH, EDWARD D.: *Sense of Conviction, Screen Memories, and Reconstruction.* Unpublished.

22. KLEIN, GEORGE S.: The Several Grades of Memory. In: *Psychoanalysis—A General Psychology. Essays in Honor of Heinz Hartmann.* Edited by Rudolph Loewenstein, Lottie M. Newman, Max Schur, and Albert J. Solnit. New York: International Universities Press, Inc., 1966.

23. KRIS, ERNST: *The Personal Myth.* J. Amer. Psa. Assn., IV, 1956, pp. 653-681.

24. KUBIE, LAWRENCE S.: *Instincts and Homoeostasis.* Psychosomatic Med., X, 1948, pp. 15-30.

25. LEWIN, BERTRAM D.: *The Nature of Reality, the Meaning of Nothing, with an Addendum on Concentration.* This QUARTERLY, XVII, 1948, pp. 524-526.

26. ———: *Dreams and the Uses of Regression.* New York: International Universities Press, Inc., 1958.

27. ———: *The Image and the Past.* New York: International Universities Press, Inc. (In press.)

28. ———: Psychoanalytic Reflections on a Meditation of Descartes. *Op cit.*

29. PIAGET, JEAN: Principal Factors Determining the Intellectual Evolution from Childhood to Adult Life. In: *Organization and Pathology of Thought.* Edited by David Rapaport. New York: Columbia University Press, 1951.

30. PÖTZL, OTTO: The Relationship between Experimentally Induced Dream Images and Indirect Vision. In: *Preconscious Stimulation in Dreams, Associations, and Images.* (Psychological Issues, II:3) New York: International Universities Press, Inc., 1960.

31. RÓHEIM, GÉZA: *Psychoanalysis and Anthropology.* New York: International Universities Press, Inc., 1950.

32. SACHS, HANNS: The Community of Day Dreams. In: *The Creative Unconscious.* Cambridge: Sci-Art Publishers, 1942.

33. WAELDER, ROBERT: *The Principle of Multiple Function.* This QUARTERLY, V, 1936, pp. 45-62.

34. ZWERLING, ISRAEL: *The Favorite Joke in Diagnostic and Therapeutic Interviewing.* This QUARTERLY, XXIV, 1955, pp. 104-114.

2

The Primal Scene and the Sense of Reality

THE PRIMAL SCENE AND
THE SENSE OF REALITY

BY PHYLLIS GREENACRE, M.D. (NEW YORK)

In this paper I present some aspects of the influence of the primal scene on the development and functioning of the sense of reality. These become evident in certain circumscribed distortions of external reality and especially in the creation and persistence of specific illusions. My conclusions are based on my own clinical experience, supplemented by the clinical reports of others and the findings of many colleagues who have done systematic work in studying the behavior of infants. Finally, I shall refer to and give excerpts from three sources: first, the account of the Wolf-man, whose infantile neurosis was published by Freud in 1914 and its later developments described recently by Gardiner (1971); second, case material from my own practice; and third, some reflections on the life and work of the painter, Piet Mondrian.

I

The term 'primal scene' is not always used with precisely the same meaning. However, it is generally agreed that the primal scene in one way or another has to do with the child's developing ideas, or fantasies, about the nature of parental intercourse.[1] The term was first used to refer to the actual witnessing, through seeing or hearing, of the sexual relationship of the parents or their surrogates. It was recognized that while the primal scene was not clearly remembered by the young child, it combined with impressions from related experiences, giving rise to various infantile sexual theories. Subsequently, the emphasis was most

Presented as the Sandor Rado Lecture for the Columbia University Psychoanalytic Clinic for Training and Research and the Association for Psychoanalytic Medicine, New York, May 23, 1972.

[1] See, Moore and Fine (1967): *Glossary of Psychoanalytic Terms and Concepts.*

often on the power of fantasy of the primal scene rather than on the actual experience. The term was then shifted to refer especially to fantasies, whether or not the actual experience had occurred.

I shall use the term, however, in the original sense—of the witnessing of parental intercourse or of some clearly related sexual event, such as birth or miscarriage. I believe such experiences to be ubiquitous, and the starting point of potent fantasies. The conditions at the time of the experience often influence the reactions to later events and so shape the theories that gradually develop throughout childhood. The direct, seemingly unelaborated memory, if presented at all, is usually updated to a later time. On analysis it proves to be a screen memory with distortions and discrepancies. If it is held to with great vehemence and thin rationalizations, it becomes an illusion, often in striking contrast to the individual's good sense of reality in the ordinary affairs of life. It is dislodged by analysis against great resistance. Derivative parts of the original experiences usually appear in the dreams, screen memories, behavior and symptoms of later life, and especially in the fantasies associated with masturbation.[2]

The exposure of the young child to adult sexual intercourse is not limited to congested living conditions, but occurs also in families of much higher social and economic status. In the majority of my analytic patients who came from relatively secure and intelligent family backgrounds, the greatest effects from early exposure to parental intercourse occurred in first, only, and youngest children. The parents of only children showed a tendency to keep the child in the parental bedroom,

[2] One wonders whether the present plethora of stage and screen demonstrations of a variety of primal scenes may not be a contagious revival, in a literal acting out, of these previously deeply buried and puzzling memories. The present background of an almost universal arousal of aggression would furnish a favorable medium for such a revival since sexual and aggressive drives are closely related in early childhood. It is interesting that masturbation is rather infrequently presented on the screen, perhaps because it would stir conflicts of a later time and more definite form.

sometimes in bed with them, over a much longer time than was true in families where there were several children. Further, these parents often romped and played with the infant in an affectionately rough manner. This intermittent acceptance of the child into the parental bed was often prolonged into the fourth or fifth year, or even later, unless the situation was interfered with by the arrival of younger siblings. This indulgent acceptance of freedom of bodily contact in the parental bed might be in striking contrast to the times when the child, awakened by unusual sounds, seeks haven with the parents only to be ejected summarily or directly punished for the intrusion.

In some affluent families where the children are early put in charge of a nurse, with whom they may also be left while the parents are away from home for considerable periods of time, the exposure to intimate sexual behavior of adults may occur when the child becomes the third member of a clandestine relationship, consummated either in the nursery itself or when he is taken to visit the nurse's home. Such a situation is described in Marie Bonaparte's (1945) article on the primal scene, and is implied as the earlier background of the two children in Henry James's The Turn of the Screw. In that eerie novel the peculiar dramatic effect of the tale arises from the pervasive uncertainty induced in the reader concerning exactly what has happened and when. When children have a very close relationship with pets or when their early childhood has been spent on a farm, the strongest impressions of sexuality may be derived from the witnessing of animals copulating, giving birth, or being castrated. Such impressions become agglomerated with real or imagined experiences regarding parental behavior, and it is difficult to determine which came first. One has only to see the extreme excitement and eagerly anxious participation of young children in the drama of birth of puppies or kittens to realize how intense and expanding is the stimulation of such a domestic event.[3]

[3] The Kinsey Reports (1948, pp. 667-678; 1953, pp. 502-509) indicated the frequency of farm children's involvement in sexual experimentation with animals during latency and under the pressure of puberty and adolescence.

The witnessing of the primal scene seems to leave an especially strong impression when it occurs early, especially before the third year. The impression left at this age cannot be readily communicated to and shared with the parents, who are in the very nature of things unusually inaccessible to the child at this time. In addition, since speech is a relatively recent and imperfect achievement, both communication and responsiveness are still largely dependent on various body contacts and nonverbal expressions. The impression of the primal scene must be deposited more in the physical components of the emotional reactions than would be true at a later age. These early body memories may be absorbed into later symptoms and often reappear in direct or converted forms in the course of treatment. They may also be absorbed into, and fixated in, peculiarly distorted forms by traumatically experienced revisions, notably in the phallic phase and especially in prepuberty. The phallic phase, with its peak in the fourth year of life, has long been recognized as the time of most sensitivity to external genital stimulations of whatever nature. Exposure to the primal scene, witnessing the birth of a sibling or the occurrence of a miscarriage, or even injury to a pet, may then have a fateful influence on the child's developing conception of the nature of sexuality. This is of special importance as occurring when the œdipus complex is already close to its height. The impression of the sexual relationship as being a sadistic act and the fear of castration have long been emphasized as significant misinterpretations which might complicate the child's later sexual development (cf., Fenichel, 1945).

When such experiences occur before the third year, however, they have been considered of lesser import as it was felt that if they came from a preverbal era (at least from the time when speech was inadequately developed), they did not emerge in a conceptualized form and could have little specific neurotic content. It was also considered that while very early experiences of the primal scene may occur, any direct coherent memory representations of them could scarcely be recovered in the course of analysis, which depends so much on verbal communication and is mainly limited to work with the neuroses. I cannot thoroughly accept the point of view that what is verbalized is the only communication useful in analytic work, even with neurotic patients. The body participates in various ways in all communications at all times, especially in emotional states. If the analyst is himself sensitive to and interested in what these accessory communications are expressing, he finds that much more is accessible to verbal representation than he might anticipate. But he must be patient and ready to make tentative, exploratory interpretations rather than depend on the very neat ones which are so satisfying as a finishing touch.

The first year of life is the time of the infant's greatest exposure to the parents' sexual behavior and it is usually assumed that the baby's reaction cannot then be clearly determined. Bernstein and Blacher (1967) have reported, however, that a specially traumatic experience may be registered explicitly even in the first six months. It is probable that except in cases where the stimulation is strong, clearly delineated, and often repeated, intense external stimulation is reacted to with increased restlessness and signs of discomfort, showing little or no differentiation between genital reaction and that of the general body activity of infantile rage. That some genital responsiveness is latent, and can be elicited even in these first six months by exceptionally strong stimulation, has been observed.

In the first half of the first year relative constancy of object representation in regard to the mother is being established; subsequently it is extended to the father and others habitually in the environment, including inanimate objects and pets. In other words, in the first year the infant has a moderate range of fairly reliable expectations from a number of external objects. Separation is going on with a good deal of uncertainty and ambivalence. At least in the first half of the first year, auditory, kinesthetic, and tactile responsiveness may be equal to or more important than vision. Within a few weeks after birth, focusing of vision occurs and is first directed toward the mother's face, as we know from the work of Spitz, Mahler, and others. This soon begins to coöperate with hearing, which elicits reactions to stimuli not immediately at hand. The reaction to parental intercourse may blend with any other arresting excitation, whether from noise, rough handling, or heightened motion. But there is a gradual increase in the pressure to *see*.

During the second year there is definite increase in the vulnerability to genital stimulation, and the excitation caused by exposure to the primal scene, or related experience, may be intense. This takes place during a period of momentous maturational change. Walking and talking are being accomplished and increase the child's range of stimulation and reactivity. Heightened bodily invigoration is evident and frequently associated with the appearance of infantile masturbation. There is a sensitivity to both general and genital excitation, and a susceptibility to genital excitation as a special responsiveness to sexual activity in others as well as situations suggesting bodily damage.[4]

The rise to the upright position in walking causes the child to see objects from new and varying angles. This occurs while the still active rate of bodily growth is such that his size in relation to the external world is rapidly changing. Freeing of his hands for exploration increases his range of manipulation and brings him into a different visual and tactile relationship with his own body as well as with the outside. The totality of these experiences contributes to the very beginning of conceptualization. In this period, too, the excretory functions are settling down into a more definite rhythm, probably largely due to sphincter maturation, while the upright position in walking and the need for ease in movement bring new elements into the infant's concern with his own excreta. They are no longer comforting quasi extensions of his body but be-

---

[4] This has recently been demonstrated in the infant observations of Galenson and Roiphe (1971). While it is possible that this excitation is somewhat increased under the conditions of the nursery observations, yet its intensity and the uniformity of its appearance are very convincing of its significance.

come impediments to be disposed of. There is a gradual shift in his emotional attitude toward them. My point here is that these bodily conditions, extensions of those that have been developing in the first year, also contribute endogenous factors to the young child's perception of what is going on in the external world and influence later conceptualization as well.

New experiences are constantly multiplying in the child's second year, and old ones are being experienced from so many new angles that reconciliations between past and present experiences are continually needed. Similarities and differences are the source of much infantile comparison, and sometimes of anxiety. Substitutions and contrasts are frequent in the developing need to establish practical dependable realities in a world that has suddenly enlarged. The seeming variability in external reality due to progressive changes in size, mobility, and posture of the child during his second year may contribute further to his recurrent need to return to the home base of the mother for repeated reassurance during his sallies into the world around him (cf., Meyer, 1936). This is conspicuous as earlier he seemed to relish some independence from the mother and largely to have overcome his anxiety with strangers. This is the stage demonstrated by Mahler and McDevitt (1968) and Mahler (1972) in their observations, and designated by Mahler as the period of rapprochement.

When speech, with its incomparable organizing potentiality and its furtherance of communication, has not been firmly established, there is a kind of rampant fluidity of sensory impressions afloat, and misunderstandings jostle for place with surprisingly acute observations. It is a time of natural ambiguity when the sounds of words may also lend themselves to what appears to be punning, but is probably uncertainty as to the distinctive meanings of words of similar sounds. At this time also transitional objects become the reliable convoy in the absence of the mother and function as an emotional stabilizer when the infant is in need. However, simple conceptualization, which accompanies the emergence of speech, has begun. Multi-

form similarities and differences may later become the source
of rich symbolism. The infant is beginning to think as well
as to observe, but is not yet clear 'which is which'. He does not
differentiate his dreams from what goes on in his room at night,
and his crib may become a kind of cage later to be compared
with, or represented in dreams as, an animal cage or prison.

Later, when parents habitually close or lock their bedroom
door at night and train the child not to intrude, the problem is
not entirely solved. The child's curiosity may even be intensified and he will progressively develop his own theories about
what is going on. He may use accessory experiences as substitutes for what he has tacitly been prohibited from seeing.
Inevitably he will react in accordance with his libidinal phase
of development at any given time. Even with an increased
opportunity for investigation, it is improbable that the young
child gets a very clear view and idea of the exact nature of the
primal scene. This depends on the actual conditions in the
parental bedroom at the time: how much light is in the room,
the position of the parents, how much of their bodies is
covered, and, especially, from what angle the young invader
approaches the bed. One might think, as many parents do, that
the child sees practically nothing before being hustled back
to his own bed, and that he soon forgets it. What he does see,
hear, and sense may certainly be confusing to him. He may be
aware of the parents in an unusual position, an impression
which is later the substance of the monsters and strange animals
that lurk in dark corners and reappear in night terrors. He may
also get the impression from stertorous breathing, moaning, or
groaning sounds that an intense struggle is going on, or that
one parent or the other is sick. The many and varied impressions depend on how this experience combines with others in
the infant's current and earlier life, as well as the state of his
bodily comfort or discomfort.

It has impressed me, however, that even when the real event
is not explicitly seen, the child frequently gets some feeling
of the sexual nature of the activity, though he may sense it

largely as a fight. I have thought that some vague awareness that the genital area is involved brings a responsive stimulation in the child's own genitals by a process of primary identification or 'mirroring'. In the second year, when there is already a susceptibility to genital arousal, this is probably associated with anal and urinary sphincter maturation and the rise of a preorgastic rhythm of response. In the fourth year, the response is greater and is associated with the genital maturation of the phallic phase.

There is a marked discrepancy between the probably almost universal witnessing of the primal scene and the widespread lack of *any* recollection of the event later on, even when other experiences of the third and fourth years may leave some clear, though usually distorted, relic in memory. The need to isolate and grossly distort the experience was conspicuous in the case of a nurse reported in my study of screen memories (Greenacre, 1949). Soon after having asserted that the parents' sexual life stopped with her own birth, this patient rather abruptly, and without realizing the inconsistency of her account, said she remembered that at age eight she had intruded on her parents when they were having intercourse, and she had been intensely frightened by the ugly look on her father's face. This was actually a screen memory for awareness of the male genitals. According to her official memory, it would have been impossible for her to see either the face or the genitals. In fact, there had been considerable sexual play with boys and she had seen a schizophrenic cousin of her father masturbating. This man had the same name as the father. The sight had frightened and fascinated her, and also excited her envy. Thus while the primal scene could not be readily acknowledged, it could not be completely repressed and broke through in an incongruous and isolated way which was inconsistent with the general alertness and intelligence of the patient.

While the first experiencing of the primal scene is probably by auditory and kinesthetic sensations, these are gradually transformed into visual scenes and pseudo memories through three routes; first, by displacement in time; second, by attribution to others than the parents; and third, by progressive modifications so that the disturbing sexual content is obscured. If the experiences are very frightening they may be repeated as nightmares or acted out in states of somnambulism. As material relating to the experienced primal scene begins to emerge in analysis, the analysand frequently complains of headaches, bursting head sensations, and visual disturbance.[5] The content of the analytic hour is usually immediately lost, whether much or little has been interpreted. On the following day, it may seem to have been dismissed as promptly as the original experience. This is repeated a number of times before the material is assimilated. If there has been a somnambulistic episode, no memory remains in the morning and knowledge of it has come from what has been told by someone else. (Such an episode resembles a small traumatic neurosis.) The deep and tenacious repudiation of the original memory is apparent also in the high degree of resistance with which any real reconstruction of the experience may be met.

This leads us to consider the phenomenon and nature of defense by denial as it joins with repression in relation to the the perception of reality, and to reality testing. The very aim of denial is the banishment of intolerable external stimulation by obliterating or erasing the source from which it came. This method of changing the unwelcome environment has always been recognized as very primitive, and its persistence beyond early infancy was first regarded as ominous, indicating a psychotic development or a severe character disturbance (*cf.*, Freud, 1924 [1923], 1927; A. Freud, 1936).

Denial was first conceived of as a modification or elimination of some part of external reality in favor of the acceptance of instinctual wishes. It was then considered as an indication of psychosis. Freud (1924) soon realized, however, that there might be a division or split in the functioning of the ego so

[5] The symptoms may resemble those accompanying the memory of an early anesthetic experience.

that the falsification of perception might exist in obsessional states side by side with the realization of the actual reality situation. This proved even more striking in cases of fetishism where the misperception—limited to the genitals due to severe castration anxiety—might coexist with a keen objective sense of reality. Such topical or focal denials might create strong illusions and be contrasted with the rather massive denials of reality which are sustained with delusion formation in the overt psychoses.

Denial as a defensive maneuver cannot be sustained alone except by the young infant. He may eliminate the external world by turning his head and eyes away (*cf.*, Spitz, 1957), by screaming to shut out noise, or by withdrawing his body or body part from offending external stimulations. Later, denial becomes an introductory step furthering repression and associated with isolation, rationalization, and displacement. The very term *denial* has been somewhat expanded and is now used with much broader basic connotations; we speak of denials of conflict, of body feelings, of superego-determined anxieties, etc.

When the very young infant cannot shut out unacceptable sound by screaming, he sometimes falls asleep from exhaustion, thus eliminating the intruding noise. As soon as he is able to focus his vision, sounds may stimulate an effort to see and he then reacts in various ways to what he sees. Strangeness is disturbing; the establishment of familiarity is a step in the direction of acceptance of reality (*cf.*, Ferenczi, 1916).

Throughout the first part of the first year, vision is the dominant factor in extending and binding together impressions from the various senses and in determining impressions from touch, handling, and hearing. Hermann (1934) emphasized the importance of skin and muscle reactions as well as internal body sensations in determining the way in which a young infant responds to stimulation from outside; he felt that these reactions may predominate over vision in the formation of the infant's later perceptions of the outer world. Bak (1953),

too, has indicated the importance of body reactions and sensations in the genesis of perversions. This formulation seems
obvious when one realizes that the infant has a small and inconstant margin of differentiation between what is inside
and what is outside. In the second year, locomotion (walking
and climbing) equals and sometimes surpasses vision in the
gratifications and anxieties of new experiences.

The earliest infantile reaction to the primal scene may be
due to its strangeness and unfamiliarity, as the infant is used to
seeing the parents in a totally different and usually responsive
position. This may be complicated by a feeling of loneliness
if there is no parental response to the infant's crying. At least
in the latter half of the first year, the infant may show a primitive pregenital type of envy or jealousy if he becomes aware
that the parents are in close bodily contact of which he is
deprived. Or he may react with fear. The former reaction is
not unlike what some pets show when a new baby is being
fondled while they are neglected. This infantile jealousy may
lead to exhaustion from crying or the infant may turn his
attention to substitute, autoerotic comforts, such as sucking
his hand or whatever happens to be nearby. In such a situation,
the denial of the external stimulation may relieve the inner
pain of jealousy. This unrelieved arousal of primitive jealousy,
combined with loneliness and helplessness, may be the dominant cause of denial of the primal scene or related sexual
situations, sometimes giving rise to negative hallucinations.
Lewin (1950) described the influence of the primal scene and
the associated denial in the genesis of states of elation ap-
proximating hypomanic episodes in the course of analysis.

We turn our attention next to the functioning of reality
testing. It evolves from and follows the development of the
sense of reality, and, in turn, interrelates with perception and
eventually with conceptualization. I would consider here the
everyday practical form of reality testing which attempts to
determine what is reliable, expectable, and at least relatively
constant in the external world. This does not include various

other types of reality appreciation as, for example, those of the artist, the inventor, the philosopher, or the mystic. The exact timing of the appearance and the essential nature of reality testing are not easily determined.[6]

Anna Freud (1965), quoting observations made by Anny Katan (1961), considers that reality testing occurs only after the development of verbalization, which to her also marks the beginning of the superego. I see a less clear line of demarcation. It seems to me that any extensive verbalization is attained with varying degrees of speed after thinking, reality testing, and the most rudimentary conceptualization have definitely begun. There are children who appear to understand and respond more or less appropriately to much that goes on

[6] In discussing reality testing, Moore and Fine (1967) make a distinction between *psychic reality* and *external reality*. They define psychic reality as the totality of a person's mental representations of his physical-instinctual life together with the mental life or dreams, thoughts, memories, fantasies, and perceptions, regardless of whether or not these accurately reflect or correspond to objective reality. External reality is understood as the sensing of the outside world of persons and things, involving time-space and causal relationships. The authors see this awareness as progressing and being organized in accord with the development of the ego and as depending on discrimination between inside and outside with the setting up of ego boundaries.

While this is a helpful schema for reference and organization of data, it does not cover some of the significant nexuses of problems of reality testing. The implication is of an absolute or at least an unchanging reality of the outer world. This may be true, but it cannot be determined as such since its sensing is ultimately dependent on human means. The latter always contain subjective elements of individual experience, relics left over from childhood which unconsciously affect the registration from the senses. In other words, we are always influenced by perceptions. We attempt to correct the individual perceptive distortions by measuring them against the perceptions of others. Still this may lead in various ways to erroneous conclusions. Group interpretations, even in groups of two, are notoriously influenced by the subjective relationship between the members. Larger groups are often even more susceptible to suggestion. Further, although the sensory stimulation may proceed in a normal manner, a temporary set of mind, even sometimes immediately environmentally determined, may influence individuals separately or together in similar or opposing directions. None of the conclusions may prove in the end to check with further experience. The question of the inevitability of the subjective intrusions into the evaluation of external sensory stimulations is one of the problems of validating human experience and scientific findings.

around them before verbalization has progressed sufficiently to be a main channel of communication. The clear attainment of verbalization is a landmark, to be sure, as it increases the facility and speed of responsive communication, supplementing the increase in range of independent exploration achieved in the success of walking. I would think, however, that the synthetic and integrative functions of the ego are implicit potentials at birth, probably depending on the degree of fineness of certain organizations in the central nervous system. Some recent observations by Janet Brown (1970) at the James Jackson Putnam Children's Center in Boston strongly suggest that difference in ego functions may be detected even within the first week after birth in infants who later appear to be especially gifted children. In one case which had been followed throughout childhood, it was significant that from the beginning the child seemed unusually independent of the mother.

In our everyday life we have to proceed with practical, approximate guidelines for reality testing. These become habitual and take their place in the second nature of common sense. In general, after the first years of childhood, reality testing proceeds first from an implicit comparison of any experience of an individual with his previous experiences; second, from a comparative checking with experiences of others; and third, from assessing whether a given experience fits into the contiguous elements in a total situation.

There is one area of common experience in which reality testing is particularly fallible and open to misperceptions and so to misrepresentations in the internalized image. This is in the appreciation of one's own body. Here internal and external stimulations may be felt in varying blends and proportions, with the body surface and special senses acting as mediators between external reality and what is internal. In the development of the sense of identity—which is a special segment in the appreciation of reality—the comparison of the appearance of one's own body with that of others is important, as this is assessed in terms of external visible attributes, i.e., size, shape, coloring, and so forth, in relation to external objects, human and otherwise. The sense of identity is further influenced by the physical sensations and the subjective attitudes and wishes of the individual. The two body areas which are most likely to suffer such distortions of perception are the genitals and the face, since they are seen less clearly on the self than on the other. In addition, they are the most complexly differentiated external parts and are more changed by highly charged emotion than is true of the body in general.

With its multiple developmental body changes and increasing experience in the outer world, the second year of life is obviously a time of heightened primitive and spontaneous reality testing. This is accomplished mostly through behavior itself, by trial and error, and through the merest beginning of rational testing which will accompany secondary process thinking. Walking itself probably promotes an appreciation of space and time in relation to the child's own activity, rather than by dependence on others. All this is then supplemented by the admonitions of parents which contribute to the beginning of superego formation.

In this developmental situation exposure to the primal scene may set in motion a widening set of reactions influencing perceptions of reality in contiguous related experiences. The consolidation of awareness of one's own body strengthens the process of separation and individuation, while the earlier primitive mirroring reaction gives way to the first wishful, imitative identifications, leading to illusion formation. From analyzing adult patients I have come to believe that the inception of an illusory phallus in girls may emerge at this time, and that it may be strengthened or corrected in the course of the later development of œdipal problems.

The situation with the boy is less clear, since the denial of the concrete possession of the phallus is more complicated and seems to require a more energetic process of denial than occurs in the reciprocal positive fantasy of phallic possession by the girl. This is probably due to the fact that the phallus is handled as well as seen when urinating. Still little boys of two may imitate girls by assuming their dress or activities. When they begin to approximate the girl's appearance by concealing the penis between the legs, is less clear; my impression is that this behavior is influenced by the observation of contemporary girls, although it actually occurs later. There is little doubt, however, that enemas given repeatedly in the first two years cause confusion about the body image in either sex.

There are, of course, other aspects of the infant's experience and the ultimate impact on him of the primal scene. The reaction to strangeness which has been so generally noted at certain times in the first year may later provoke some pleasurable excitement mixed with fear. This leads to the spirit of adventure in later life. However, when the child or adult meets a situation so strange that he has nothing with which to compare it, the stimulation is overwhelming and a shock reaction occurs. The intensity of the shock depends on the degree of helplessness and the availability of external aid; the reaction may be flight-fight, or freezing.

Some primal scene experiences are of this nature to the young child. The parents are seen or heard in so grotesque a way as to be only faintly recognizable, their appearance and behavior contrasting markedly with that ordinarily seen by the child during the day. In the first two years the infant may be overwhelmed by this situation. But in the second year, when there is a more complex and differentiated psychic and bodily response, the reaction may be flight in the direction of what is familiar (e.g., touching the mother), or immobilization with some change in the state of consciousness, such as confusion, or partial or total rapid denial of the experience. Although these reactions may occur at any time in life in response to overwhelming situations, they are more frequent in childhood when experiences in the night, and the dream, are not easily separated from daytime experiences. At night everything is more confusing, and bodily reactions participate even more in perceptual disturbances.[7]

[7] The economics of situations of overwhelming loss were described succinctly by Fenichel (1945).

II

There is a special form of denial which, with such accessory defensive paraphernalia as repression, isolation, and displacement, becomes so strengthened that it forms a wall, illusory, yet built as though for permanence. It presents itself in various proportions, symptoms, and character traits, and is usually more or less accepted by the patient. Not many patients directly complain of it although the sense of restraint and lack of spontaneity may be somewhat troubling. Although it arises out of the fear of being externally overwhelmed, it fundamentally serves the function—of which the individual is not much aware—of keeping him from being overcome by his own primitive instinctual drives, both aggressive and sexual.

This wall has usually been built in gradual stages from early childhood, and sometimes marked by crises. The original shock reactions are related to, and sometimes combined with, experiences of awe, but often have arisen out of more painful experiences in which anger has been more specifically aroused. The primal scene itself may have been associated with a shock reaction, or less severe reactions may have become confluent with severe responses to other traumata. Here there are two general categories: those which have involved estrangement from or loss of one parent or the other very early; and those which were associated with overwhelming violence to the infant's own body. Among the latter I would include operations, whether with or without anesthetic, febrile illnesses with deliria, and even the attacks on the infant's body through the use of repeated enemas.[8] Certainly the strongest walls of denial are those that have been re-enforced by operation on, or induced painful manipulation of, the genitals themselves, even when undertaken for therapeutic reasons.

[8] Looking back over my own early cases, I have been impressed by the frequency of tonsil- and adenoidectomies without preparation and especially the severe reactions to mastoid operations requiring frequent and painful dressing. Fortunately, many of these situations have been ameliorated through the use of antibiotics, as well as by the understanding of the need for special maternal care throughout such periods.

Actual primal scene experiences and related actual traumatic events in the first two or three years of infancy seem to furnish the nucleus or foundation of denial. One suspects that this foundation may rest upon an externalization of the stimulus barrier. There is a fear of wildness (or violence), sometimes associated with fear of psychosis, which is not justified by other elements in the character formation. Such wildness seems also to represent the content of masturbatory fantasies, which have been isolated largely out of fear of castration. The basic foundation of the wall is re-enforced by later crises, which bring with them superego re-enforcements at different times throughout childhood and even into adolescence. In the cases I have seen there has been a history of severe provocative tantrums mostly in the third or fourth year.

The nurse-patient mentioned above had earlier developed a firm illusory retaining wall which began to crumble under the impact of her hospital training. At the beginning of analysis she presented a dream and then sometime later brought in a sonnet she had written early in her nursing career. In the dream she was going in and out of places in Rockland County and questioned whether she would stay and work there. Her associations were to whether or not she should stay in analysis since she had already attempted it unsuccessfully with another analyst, or whether she might prefer to live in the country as her friends did. At the time I did not recognize the masturbatory confession in the dream, or her fear of wildness and psychosis, as this was later revealed in her memory of the schizophrenic cousin's masturbation. This memory had been amalgamated with the primal scene experience and deposited, as it were, in the distorted, ugly expression of the father's face.

In the sonnet the patient described her wall: 'I built a wall of thoughts in even row / Like bricks they were to be, so firm and strong / Protecting me from laughter and mad song / And echoes of a fear that would not go.' The rest of the sonnet expressed the incipient failure of this defense and her need to find a new vision and hope in her life.[9] As in other patients with early primal scene experiences and a propensity for wall-building, there were severe tantrums, remembered as occurring around the age of four, associated with such prolonged breath-holding that the child appears to be on the verge of losing consciousness.

The Wolf-man's wall was of lighter weight. It was an illusory veil that enveloped him when he came to Freud for treatment at the age of twenty-four (Freud, 1918 [1914]). Practically immobilized by his obsessions and compulsive rituals, he summed up his complaints by saying that the world was hidden from him by a veil. This had only once been torn—on the occasion of his passing a bowel movement as the result of an enema, and for a time after this he could see the world clearly. The idea of a veil had not always been disturbing. He had been born with a caul and on Christmas Day, facts which marked him as a special child of good fortune.

On his fourth birthday, however, his neurotic troubles had emerged in an anxious dream. His window opened suddenly revealing seven white wolves outside, seated in a walnut tree and staring fixedly at him. The spontaneous opening of the window was a dream projection and repetition of opening his eyes on awakening; the staring of the wolves similarly reflected his own staring gaze at his parents involved in sexual, animal-like behavior so strange that it induced a feeling of alienation. The opening of the window was related, too, to the tearing of the veil by the defecation which permitted him to see better. This temporary clearing of the vision resembles the brightened effect of repressed emotion in a screen memory. The veil was being restrengthened, as subsequently it seemed to hide him from the world as well as the world from him.

The original reality of the caul, which had become a symbol, joined with the actuality of the nuclear primal scene experi-

---

[9] The clinical details of this case are given in my article on screen memories (Greenacre, 1949).

ence which had occurred when the patient was an infant of about one and a half years. This first experience, dormant but fairly well constellated in the infant mind,[10] was given a new stimulus and significance when at the age of three and a half the little boy was seduced by his sister who was two years older. She may have exposed herself; at least he wished to investigate her body as well as his own. It seems probable from a dream which occurred in the course of his analysis that the *veil* then took on the added meaning of representing both his own foreskin (as it had his eyelids) and his disturbed vision of his sister's genitals. He spoke of wanting to tear off her coverings or *veils*. At this time he was already under the influence of castration threats and fears connected with his masturbatory activity. Subsequently he developed rages, at times quite severe, which continued until the age of eight. These states may have contributed to the feeling of the veil, since such rages culminate, like masturbatory states, in a condition of a glazed blurring of contact with the external world.

The veil, as such, disappeared during the first period of treatment by Freud; or perhaps more accurately, it was so diminished as to be no longer complained of. The patient was generally better but he still suffered from anxiety which appeared to him as a fear of 'losing his reality'. By this he seemed to mean a possible breakthrough of wildness in behavior or violence in thought. In general, through the years that followed his treatment by Freud, he seemed steadied so long as he had at least some supporting contact with Freud or, in later years, with Dr. Brunswick and Dr. Gardiner. Without this, his veil might have thickened into a retaining wall, as a protection and a restriction. Its main protection was against his own inner primitive instinctual drives.

His pursuit of women and his marriage itself appear more as efforts to give structure to his life than as well-developed love

10 In 1923 Freud offered a tentative revision: 'Observation of his parents copulating or observation of them together' occurred at one and a half (Gardiner, 1971, p. 262,n.).

relationships. They were apparently hedges against loneliness, the nagging urge to masturbate, and disturbing masturbatory fantasies. Though he genuinely missed his wife after her suicide in 1938, and grieved for her in a prolonged obsessional way, he seemed to feel this loss largely as a threat to the maintenance of his sense of reality, which was more than ordinarily dependent on viable relationships.[11] At this time, the time of the *Anschluss,* he was also bereft of the possibility of contact with Freud, who had given him emotional lifeblood. Freud had also been an extraordinarily satisfactory replacement for his own father, who had died a short time before the Wolf-man first sought psychiatric help.

His obsessive-compulsive condition had improved greatly after his first period of treatment with Freud from 1910 to 1914 and the veil was not then a matter of complaint. Two subsequent periods of disturbed behavior did occur, as he had always anxiously anticipated. The first of these came in 1926. A visit to Freud, in which he saw his benefactor in a depleted state after his first mouth operation, may have added to other circumstances in precipitating the disturbance, essentially a severe panic with increasing obsessional preoccupation with the condition of his nose. It was clearly a reactivation of a morbid concern with the pimples on his nose in adolescence. But now his obsession was more severe and unremitting, and led to the illusion that one of the pimples had broken leaving a hole which might be incurable. He carried a pocket mirror with him and was constantly examining the 'hole'. He also developed a paranoid-like attitude toward one of the doctors

[11] He expresses this clearly in his later written account. 'The question kept hammering away in my mind: How could Therese do this to me? As she was the only stable structure in my life how could I, now suddenly deprived of her, live on? It seemed to me impossible.' He had met her a year or two before he first consulted Freud. She was a nurse in a sanitarium when he was under Kraepelin's care. Their mutual ambivalences had made for a painful and rather dreary love affair. His own ambivalence, due in large measure to his struggle with his passive feminine attitude, had been helped by his treatment with Freud, which had allowed him to take a more decisive attitude. (See, Gardiner, 1971: *The Wolf-Man,* pp. 49-65, 74-80, 122.)

whom he had consulted and whom he now felt was persecuting
him.[12] The hole was an illusion, probably of an anus vagina,
and may be considered as the male equivalent of the development of an illusory penis in the female. Both are severe distortions of body reality but are not necessarily indicative of
psychosis.[13]

This period of illness was treated by Dr. Brunswick and a
diagnosis of paranoia was made. The patient was angry with
Freud for seeming to desert him and at first presented Dr.
Brunswick with a wall of unyielding silence. Once this was
penetrated, the symptoms yielded to five months of treatment.
His condition later on indicated that these ideas had not
been truly delusional but rather parts of his extreme anger and
depressive need for punishment.[14] It is significant, however,
that this paranoid-like panic had been preceded by a considerable period in which the Wolf-man, always interested in painting, had undertaken to do a self-portrait. He had then spent
many hours looking at himself, especially his face, in a mirror.
This almost surely rearoused old problems of blurred staring in
connection with the primal scene, and especially of looking at
his sister's genitals and comparing them with his own, which

[12] In consideration of the question of paranoia in the Wolf-man's case, one
should remember that his favorite uncle, who had played with him most in
his childhood, had suddenly disappeared after an acute paranoia had developed.
After a period of hospitalization he had been sequestered on his Crimean
estate. Although he was supposed to be living comfortably there, in 1909, just
at the time the Wolf-man was seeking help for himself, he heard of this uncle's
lonely and gruesome death, his body actually gnawed by rats that infested the
place. A fearful identification with this uncle may have colored the Wolf-man's
symptoms at this time.

[13] Jonathan Swift, whose Gulliver's Travels betrays so clearly the author's
preoccupation with both genital and general body changes in size, was repeatedly troubled by the size of the pores in the skin. He was a great show-
man himself who hid parts of his life behind a series of veils so adroitly that he
created mysteries which have never been solved. In the fading state of increasing
senility, he stood repeatedly before a mirror as though studying himself and
saying, 'I am who I am!'.

[14] The full account of this appears in A Supplement to Freud's 'History
of an Infantile Neurosis' in The Wolf-Man (Gardiner, 1971, pp. 263-311). It
was originally published in the Int. J. Psa., IX, 1928, pp. 439-476.

could only really be seen clearly in a mirror. This became evident in his second break-through of wildness.

This disturbance was not nearly so severe as the first one had been and occurred in 1951 at sixty-five when his wife had been dead for thirteen years. He was retired and was beginning to feel the greater impact of loneliness without work and with a mother rather than a wife at hand. He again turned to painting as an expressive outlet. Actually, the break-through consisted of only an episode and had the quality of a piece of acting out, but it was still vivid in his mind when he related it to Dr. Gardiner some five years after its occurrence.[15] On a certain day he awoke with a headache and despite his mother's cautioning that he should remain at home, he felt impelled to go out and paint. He must already have been in an altered state of consciousness, related to somnambulism, for without realizing what he was doing, he wandered into the prohibited Russian zone in Vienna. Overcome by thoughts of his childhood, he did not realize that this was forbidden territory. As the light of day changed from bright to somber, he shifted his position and sat painting a picture of a house which 'really consisted of only a wall in which one saw black holes instead of windows', completely bombed out (Gardiner, 1971, p. 329). As he sat there lost in dark romantic feelings, he was overtaken by Russian soldiers who took him into custody under the suspicion that he was spying. He was held for two and one half days under conditions which sound like a milder version of Kafka's account of The Trial. He was then released without any realistically alarming sequelae.

His mother repeatedly referred to this incident as an 'act of madness which no one can understand'. He himself felt that it was similar to other brief periods of depression, especially to the time of his nose problems. He felt that he had lost control of himself and lost his hold on reality in acting in this dangerously mad way, and for weeks afterward he was filled with

[15]See, The Wolf-Man's Description of the Episode of the Painting in *The Wolf-Man* (Gardiner, 1971, pp. 331-334).

self-reproach. To me it seems pretty clear that this episode was an acted-out condensation of the primal scene and the seduction by his sister, which were combined in the early wolf dream at the age of four and played so large a part in his prolonged obsessional frenzy twenty-two years earlier. After the episode was over, he realized that it had occurred on the anniversary of his sister's suicide. At the time of her death he had been unable to mourn, but later he had had a displaced acting out of his grief when he impulsively visited the grave of a well-known poet and found himself weeping copiously. His sister had been an aspiring poet.

The intensity of his self-reproach and his guilt feelings, with the need to flirt with punishment, may be an indication of the persistent strength of his curiosity, jealousy, and rage at being the less effective, the diminished one in both experiences. At the same time his need to repeat and master through painting the horror of the blacked-out windows represented the castration threat involved in what he saw dimly but elaborated and imagined as his mother's and sister's genital orifices, and possessed himself in his own unseen anus.

The walls of defense founded on early infantile denial may take on various forms and textures as they progressively incorporate new ingredients from the experiences which go into their construction, not only in infancy but throughout childhood and adolescence. The first patient, the nurse, had built a wall of brick and stone. The Wolf-man had a tenacious veil as his wall, at one time extended into a wall of stubborn silence. Another of my patients had an illusion of being enclosed in a lucite cube through which she could see but not be touched. Still another managed an even more illusory wall by automatically unfocusing her eyes, very much like the closing of a shutter on a camera (Greenacre, 1947). This reminds us also of the Wolf-man's original dream in which the opening of the dream window was the externalization of his opening his eyes. When the experience is overwhelming, early, and often repeated, the wall foundation is likely to be the more intractable. But the wall, in whatever form, is built to restrain wildness, to hold in check impulses felt as though of murderous rage, or nearly uncontrollable sexual impulses. These, probably generally, are more explicitly expressed in masturbation fantasies, which are in turn feared.

The life and work of Piet Mondrian present another form of the wall, modified in an extraordinary way in accord with the demands of this talented artist. We have no carefully documented psychoanalytic case study, but the man himself has provided revealing records: the paintings he left; his own autobiographical sketch written at sixty-nine and published posthumously under the title, Toward a True Vision of Reality; and his essay, written at forty-seven, Natural Reality and Abstract Reality. Although these are so impersonal as to seem aseptic, they are very revealing. Supplemented by the monograph of his friend, Michel Seuphor (n.d.), they give facts pertinent to this study.

Mondrian decided to become an artist at fourteen and from then on pursued his course with a single-minded devotion to the goal of purifying his vision, to free it from all subjectivity of emotion. He started out as a realist, painting landscapes, houses, a single church or windmill outlined against the sky. He even did a few portraits. But he passionately hated motion of any kind and found people in action the most disturbing of all. They soon were omitted. Even immobile cows in flat meadows were sacrificed. He loved flowers but they must appear singly and not in 'ensemble', i.e., in relation to each other. He turned to trees, painting them at first usually singly, stately, and dignified. Later, they appeared with twisted, tortured limbs as though arrested in a state of agonized motion. He experimented with the effects of light, painting the same scene either by the strongest sunlight or by moonlight. Fascinated for a time by the ever-changing sea and sky, he found that they too suggested more motion than he could tolerate.

He stated that he saw with realist eyes past beauty or (ordinary) reality of man, and that pure reality must be painted
without the infiltration of *any* subjective feelings or conceptions. Since particular form and natural color evoke subjectivity,
he felt he must reduce his pictures to the elements of form and
primary color alone. Ultimately he felt that the only really
constant relationship is expressed in the right angle; that the
two fundamental forces of nature are expressed in the horizontal and the vertical meeting in the perfect right angle.
(Parenthetically one wonders here whether he was making an
effort to harmonize night and day.) Space, uncluttered, was
the background on which he could create the equivalence of
these two factors. He was clearly eradicating the family circle
and any of the comforting rounded forms of life and human
contact. It is not hard to see that he must have felt the danger of
an overwhelming force of aggression in himself and the need
of strong containing walls both in life and in his painting.

He began to paint walls themselves, first of rather warm
reddish brick in patches, perhaps the indistinct walls of a house
in the half light in which the right angle of the joinings of the
bricks stood out like small right-angled crosses, sometimes em-
braced by incomplete ovals. Later, the texture of the brick
faded and the ovals disappeared while the little crosses became
prominent in irregular patterns as though spattered in space,
still suggesting motion and emotion. Next, the crosses extended their linear arms to join each other to create rectangles
of varying sizes and distribution, each enclosing its own
primary color. He is said to have spent hours arranging and
rearranging these to form a pattern which would have absolute
balance, in which nothing would be loose or open-ended. This
search for perfection in both expression and strong containment of the primordial forces progressed through various stages
until it reached the compositions of infinitely precise rectan-
gular forms, for which the painter became famous in his later
years. In fact, in the end his painting barely escaped disappearing into the eternal harmony of a pure white unmarked space.

Surprisingly enough, in the last two or three years of his life, these purified architectural forms began to break up again. His last two paintings showed varied linear groups of small imprecise forms of assorted colors jostling each other in obvious motion and were labeled by their author, Broadway Boogie Woogie and Victory Boogie. These were painted at the age of sixty-nine in New York in 1941 or 1942.

His paintings seemed to reflect, to an unusual degree, what was going on in his own attempt to live. There was an increasing effort to extricate himself from particular personal relationships and to live in a perfectly balanced cosmic harmony. This seems another form of the rebel's search for a utopian existence. He insistently fled from motion and emotion as though these were the devils of darkness. His studio, bare and painted white, appeared more suitable for a monk or a surgeon than a painter. He could not stand even the intrusion of books.

Mondrian was a rebel in a life-long struggle with his father, who is described as a sententious tyrant, a Calvinist schoolmaster who wished his son to become a teacher. The boy's determination to be a painter came with puberty, but he succumbed to his father's will to the extent of qualifying to teach drawing. His further decision at twenty to go to the Academy of Fine Arts alienated him from his parents and his home, to which he never returned voluntarily except for the briefest visits.

During the next few years at the Academy, and after, in order to earn his living, he did copies of pictures, illustrations for scientific books, some portraits, and occasional teaching. He was an amiable, friendly young man, markedly shy with women. His appearance was arresting partly because of his large and luminous dark eyes, which are conspicuous in his photographs and in a series of self-portraits. He was then obsessionally worried about possible blindness and according to his younger brother, he tried to deal with this anxiety by ridiculing himself in regard to it.

In this general period there were two break-throughs of wildness in behavior, both of which were symbolically self-destructive. On one occasion while visiting in Cornwall at the invitation of one of his women students, he leaped into the sea from a high overhanging rock. He succeeded in swimming ashore, but fatigue and the immersion brought on a severe attack of pneumonia, from which he recovered slowly. The other eruption of wildness was repeated several times. He painted a number of self-portraits which required his studying his face in the mirror. But when the portrait displeased him, as it usually did, he would destroy it by shooting it with a pistol. A fellow painter who participated in these acts saved one of the offending portraits and wrote on it a quotation which translated means: 'So I take the risk of thrusting myself into the world, and I wait calmly until destiny, which eternally pursues us, lifts my desire to the point of self-confidence'.

In his journey away from home, Amsterdam had been the first stop and Paris the second. He was then in the stage of seeking relief from the varying shades and combinations of color in nature by adopting the use of primary colors alone. He was also seeking an intellectual style which would be loved for itself alone and eternally. In 1914 he was summoned home by the illness of his father but this visit was lengthened to the duration of World War I, which broke out just at this time.

Perhaps the pressures of the time accelerated the changes going on in him. At this time his renewed interest in the sea brought out the idea of horizontal and vertical forces as the basic and eternal principles of life. As soon as the war was over, he returned to Paris where he remained until 1938. This was the end of the period of the first great changes in his painting.

Throughout these years, he had lived a generally ascetic life, but he made a number of friends, began to publish articles, and to take a definite place in the world of painters. He knew many women, some of whom had been his students. He suffered compulsive infatuations which never lasted. He was intensely fond of dancing and felt it a treat to be taken to a well-known dance hall. Otherwise, he danced alone in his studio with his small red painted phonograph. A friend who watched him considered him ridiculous, was embarrassed, and understood why women did not wish to marry him. When he was approaching sixty and had begun to take dancing lessons, he would pick out the prettiest girl on the dance floor, but was as stiff as a ramrod, attempting only vertical and horizontal movement. He was bitter that his country had banned the Charleston; if this ban continued he would never set foot in Holland again. He thought the Charleston was a 'sporting dance', contrasting it to erotic dances. Since the partners always kept a certain distance from each other and spent so much energy in doing and keeping track of the steps, he was assured they would have no time for thoughts of sex.

He had planned to come to the United States, but stopping too long in London en route, he was caught by the Second World War and did not arrive in New York until the fall of 1940. Here his paintings underwent another radical change. The precise black lines, enclosing rectangles of pure color, melted away and were replaced by thicker lines of a succession of small segments of various colors. These were the Broadway Boogie Woogie and the Victory pictures. Whether the Victory was for life or for death is hard to say for he died soon afterward of pneumonia.

Obviously, this is the story of a talented man who had from childhood struggled against both sexual and aggressive drives. Nor is this strange when one considers that probably from his earliest years he suffered from extreme stimulation. For he was the oldest of five children born to the sternest of Calvinistic fathers, who was a headmaster in the school. The children came in about ten years and there was every chance that this oldest child had multiple primal scene experiences as well as awareness of the birth of the younger siblings, certainly a situation which inevitably would compound œdipal jealousy, and sibling jealousy and envy. His symptoms themselves bespoke the extremest sensitization to movement and noise; his infantile anger was expressed in his wish to keep all objects, whether animate or inanimate, separated from each other. Not even flowers should be seen with intertwined stems. He seemed to have taken into his body the multiple and unorganized as well as rhythmic motion around him, and to have attempted to convert it into a cosmic rhythm which would be perfect and eternal, and to project this in his painting. His fascination with dancing with his whole body in a state of stiff erectness proclaimed, unknown to him, the displacement of genitality to the total body self. He was ultimately unable to live according to the art form he had created, in which motion and emotion would be walled safely into rectangles. But he had only a brief period of freedom before he died.

CONCLUSION

The primal scene and related experiences have pervasive effects on a child's later life and character, especially in shaping the manifestations of both sexual and aggressive drives. The effects are powerful in the first months of life when the infant's separation from the mother is scant and the primal scene is apt to be a most intimate and repetitive experience. At that time sexual and aggressive responses are not differentiated, and other uncomfortable stimulation from any source may initiate a lasting tendency to respond with action.

Disturbances in the sense of reality are more specific and differentiated during the second year when rapid maturational changes produce drastic shifts in the infant's contact with the outer world, resulting in disturbances and contradictions in his perceptions. The primal scene may then be an overwhelming experience in its strangeness, arousing infantile reactions of loneliness, alienation, or of feeling overwhelmed, accompanied by changes in the state of consciousness. Under other, less severely bewildering conditions, it excites acute and primitive jealousy to the point of infantile rage.

Defense by primitive denial is then set in motion, followed by repression and isolation and, at a later time, by rationalization. Denial, however, is both strong and insidious, and tends to be a widening and inclusive defensive maneuver which infiltrates many other relationships in later life, permitting opposing perceptions to endure in juxtaposition. Together with the defensive mechanism of isolation, denial forms the basis of tenacious walls of containment which both support and restrict the developing character of neurosis.

REFERENCES

BAK, ROBERT C. (1953): *Fetishism.* J. Amer. Psa. Assn., I, pp. 285-298.

BERNSTEIN, ANNE E. H. and BLACHER, RICHARD S. (1967): The Recovery of a Memory from Three Months of Age. In: *The Psychoanalytic Study of the Child, Vol. XXII.* New York: International Universities Press, Inc., pp. 156-161.

BONAPARTE, MARIE (1945): Notes on the Analytic Discovery of the Primal Scene. In: *The Psychoanalytic Study of the Child, Vol. I.* New York: International Universities Press, Inc., pp. 119-125.

BROWN, JANET L. (1970): *Precursors of Intelligence and Creativity: A Longitudinal Study of One Child's Development.* Merrill-Palmer Quarterly of Behavior and Development, XVI, pp. 117-137.

FENICHEL, OTTO (1945): *The Psychoanalytic Theory of Neurosis.* New York: W. W. Norton & Co., Inc.

FERENCZI, SANDOR (1916): *Contributions to Psychoanalysis.* Boston: Richard C. Badger, pp. 181-184.

FREUD, ANNA (1936): *The Ego and the Mechanisms of Defence.* New York: International Universities Press, Inc., 1946.

——— (1965): *Normality and Pathology in Childhood.* New York: International Universities Press, Inc.

FREUD (1918 [1914]): *From the History of an Infantile Neurosis.* Standard Edition, XVII, pp. 7-122.

——— (1924 [1923]): *Neurosis and Psychosis.* Standard Edition, XIX, pp. 149-153.

——— (1924): *The Loss of Reality in Neuroses and Psychoses.* Standard Edition, XIX, pp. 183-187.

——— (1927): *Fetishism.* Standard Edition, XXI, pp. 152-157.

GALENSON, ELEANOR and ROIPHE, HERMAN (1971): The Impact of Early Sexual Discovery on Mood, Defensive Organization, and Symbolization. In: *The Psychoanalytic Study of the Child, Vol. XXVI.* New York/Chicago: Quadrangle Books, pp. 195-216.

GARDINER, MURIEL, Editor (1971): *The Wolf-Man.* By the Wolf-Man. With A Case of the Wolf-Man by Sigmund Freud, and A Supplement by Ruth Mack Brunswick. Edited, with notes, an introduction, and chapters by Muriel Gardiner. New York: Basic Books, Inc.

GREENACRE, PHYLLIS (1947): *Vision, Headache and the Halo. Reactions to Stress in the Course of Superego Formation.* This QUARTERLY, XVI, pp. 178-188.

—— (1949): A Contribution to the Study of Screen Memories. In: *Trauma, Growth and Personality.* New York: International Universities Press, Inc., 1969, pp. 188-203.

HERMANN, IMRÉ (1934): *Vorläufige Mitteilung: Urwahrnehmungen, insbesondere Augenleuchten und Lautwerden des Inneren.* Int. Ztschr. f. Psa., XX, pp. 553-555.

KATAN, ANNY (1961): Some Thoughts about the Role of Verbalization in Early Childhood. In: *The Psychoanalytic Study of the Child, Vol. XVI.* New York: International Universities Press, Inc., pp. 184-188.

KINSEY, ALFRED C.; POMEROY, WARDELL B.; MARTIN, CLYDE E. (1948): *Sexual Behavior in the Human Male.* Philadelphia and London: W. B. Saunders Co.

—— —— ——; GEBHART, PAUL H. (1953): *Sexual Behavior in the Human Female.* Philadelphia and London: W. B. Saunders Co.

LEWIN, BERTRAM D. (1950): *The Psychoanalysis of Elation.* New York: The Psychoanalytic Quarterly, Inc., 1961.

MAHLER, MARGARET S. (1972): *Rapprochement Subphase of the Separation-Individuation Process.* This QUARTERLY, XLI, pp. 487-506.

—— and MC DEVITT, JOHN B. (1968): *Observations on Adaptation and Defense in Statu Nascendi. Developmental Precursors in the First Two Years of Life.* This QUARTERLY, XXXVII, pp. 1-21.

MEYER, ALBRECHT (1936): *Das Kleinkind und seine Umwelt.* Ztschr. f. psa. Päd., X, pp. 93-102.

MOORE, BURNESS E. and FINE, BERNARD D. (1967): *A Glossary of Psychoanalytic Terms and Concepts.* New York: The American Psychoanalytic Association.

SEUPHOR, MICHEL (undated): *Piet Mondrian.* New York: Harry N. Abrams, Inc.

SPITZ, RENÉ A. (1957): *No and Yes. On the Genesis of Human Communication.* New York: International Universities Press, Inc.

3

THE
SENSE OF
REALITY

THE SENSE OF REALITY

BY GREGORY ZILBOORG (NEW YORK)

I

The psychopathologies of the past were all aprioristic. Even those of Greek and Roman medicine, which appeared strictly empirical and clinical, were founded on a priori standards. They took it for granted that there was a right, a correct way of thinking. Any departure from the preconceived intellectual norm was considered pathological. These deviations would not be noticeable, of course, until they became gross enough and too obvious to escape even the man in the street. Historically, rationalism, or intellectualism, was not the only standard in psychopathology. It was also assumed that man naturally follows the good and, if he should turn to evil, he becomes abnormal. In other words, depending upon the prevailing criterion, mental illness meant being irrational or bad, or both. Even today, although the common prejudice against mental diseases is no longer officially upheld by medicine, the general public is still diffusely of the opinion that a mentally sick individual is an irrational, bad, weak or degenerate person. In point of fact, it is difficult if not impossible to define proper reason, good or strong character, health, or degeneracy, but they are taken for granted.

This a priori attitude is not limited to psychopathology and does not make it, though some would argue to the contrary, an unscientific system of speculations about the behavior of man. The biologist or physiologist, for example, deals with living tissues. He takes life for granted. He cannot define it very well, or even describe it adequately. He does not doubt that all his colleagues know, in the same way that he does, what life is; or better, he supposes that none of them knows any more than he, and they all proceed with their studies of life and living tissues, unembarrassed by their fundamental ignorance.

Read before the New York Psychoanalytic Society, April 30, 1940.

The same may be said of the physicist who deals with such fundamentals as force and matter. The major difficulty in a science is not the fact that it is frequently constructed on so called common sense assumptions of good, evil, reason, life, force or matter. The problem lies in how it deals with them. If, for instance, one accepts the inevitability of gravity, everything from a soap bubble to an aeroplane might be considered an illusion; since nothing can violate the law of gravity, anything that seems to deny it does not really exist, or is of the devil. On the other hand, the same respect for gravity might lead to the assumption that the contradiction is only apparent and we might proceed to investigate how the bubble circumvents the manifestations of gravity without violating the basic natural law.

This elementary and perhaps obvious principle of thought admits of mention because it is so often overlooked when we consider such a discipline as psychopathology, which is not an experimental science but is rather observational and descriptive. Paradoxical as it may seem, many a priori assumptions in psychopathology have proven psychologically correct, although their content has undergone considerable modification in the course of centuries. Irrationality is still accepted as a criterion of severe mental illness but we have learned to mistrust our absolutistic attitude towards what is rational. We study the thoughts and behavior of the psychotic and endeavor to discover the basic psychobiological rationale for the allegedly irrational reactions. That a mental disease may be an expression or result of sinfulness we still readily admit; but instead of endowing the concept of sin with an absolute, almost objective value which was the practice of the Catholic psychiatrist of the fifteenth century, or even the Protestant of the Nineteenth like Reil, we bear in mind the deeply subjective, mostly unconscious sense of sin which is the burden of the pathologically depressed patient. We call it the sense of guilt. We might call it the patient's private sin. When we consider a neurotic character or a schizophrenic, we still understand him to be a weak or evil character, though we have partially divested ourselves of that sermonizing attitude which casts the shadow of opprobrium on the patient. We speak more euphemistically of a social maladjustment, aggressive impulses and weak ego organization.

These are not superficial parallels. One wonders to what extent we still pass judgment on the patient. Is it not here that lies what the physicist calls the element of uncertainty? Does not our human equation still contribute a number of subjective, evaluative attitudes towards the psychopathological phenomena which we are studying with what appears to us the most dispassionate detachment, a detachment we like to call objectivity? Upon the answer which psychology may ultimately find for this query will depend the future status of mental sciences: whether psychology and psychopathology will at length become strictly scientific disciplines or return to the domain of pure philosophy and become again the prey of prejudice and speculative flights. The question seems not only basic but timely, if not really urgent, for the development of psychoanalysis within the last one or two decades has brought us face to face with it. We must now expect either that psychoanalysis will find a scientific answer or, if no solution is forthcoming, the psychopathologist will rightly turn away from psychoanalysis as one would abandon an unfinished dwelling whose architect insists that for some reason there need be no roof. The problem is put here so sharply not because I presume to have an answer. I have not. But there is hope that, if we take cognizance of certain salient facts, we may open an avenue which will lead us to a solution of the difficulty.

II

There was a time when psychoanalysis was primarily interested in subjective symptoms—anxieties, depressions, hysterical paralyses. It has also concerned itself with certain incapacities which permit a lesser subjective awareness of illness—hypomanic or depressive states, or neurotic behavior. It discovered the unconscious and for a period concentrated on the intensive analysis of the unconscious content of sexual trends and on the

detailed study of dreams. As soon as the extent and activity
of the unconscious sphere was established, it was recognized as
part and parcel of the total functioning of man's mind; the
concept of unity in psychological life suggested itself. The con-
tour of the psychic apparatus began to take shape before Freud's
mental eye. Further analysis of the ideational content of the
unconscious was by no means abandoned but the center of
attention was shifted a little and an additional problem arose:
what are the characteristics of mental functioning? As early
as 1911 Freud published his Formulations Regarding the Two
Principles in Mental Functioning. Using as a point of departure a thought expressed a little earlier by Pierre Janet that
every neurosis alienates the neurotic from actuality, Freud
sketched in broad but poignant lines the developmental road
from the pleasure principle to the reality principle. He concluded: 'Just as the pleasure-ego can do nothing but *wish*, work
towards gaining pleasure and avoiding "pain", so the reality-ego
need do nothing but strive for what is *useful* and guard itself
against damage. Actually, the substitution of the reality-
principle for the pleasure-principle denotes no dethronement
of the pleasure-principle, but only a safeguarding of it.' [1]

Freud was not unaware of the fact that the process of testing
reality was complex, often tenuous and fraught with uncertainties. Turning to the unconscious, he stated: 'There is a most
surprising characteristic of unconscious (repressed) processes to
which every investigator accustoms himself only by exercising
great self-control; it results from their entire disregard of the
reality-test; thought-reality is placed on an equality with external actuality, wishes with fulfilment and occurrence, just as
happens without more ado under the supremacy of the old
pleasure-principle.' [2] The importance of psychic reality thus
became apparent but this phenomenon, though familiar to all
students of analysis, has not been sufficiently correlated with
the process of reality testing. It is recognized as an empirical

[1] Freud: *Formulations Regarding the Two Principles in Mental Functioning.*
1911. Coll. Papers, IV. p. 18.
[2] *Ibid.,* p. 20.

finding of fundamental clinical significance but, as we shall presently see, it is not integrated with the whole problem of psychological functioning in the direction of developing the sense of reality. Freud did not confine himself to the statement of this finding or to a cursory glance at the use to which it should be put in our clinical work. After he had formulated his topographical concept of personality and prepared himself to review and revise his conception of anxiety, he returned in 1924 to certain implications contained in the phenomenon of psychic reality. Writing on The Loss of Reality in Neurosis and Psychosis, he described the manner in which the neurotic abandons his claim on certain aspects of reality and puts restrictions on the id, whereas the psychotic 'in another, a more lordly manner, creates a new reality which is no longer open to objections like that which has been forsaken'.

> '. . . Neurosis does not deny the existence of reality, it merely tries to ignore it; psychosis denies it and tries to substitute something else for it. . . . It is hardly possible to doubt that the world represents the store-chamber from which the materials or the design for constructing a new reality are obtained. But the new phantastic outer world of a psychosis attempts to set itself in place of external reality. That of neurosis, on the contrary, is glad to attach itself, like a children's game, to a part of reality—some other part than the one against which it must protest itself; it endows it with a special meaning and a secret significance which we, not always quite correctly, call *symbolical*. Thus we see that there arises both in neurosis and in psychosis the question not only of the *loss of reality,* but of a *substitute for reality* too.' Freud also stated: 'A reaction which combines features of both these is the one we call normal or "healthy"; it denies reality as little as neurosis, but then, like a psychosis, is concerned with effecting a change in it.' [3]

The consistency of these conclusions and their implications should be noted for further reference. Freud said in 1911:

[3] Freud: *The Loss of Reality in Neurosis and Psychosis.* 1924. Coll. Papers, II, pp. 279–282.

the reality principle seems to have come about not in opposition to but in order to safeguard the pleasure principle. To put it in our more recent terminology: the ego as an institution of the personality at no time loses its need or purpose to find adequate outlets for the id. Freud said in 1924: the constant loss of reality (relative weakening of the ego and corresponding strengthening of the id) and establishment of substitutes for reality are common to neurosis and psychosis and healthy normal states. Apparently it is a matter of quantitative relationships; it is a matter of the ego's strength in the job of keeping the id properly harnessed and bridled—not in order to bring it to a standstill, for this is impossible without a lethal exodus, but to make it walk rather than trot, to make it trot rather than gallop and to make it pull the ego along the road without fits and starts and with as few jolts as possible. It is also a matter of the ego's ingenuity in mastering and cajoling reality.

After forty years of investigation, psychoanalysis finds that the major part of its attention is drawn to the functions of the ego in relation to reality. Neuroses and psychoses are no longer looked upon as mere manifestations of repressed impulses and ideas but as forms of adjustments to reality. Psychoanalysis is not occupied solely with symptoms as such and with the ideational content of the unconscious. The symptoms reveal themselves as accidental by-products which are sloughed off when the real core of the personality difficulty is properly attacked. We have made more than a little headway in our study of the defenses used by the ego, of its synthetic and integrative functions in relation to the various units of the personality, but the ego's actual manipulation of reality has hardly been taken into consideration. Our interest seems to have skipped over this particular aspect of the problem.

We may properly wonder why imperceptibly we turned away from a better understanding of the rôle of the ego in the problem of reality and instead concentrated on the biological and cultural forces that throw their impact against the ego. That we should be aware of these external forces is obviously of utmost importance, but the question is whether we can understand their real significance as long as we do not fully know which of them are external and which merely externalized formations of the ego. The whole problem would be immeasurably simplified if we were able to establish once and for all what reality really is. We could then take it as an established datum, invariable under certain conditions, and proceed with our deeper investigation of the ego. Unfortunately, reality is one of the unknowables in science; it is for abstract philosophy to speculate about it. We must take it for granted in the same manner as the physiologist takes life for granted. We may, as we always do, call it diffusely the outer world, but we can also proceed to look at it from the standpoint of the ego and see what psychological components enter into the formation of our concept of it.

III

We envisage and always evaluate the relationship between the ego and reality by determining how much true interest we have in reality, that is, with how much libido we invest the object. The concept of cathexis proved to be so useful and convenient that we overlooked the essential characteristic of the process of investing objects (persons or things) with libido. This process certainly does not mean that a particular amount of libido, like so much ethereal substance, actually flows in space and time, invisibly but materially, from the individual to the object. It means that our psychic or perceptive apparatus bears an image of the object, not a photographic image, but something we call the representation of the object and, once within our psychic apparatus, this representation is invested with libido and in some unknown way correlated with our sensorimotor system. We are then able to feel and act in relation to the object. The representation is not a primary and spontaneous result of our psychic activity, but takes time both phylo- and ontogenetically to develop. In the beginning the images of the outside world do not produce representations; they remain

images and are taken for the objects themselves. Thus the
dream has equal weight with reality. As a recent German
writer puts it, this status of the image signifies not a lack of
discrimination but a 'de-realizing' of external phenomena which
are regarded by the primitive man simply as appearances that
seek to report something to the individual, while the individual
actually fills the world with his own images.[4] This is the animistic stage of primitive people and of children. The libidinous charges are concentrated not on the images of things but
on the fantasies generated by them. This is the quintessence of
psychological reality which ideally conceived is totally dereistic
and animistic.

If we now try to conceive an equally ideal realistic state, one
in which the psychic apparatus is guided only by the reality
principle, we shall have to construct an individual who is never
disturbed by any fantasy and who sees things only as they
allegedly are and does not elaborate upon them. Such an individual, whose total energies are directed towards things, or their
representatives, will actually have no desires, no feelings, no
sense of contradiction. In his eyes the outer world will continue to function in its own way and he will have no impulse
to alter it. Such a hypothetical man, devoid of the discomforts
coming from the id and the inconveniences imposed by the
superego, is no individual at all. One may conceive of his
existence only as an abstraction without meaning.

Human beings function somewhere between these two absolute states of animism and realism. Naturally, there are infinite
gradations between them, imperceptible transitions, mixtures
of one with the other in a great variety of proportions.
Nietzsche sensed this in his concept that any distinction between
reality and appearance is purely arbitrary and destroys the unity
of mental life. 'His emphasis therefore was upon mental attitudes and experiences as primary events, while sensory reactions
were of secondary importance, since in each situation psychic

    [4] Lipps, H.: *Die Wirklichkeit bei den Naturvölkern.* Fortschr. Deutch. Wiss.,
XV, 1939, pp. 353–354. *Cf.* Psychological Abstracts, XIV, No. 3, March, 1940,
p. 152.

unity prevailed in the man-environment relationship.' [5] Psychic unity cannot be defined in any absolute terms. It is probably that state of the psychic apparatus which we call 'healthy' and which Freud referred to as a certain combination of loss of and substitution for reality.

This psychic harmony is subject to a variety of disturbances which are not strictly pathological. The child who begins to enjoy playing with toys is an illustration in point. It takes toy after toy with apparent realistic interest. It plays with the toy a while, then discards or breaks it. Broken or unbroken, the plaything is abandoned without regret and the child turns its attention to something else. This phase of childhood development is a definitive one and lasts for a considerable period, probably until the termination of the latency period. Its outstanding characteristic is the alternation of apparently intense interest in the object and complete indifference to it. Because the child displays great keenness of observation and a sense of detail during this period, one at first gains the impression that it is now fully attached to reality and then back in its semi-animistic state. Closer inspection reveals a different psychological picture. 'It would be incorrect to think that he [the child] does not take this world seriously; on the contrary, he takes his play very seriously and expends a great deal of emotion on it. The opposite of play is not serious occupation but—reality. Notwithstanding the large affective cathexis of his play-world, the child distinguishes it perfectly from reality [I would say its play is different from reality. It is questionable whether the child really distinguishes reality so perfectly. G. Z.]; only he likes to borrow the objects and circumstances that he imagines from the tangible and visible things of the real world.' [6] The child seems to strive not for mastery and control over reality but for a kind of temporary self-assertion over the object and

[5] Wagner, K.: Über die Grundlagen der psychologischen Forschung Friedrich Nietzsches. Ztschr. Psych., CXLVI, 1939. Cf. Psychological Abstracts, XIV, No. 4, April, 1940, p. 174.

[6] Freud: The Relation of the Poet to Day-dreaming. 1908. Coll. Papers, IV, p. 174.

appears to have no other goal than to enjoy the grasping. It is easy to discern a hungerlike need to 'take it all in' and a certain distractibility which are similar in psychological tone to hypomanic states and the other typical attitudes of oral incorporation. One is tempted to say that in this period the child constantly takes bites out of reality; it is tasting rather than testing. It does not synthesize and correlate realities well until later when the anal cathexes of the latency period become integrated with the ego and the superego. Before this integration takes place the individual functions not on the level of reality but on that of the concrete. If I may be permitted, I should like to say that the child is concretistic, not realistic.

The same attitude comes clearly to light in schizophrenics who seem to see and observe certain things quite well but somehow do not endow their relationship to the object with any affective tone. They drop it as easily as they pick it up. The nonpsychotic, schizoid person also lives under the domination of the concretistic attitude, which at times is very deceiving. Recently Helene Deutsch mistook it for a truly realistic attitude and considered it typical of Americans. The patients she cited appeared to be schizoid personalities and incipient schizophrenics, characters by no means confined to this side of the Atlantic. The lack of affective tone in such cases is easily understood in the light of the fact that oral incorporative reactions are closely associated with the animistic phase. Under these conditions there exists no true object representation that one holds and invests with libido; there is only an image of the concrete, not of the real. The sense of the concrete is orally destructive, whereas the sense of the real is retentive and constructive. Any destructive drive which cannot be mastered because of outside circumstances or inner disability reduces the contact with reality and leads to the reassertion of the animistic reactions, impoverishment of the ego and sometimes a nihilistic attitude toward the world or one's own self.

The sense of somatic unreality in certain profound depressions and schizophrenias, depersonalizations, ecstatic states of conversion, or other mystical experiences come to mind to illustrate this psychological condition. I once observed the phenomenon *in statu nascendi*, where the process revealed itself with utmost clarity.

The patient, a man in his early thirties, appeared dull and depressed, blocked and retarded. He kept his eyes closed and, when presented at a staff meeting, he hardly responded to any of the questions put to him. At one point he seemed to be aroused from his semimutism. He opened his eyes and, looking away from the people in the room, his gaze fixed as if on a very distant object, he said that he did not know exactly what was happening, that things appeared close at first, then moved farther and farther away. His eyes became half shut as if trying to focus on a vaguely perceived and remote object. He was silent for a moment, then went on to say that things disappeared. His eyes filled with tears but his face remained masklike. At this point he said that he could hear a voice coming from the distance. He slumped into the state and posture which he had displayed throughout his stay in the hospital. He made no attempt to dry his tears.

The patient's representation of his parting with reality in terms of space is in itself not unusual; it is rather a universal propensity of human psychology. The striking features are the precision with which the patient described the transition to the loss of reality and the attempt to retrieve it by means of turning in the direction of an animistic condition which appeared in the form of a hallucinatory projection. On the borderline of this transition, one could observe the loss of affect, or rather the schizophrenic modification of it. The tears appeared just as he was psychologically losing his last hold on the object but at the moment it was gone from him his eyes closed, as if he did not need to try to look any longer. His tears were left to run down his cheeks as if he were no longer aware of them, for they or the feeling they expressed belonged no more to his world.

This schizophrenic episode illustrates but the extreme form of a process which is constantly operative under a variety of nonclinical circumstances. We know that the loss of reality is accompanied, if not caused by a considerable reduction of ego functioning which is always intertwined with strong aggressive impulses. In Chekhov's play, Three Sisters, the old army doctor, Chebutikin, is a kindly, somewhat gruff, garrulous and sentimental old man; he drinks. We find him at the basin washing his hands. The wine clouds his mind a bit and leads him into the following somewhat surly soliloquy:

> 'The devil take it all . . . smash them all. . . . Here I am thinking that I am a doctor and that I can treat folks for all sorts of afflictions—yet I don't know a thing about medicine. I have forgotten everything I ever knew. I don't remember a thing . . . not a thing. . . . Damn it. . . . Last Wednesday I was called in to see a sick woman. Well, she died and—it is my fault that she died. Yes, sir. Some twenty years ago, I must have known a little, but I don't remember anything. I am not even a man but merely make believe that I am one, just make believe that I have hands and feet and a head too! Mayhap, I don't exist at all but it only seems to me that I walk, eat, sleep. (He weeps.) Oh, if only I would not exist. Damn it. The other day I was in the club; they talked about Shakespeare and Voltaire. I never read those fellows—but I made a face, as if I did. The others too did exactly the same thing as I did. Dirty—plain low and dirty—and that woman whom I killed last Wednesday came to my mind—everything came back to me and I felt low and dirty and went and got drunk.'

The old doctor dries his hands and goes out into the adjoining living room. Paying little attention to those present, he picks up an old porcelain clock, a family heirloom, and begins to examine it with utmost care. Suddenly it slips from his hands and falls to the floor. There is general consternation. The doctor takes a good look at what has just been a good clock and proclaims with humble solemnity, 'Busted to pieces', as if this were the logical outcome of his righteous and self-humiliatory disgust. And natural outcome it was. The aggressive impulses aroused by the death of his patient and the consequent sense of guilt were turned on himself and produced an intense conflict. For a moment he had quasi-suicidal fantasies which led him to a denial of his own existence, but this solution his sufficiently strong ego would not permit. His aggression was again everted to the outer world. Displacement of the aggression to the porcelain clock is but a neat attempt to drag the world into perdition, even as a moment before he had tried to drag his own ego; at the same time it is probably an attempt on the part of the persisting ego to test its ability to master.

Drunk as the old doctor was, he represents a more or less normal reaction: he escaped the total loss of reality by managing to pick up and to master a substitutive part of it, thus restoring his waivering ego to a new sense of strength and reality. That the final stage in this brief drama presents a symptomatic act does not make it really pathological since it was a mere slip, an 'accident', rather than murder or suicide.

A so called normal reaction, however, need not necessarily run this course. The aggressive impulse may put the individual a step farther away or deeper down, and 'healthy' adjustment may be achieved by way of, for example, a simple religious fantasy which is the animistic level. It is 'healthy' even though it sacrifices a great deal of reality. A very nice instance of this type of adjustment is found in a scene from Dostoyevski's Brothers Karamazov. Dmitri is the quixotic and reckless, half-fallen nobleman, half-risen bourgeois. Tense and hectic, he sits in a carriage trying to engage the driver in conversation. The driver is one of those humble and gentle peasants of old Czarist Russia who carries the burden of life in a Christlike manner of nonresistance. He has borne oppression for so many generations that he represses even his awareness of protest. The official serf of the previous generation and the actual slave of the generation of the Karamazovs, he is not very communicative, but Dmitri continues to prod him and the driver finally speaks:

'You see, Sir, when the Son of God was crucified and died,
He came down from the Cross and went straight to Hell, and
He set free all sinners who had been suffering there for many

years. Hell began to groan, for it thought that this meant no more sinners would be sent there. And Jesus spoke: "Oh, Hell, don't groan. Thou shalt not remain empty; there will be sent to thee all sorts of noblemen, rulers, judges and rich folk and thou wilt stay filled even as thou hast been for ages, until the day when I come again." This is the truth, Sir; this was the word.'

The appealing simplicity of this belief in a hell that is alive, endowed with thought and voice, is characteristic substitutive reality in such a case of apparently relentless, although unconscious hatred. The 'healthy' submissiveness of the ego takes the form of serene humility, denying and repressing the very existence of the cheerless reality and the protest against the need to make a living by driving reckless, rich drunkards from brothel to brothel. This submission could be reached only by creating a new religious reality which is achieved by means of a double identification. The philosophic driver identifies himself with the Christ, crucified and kind, and with the Hell which is going to torture the rulers, the noblemen, the judges and the rich—all those who are (unconsciously) held responsible for the stark fate of the peasants, the humble sinners released from Hell by Christ's own hand.

This normal adaptation by means of what Freud once called an 'illusion' is actually a substitutive reality. One is inclined to agree with René Laforgue when he said, 'I don't follow Freud when he calls religious belief an "illusion". It is only from a certain level of our ego development that religious belief appears to us an illusion, exactly in the same manner as some of our scientific beliefs of yesterday, and also of today.' [7]

It is obvious that in the so called normal states in which the sensorium is clear and the sense of gross reality is unimpaired, the ego, the central apparatus for realistic synthesis, possesses a sense of reality quite different from that which we seem to

[7] Laforgue, René: *Relativité de la Réalité; Réflexions sur les Limites de la Pensée et la Genèse du Besoin de Causalité.* Paris: Les Éditions Denoël, 1937, p. 64. (Trans. published by Nerv. and Ment. Disease Monographs, New York, 1940.)

assume. Our assumption, never clearly formulated but clearly pervading our attitudes and clinical writings, is that a true reality exists which, if we are to remain psychologically healthy, we ought to learn to perceive and to evaluate lucidly and factually. Our assumption does not seem to correspond to the true state of affairs. Each so called objective fact is actually a composite made up of the image of the object and a variable number of nihilistic and animistic qualities as well as direct projections of our fantasies into the image. In other words, when the image, a concrete, purely perceptive affair is incorporated orally, it becomes in the course of our ego development the prey of our anal-sadistic drives. It is engulfed as it were in a struggle which produces progressive combinations with these destructive drives, identifications, self-preservative reactions, projections and magic animation, all of which form a psychological alloy called object representation. The narcissistic or egotistic elements undergo a corresponding change which we call love. Our relationship to the object representation we call object love. The status of the representation and object love are constantly maintained through the eternal need for perceptive, concretistic reactions—that is, contact with and interest in the outside world.

The sense of reality is, therefore, not the static result of a certain psychological developmental process but is a fluid, changeable and, one is tempted to add, inconstant as well as inconsistent quality of the psychic apparatus, a quality that permits us to master and modify the concrete, to make it 'useful' to us. This usefulness depends upon the very inconstancy or the pliability of the sense of reality which guarantees its functional ability. It depends upon those instinctual elements which generate psychological reality and which become an integral part of every new object representation formed.

Perhaps the simplest example of this is our reaction to such an object as a picture. We never speak of a picture merely as a picture. We always speak of it or at least perceive it as 'beautiful', 'powerful', 'convincing', or 'weak', 'disturbing', 'indifferent', 'disgusting'. We always combine our awareness of the picture, the image of it, with a number of animistic or sado-masochistic projections, and only in this combination does the picture become an object representation. Only then do we form a sense of reality.

IV

True scientific investigation, both theoretical and clinical, must consider the component of animistic projection of the object representation as a most potent element of uncertainty. It is highly subjective in its unconscious constellations and, coming as it does from the id, it carries a strong affective tone which adds to uncertainty. This feature of our sense of reality, although couched in different terms and approached from a different angle, led Laforgue to speak of the relativity of reality. The elements which make for this relativity have also another feature which we must bear in mind if we are to understand the functioning of the sense of reality at any given moment. In so far as our sciences are created by man, they cannot help but be colored by those psychological realities which are projected as animistic trends into the scientific constructions. Every time a body of knowledge is systematized, every time a scientific theory is formulated, the animistic projections are smuggled in and acquire the authority and weight of the scientific system itself. We are never able to rid ourselves of this body of animistic elements but, unless we recognize them and evaluate them accordingly, it will be impossible for us to discount the uncertainty and to increase our approximation to valid understanding of our observations. This is particularly true of mental sciences in which greater complications arise from the fact that the ego, which is the chief transmitter and regulator of knowledge, is called upon to perform a double task. It must investigate the animistic and projective factors which are the main sources of error; yet these very same elements present the foundation for the ego's existence and the guarantee for its functioning; they are the connective tissue supporting the nuclei of the ego.

It is incumbent upon every psychological investigator who

deals with the unconscious to understand the psychology of his own method. Unless he does so, scientific research is impossible or it becomes a mere displacement reaction as in every compulsion neurotic symptom. The work of research will then serve a biphasic purpose—a flight from the understanding of the animistic projective elements and at the same time a gratification derived from the vicarious manipulation of them. Sciences rise and fall through the centuries because of this characteristic, and one may say with Laforgue that 'despite appearances to the contrary the majority of intellectuals and scientists are still today more or less on the religious level of thought'.[8] I understand by 'religious' not the ceremonial elaborations of religion but its essential animistic content.

That the animistic drive is always present and is at times of intense power is revealed by the lives of certain scientists. They preoccupied themselves for most of their lives with concrete, seemingly 'realistic' subject matter, but in the course of years began to behave as if they never had learned much from their investigations. As the cohesion between the integral elements of their ego began to loosen (as a result of biological involution or a severe neurosis), they fell into the pit of a purely animistic world. Oliver Lodge turned from physics to commune with the dead. Charles Richet, a physiologist of great repute, spent his later years in the same preoccupation. Auguste Comte, the positivist and logician, became a mystic.

What is true of the individual scientist is true also of the various systems of thought which have dominated our sciences at various periods of history. Whenever animism with its projections claimed a part of the outer world, that part remained totally inaccessible to scientific investigation. The Egyptians are a case in point. Despite the relatively advanced state of their science they were unable to study the sun. Saussure in his excellent work on the Greek miracle called attention to the fact that 'In Egypt the sun was the chief divinity, Rha Amon and later Rha Aton. Like any father or father symbol, it was taboo, just as Jehovah was to the Jews. One recalls in this

[8] *Ibid.*, p, 87.

connection the commandment, "Thou shalt not create any image of thy God". Consequently, the Egyptian calendar was calculated not in relation to the sun but to the star of first magnitude, Sirius.' [9] There is an interesting and potent inference in this phenomenon: any magico-religious animism or its philosophic equivalent diminishes our curiosity, stunts the drive to master the world through learning what it is, reduces the passive sense of reality, which is the ability to perceive, and thus inhibits or dissolves the dynamic force of our sense of reality. This may explain the romantic fascination as well as the scientific sterility of Platonism or philosophic idealism in general.

It is worth pondering over this subject for a while. The idealist is basically an animist; he knows of no other reality than the ideas of things. His ego, like any 'primitive ego, puts itself in the center of the universe and believes itself to be able by its actions to set into motion all events of life, those which are desired as well as those which are feared'.[10] In other words, Platonisms or idealism make man's reasoned will the alpha and omega of the system of the universe. The outer world, not the one populated with his animistic projections, presents little interest for him. He is more concerned with how to make men behave and live within the sphere of his projections. Consequently Plato's chief preoccupation was not science but political sociology. Man, the center of the world, feels most central and most magically potent within the sphere of public activity; it gives him the strongest illusion of omnipotence. Platonism is essentially a religious system couched in political terms. Its reality is a purely individual, private reality which Plato tried to translate into terms of sociological constructions. One might express surprise that despite the preëminently religious nature of Platonism, it not only proved unacceptable to Christianity, the most powerful religious system of our civilization, but it was actually rejected and is still being combatted with utmost violence. From the standpoint of consistent monotheism, Plato

[9] *Ibid.*, p. 61.
[10] *Ibid.*, p. 94.

is totally unacceptable not because of his animistic ideology but because, having placed man in the center of the universe which was his Republic, Plato made peace with his homosexuality. He extolled its manifest sensual form and brought it down straight to earth in its socialized cultural form. He wanted the fathers, the wise, good and omniscient fathers, to rule his Republic and the sons to follow in simple, serene obedience, not in fear but in a blessed state of welcome passivity. In making the idea of the State and supreme reason his sublime authorities, Plato forgot God. Again citing Laforgue, one should not overlook that the prerequisite, the quintessence of established religious belief, is the surrender of one's omnipotence to the Godhead, the Father. 'It is only God who is omnipotent, but man gains or loses his right to protection from God depending on whether his behavior is good or bad.' [11]

Modern monotheism leaves to us the outer world, permits us to deal with it at will, grants us a moderate degree of the sense of reality—provided we give up our aggression and preserve our passivity. The primitive anthropocentric drive, never fully given up by any individual, finds itself best accommodated and least thwarted in the atmosphere of established monotheism. These circumstances may involve no sacrifice to the adult sense of reality, because religion is taught from childhood and the individual does not rise fully to that synthesis of ego formation which develops a sense of reality. On the other hand, if a sacrifice is offered, the individual is fully repaid by the libidinous gratifications tendered on the magic, narcissistic level. In either case, however, a certain balance of forces is established within the ego, a sense of harmony which in itself serves as a very restrictive force both on the libidinal development and on the sense of reality. In this orientation uncertainty in psychological investigation assumes considerable dimensions and the development of mental sciences becomes inevitably impeded. In some respects it even stops and our knowledge becomes static. This has been the status of mental sciences wherever

[11] *Ibid.*, p. 94.

and whenever the Thomistic edition of Aristotelianism has prevailed. Even in the Protestant world the mere deviation from
formal dogma and the establishment of heresy have not
removed the impedimenta of animism. The whole history
of the controversy between the somatologists and the psychologists demonstrates this point conclusively. The somatologist
left his animistic world undiscussed and untouched, while the
proponent of the naïve psychogenesis of mental diseases merely
claimed more territory for his animism and continued to
reduce mental sickness to sin.

The struggle for and against the assertion of one's animism
is universally one of the most decisive factors in the development of human thought and man's knowledge of himself. It
is a force always present in our work and, therefore, our culture, and it can be recognized in every walk of human endeavor.
We submit to it either under cultural pressure or under the
pressure from within. Darwin first omitted to mention the
Creator in his Origin of Species and was severely criticized.
Huxley urged him not to pay any heed to the attacks but
Darwin admitted the Creator to his second edition. The
important fact is not whether Darwin was convinced that his
was a serious omission, or whether he merely decided to make
an insincere bow to bigotry. The point is that Darwin did not
have sufficient courage. Perhaps Huxley would have lacked it
too had he been the author of the Origin of Species. This lack
of courage in Darwin, as in Galileo, cannot be disposed of with
the reprobatory epithet, 'cowardly'. It is but a sign that somewhere both Galileo and Darwin had a lingering feeling that
the 'world' was or might be right.

Wagner, as Nietzsche reminds us in a tone of morose sarcasm,
started with enthusiastic hopes to write as his first opera a
hymn of rebellion and hedonistic freedom. It was to be called
Luther's Wedding. He never wrote it. He ended his work
with the pious purity and mystic humility of Parsifal.

It is difficult for man to learn to get along in life without a
father. In fact, it is not possible for him fully to achieve this
independence. 'In the measure that he is obliged to act with-

out a father and without absolute values, that is with a sense of relativity, he becomes perhaps reconciled to death, which we have not yet learned to face rationally by pressing it into our service.' [12]

The basic difficulties of our scientific approach to the world are the same as the difficulties encountered in the development of the sense of reality. These stumbling blocks are of particular and detrimental moment in the growth of mental sciences. If we reduce them to a simple dogmatic enumeration they are: (1) the constant pressure of our idealized hedonism which forces us to perceive man as the most unique phenomenon of nature; (2) the animistic trends which are endowed with sufficient dynamic initiative to keep the ego in check and always threaten to overrun it; and (3) the projections of both the anthropocentric and animistic fantasies into the outer world, thereby forcing the ego to perceive these projections as if they were the outer world and not merely an integral, supportive component of that world.

The development of scientific attitudes tends to control the influence of those impedimenta, but at times these attitudes themselves fall victim to the forces they seem to combat. The sense of reality is again impaired by too great an admixture of psychological reality which weakens the useful value of the object representations. We can see in a more specific way how this process works in the field of psychology.

V

Psychology has made a definite effort to find for itself a place, no matter how modest, among the natural sciences. For a time, before the discovery of psychoanalysis, it assumed the guise of a materialistic discipline and always wore the uniform of anatomy and physiology. That this was only a mask is obvious. By reducing psychological processes to structure and physiological function, psychology actually set aside the whole problem of psychic activity and left it where it had always been—

[12] *Ibid.*, p. 65.

in the domain of idealistic or animistic philosophy. The real incorporation of psychology into natural science was brought about by psychoanalysis. This fact is true whether the official representatives of natural sciences fail to recognize it or summarily reject it. Under the influence of Darwin, and perhaps even more under that of Lamarck, a theory of evolution of the psychic apparatus was evolved. Man was removed as it were from his anthropocentric animistic throne, or at least the throne was given a very disrespectful, revolutionary jolt. 'By putting concrete problems concerning the development of human consciousness out of the elementary needs of organic life and up to its highest rational manifestations, modern naturalism claims to have actually and definitively incorporated man into nature. Reason itself, as manifested in science, is then only a continuation of the natural evolution of the animal world, the latest stage of adaptation of living beings to their environment; and all the forms of thinking on which idealism constructs its systems are products of the natural reality and, as instruments of adaptation, dependent both on their natural object-matter and on the natural organization of the living beings who use them.' [13] The claim that man in his totality belongs to nature evoked a double opposition. Confirmed idealism would not accept any such 'humiliation' of man. Opposition to the claims and scientific inferences of psychoanalysis can be easily understood in the light of the ego's inability or extreme reluctance to give up the sense of exclusiveness in relation to the world.

The motivations that led biological sciences to raise strict objections to psychoanalysis are less obvious. At first these objections seem to grow out of a candid wish to be strictly scientific and to avoid anything that appears to spoil by allegedly idealistic intrusions the realistic air in which science operates. Closer psychological inspection of the situation offers a somewhat different picture. It has been repeatedly emphasized that natural sciences were willing to accept man and to include

[13] Znaniecki, Florian: *Cultural Reality*. Chicago: The University of Chicago Press, 1919, pp. 3-4.

him within the realm of their endeavors only on the condition that the true operation of his psychic apparatus, with the exception of formal logic, be left to the speculative and affective fields, the idealistic philosophies, theology, metaphysics and that vague and chameleonic little idol called common sense. Science resisted and still resists the introduction of man in his totality as subject matter, not on scientific but on purely idealistic grounds. These idealistic grounds, as we have seen above, are the same anthropocentric, animistic ones that operate in other human attitudes. It would appear that philosophy and religion rejected psychoanalysis in the manner of a hysteric who, unable to accept certain libidinous claims, rejects them as foolish and bad fantasies which have to be repressed. The scientist completed the same process of rejection in the manner of the compulsive neurotic who isolates a given number of libidinous claims and treats them as foreign to his own self-conscious, voluntary, free activities.[14]

Whatever our formal claims for understanding and working with and on reality, the sense of reality is always marred by the ego's own fears of giving up not its realistic but its libidinous, animistic propensities. We cannot overlook this fact in the development of our own scientific peregrinations and vacillations in the field of psychoanalysis. That is to say, there is no reason why we should not expect ourselves to be involved in the same struggle and frequently in the same confusion as to a clear appreciation of reality and as to the limits of our ability to develop any degree of such appreciation. Involved we are indeed, even more than we realize and much more than the disciples of other sciences. For psychoanalysis the question which has become the cardinal problem of our work happens to concern our relationship with the outside world and the working of the apparatus within us which deals with this relationship. In many if not all productive sciences

[14] I am indebted to Dr. David M. Levy, who in discussion of this paper called my attention to the work of James K. Leuba. The statistical conclusions of Dr. Leuba regarding religious beliefs among various scientific groups seem to corroborate the point of view arrived at here through purely psychological analysis.

this question is not even raised; no other discipline depends so much upon a sober approach to the problem and no other discipline is so much in danger of serious breakdown if it does not effect an adequate approximation to a solution. We ought to appreciate fully the importance of this point. The fact that psychoanalysis may fail of solution and end in scientific dissolution is in itself not important because no science will survive if it fails to do what it is supposed to do. Though we may still use the word 'lunatic', astrology, so prevalent for centuries, has disappeared from the community of scientific systems and no one regrets or feels its absence. Of greater danger is the anxiety of those who, identified with a given science, try to save it by artificial means. The danger becomes more serious if these means prove to be dogmatic and consist of all the unconvincing but very stubborn methods of conceptual manipulation which never prove anything and never save anyone. For conceptual manipulations, particularly in a problem concerned with reality, by their very nature deal with absolutes and not with empirical and pragmatic relativities and they are bound to become more scholastic than enlightening. We may speculate a great deal about ego structure, ego weakness and ego strength, visualize a variety of mathematical permutations even greater than the Newtonian binomial complexities, and yet come not one inch closer to a better understanding of the sense of reality. One need not pursue the argument at greater length. It suffices to recall that any conceptual thinking is dereistic and leaves little room for the productive elucidation of a problem. In recent years, psychoanalysis has begun to show here and there trends towards such conceptualization. These trends are not necessarily signs of the failure of psychoanalysis itself; they are indications of the difficulties of the problem and the strength of our own resistances when we begin to test reality.

I do not wish to suggest that psychoanalysis in its totality has become conceptual, but there is no doubt that the humorous remark of Freud in which he called metapsychology 'the witch' contains more than a grain of truth. Any attempt to preserve psychoanalysis on the sole foundation of metapsychology, which is the tendency in many quarters, would lead inexorably into more animistic projections and to less enrichment of the reservoir of scientific object presentations. The scientific position of psychoanalysis was vouchsafed not so much by its conceptual richness as by its empirical naturalism. It is close kin to truly natural sciences, to biology in the broadest sense of the term.

Once the problem of the sense of reality is confronted and once the major problems of psychopathology have become questions of ego functioning and adjustment to reality, it is inevitable that social or cultural reality should become one of the most important fields of our investigation and the most fertile testing ground of ego adaptation. It is not necessary here either to emphasize the importance of cultural factors or to recite the history of their inclusion in the orbit of our observation and study. Cultural anthropology and psychological sociology of today owe their impetus and their findings to psychoanalysis. It is interesting in this connection to mention as an example the original opposition to Totem and Taboo. Kroeber recently returned to this contribution of Freud [15] and, twenty years after his original attack on the little book, admitted its importance. In the light of what was learned by anthropologists in the last decade, he accepts a number of Freud's assertions which he had originally rejected, but he is still reluctant to consider Freud's topography of the personality as valid—in other words, the naturalistic approach to the genesis of what we call personality still arouses considerable opposition. Herein lies the most important source of our difficulties. Cultural reality, like any other reality, is a product of our general development. The termites, the bees, the ants also live in a social unification and also actively maintain their communal unity with a great deal of tenacity; but they are not human and therefore they do not talk or write and tell what they have performed; and they do not claim any special and unique credit for their biosociological performance.

It is a very interesting coincidence, one of the many coinci-

[15] Kroeber, A. L.: *Totem and Taboo in Retrospect.* Amer. J. of Soc., XLV, No. 3. November, 1939, pp. 446–451.

dences in this history of thought, that culturalism began to assert itself as the source of the many answers to questions about the human mind almost simultaneously with the beginning of psychoanalytic studies of the ego. Like many other systems of thought it proved a double-edged sword. It cut into the solid darkness of many a problem but it also cut the psychological solidity of many an analyst.

Let me quote a characteristic passage or two from one of the best exponents of culturalism. 'History of culture', says Znaniecki, 'is the only field in which we can follow directly and empirically at least a part of the evolution of the human "mind" and the only theory of mind which can be directly based upon empirical data is therefore a theory which takes mind as a product of culture.' [16] 'If therefore modern thought intends to avoid the emptiness of idealism and the self-contradictions of naturalism, it must accept the culturalistic thesis. . . . It must maintain against naturalism that man as he is now is not a product of the evolution of nature, but that, on the contrary, nature as it is now is, in a large measure at least, the product of human culture, and if there is anything in it which preceded man, the way to find this leads through historical and social sciences, not through biology. . . .' [17]

While these lines were not written by a psychoanalyst, they express many a claim brought forth in the course of the history of psychoanalysis by some of those whose relation to analysis is indisputable. These claims are partly reminiscent of the old dictum: *Tempora mutantur et nos mutamur in illis.* But the fact that we change the times does not necessarily imply that we change because of the times. One reason is most frequently put forward as to why culture should be considered a phenomenon apart from the rest of the world and why it should be taken as a self-made, self-sustained and self-improving entity. This reason is very illuminating and of particular value for the topic under discussion. It is that culture is supposed to make man, and man is supposed to have made

[16] Znaniecki: *Op. cit.*, p. 15.
[17] *Ibid.*, pp. 21–22.

culture. Something extrabiological, extranatural, is founded and man is considered part and parcel of his own creation. He is placed over nature, outside of his purely biological, purely natural status. We recognize in this cleavage from biology not so much an unscientific denial of biological forces, but a forceful assertion of the independence of the human psychic apparatus from everything except the creations of man himself. Theoretically such a premise would suggest a restitution of the animistic, idealistic world at the sacrifice of a good part of realistic orientation. The validity of this inference is subject to denial and its implications to rejection in the same manner and with the same intolerance as the somatologist rejects any suspicion that deep underneath he really has a purely animistic view of the psychic apparatus. Fortunately, it is not necessary to test this attitude by means of purely formalistic logic. The fact is that the culturalist definitely deals with such purely idealistic data or goals as cultural progress, ultimate achievements and justice. He cannot help but be a reformer. As soon as pure culturalism is espoused, one hears of ultimate truth not so much about man as for the sake of man, and one 'should not forget that for a number of people today truth has more the character of religious faith than that of scientific evidence'.[18] In addition to these idealistic components which are of general nature, we find the tendency to lift man to exalted heights. As Karen Horney aptly puts it, 'when the "ego" is no longer regarded as an organ merely executing or checking instinctual drives, such human faculties as will power, judgment, decisions are reinstated in their dignity'.[19]

There is yet another trend which enables us to test exclusivistic culturalism for the presence of animistic projection and anthropocentric idealism. This is the denial of the totality of the biological forces which are responsible for the formation of the psychic apparatus, the denial of the theory of instincts

[18] Laforgue: *Op. cit.*, p. 64.
[19] Horney, Karen: *New Ways in Psychoanalysis*. New York: W. W. Norton, & Co., Inc., 1939, pp. 10–11.

as well as the rhythmic, spontaneous repetitiveness of psycho-biological reactions. In other words, culturalism in psychology seems to be derived from the same reactions as those other systems of thought which are unable to arrive at a true synthesis of the magic animistic components of the ego with the images of the concrete outside world. Having arrived at a point at which we are confronted with the fundamental problem of the sense of reality, it is psychologically inevitable that there be a convergence of all the lifelong conflicts with regard to how much absorption of the concrete the ego may permit at the expense of its own dependence on the magic projections.

This problem cannot be easily solved. It may never be solved. When psychoanalysis had to face the task of acknowledging the existence of the unconscious, it met the same difficulties. It seemed impossible for the omnipotent ego to recognize the existence of something that deprived it of a large part of its potency. However, when the ego learned that the unconscious could be reduced to a secondary position, where it could be recognized, understood, mastered, the ego began to show a willingness to let that unconscious be. The same is true of our aggressive impulses and anxieties. The ego finally learned to accept them only because it was convinced at length that it could dominate them, observe and hold in check these intruders into the harmony of life. When the problem of reality arises, the ego seems to be truly at a loss. The overwhelming magnitude of the macrocosm is so frightening that the ego has to fall back on the only resting place that once gave it comfort and a sense of well-being—on the genetically oldest and the strongest stage of animism from which and from the elaborated projections of which sprang that complexity called culture.

To surrender this support for the illusory hope of discovering its component parts is difficult for the human ego; it may never surrender it in sufficient measure and degree. The sense of reality is therefore bound to remain shifty, uncertain and in an eternal state of that unstable equilibrium which vacillates between knowledge and revelation and which at one and the same time produces health and generates disease.

4

FOLIE

A

DEUX

FOLIE A DEUX

BY HELENE DEUTSCH (BOSTON)

We understand by *'folie à deux'*, in the strictest sense of the term, the transference of delusional ideas from a person psychically ill to another person psychically healthy, who then accepts the delusional system of the ill person and assimilates it into the content of his own consciousness. It is not yet completely clear to us what enters into the psychological genesis of the induction, in addition to dispositional factors, close companionship, and all the other factors through which *folie à deux* is known to arise. The deeper psychological mechanisms which result in the psychic dependence on and identification with the primarily diseased person must still be subjected to analysis in every case.

In addition to the individual adoption of the psychic contents by one person from another, we also find the process as a mass phenomenon, where entire groups of psychically healthy people are carried away by psychically diseased members of the group: world reformers and paranoiacs, for example. Indeed, great national and religious movements of history and social revolutions have had, in addition to their reality motives, psychological determinants which come very close to the pathological processes of *folie à deux*.

In this presentation, I have limited myself exclusively to clinical observations and have chosen from among a number of cases, a few in which I shall make a special attempt to clarify the differences between hysterical and psychotic forms of *folie à deux*.

I

Many years ago, while associated with the Viennese Psychiatric Clinic, I published a summary of a number of cases of *folie à deux*,[1] and I shall take from this publication one case which affected a group of three members of the same family:

In 1918 there was admitted to the Psychiatric Clinic in Vienna a family, consisting of a mother, a daughter, and a son, all suffering from the same symptom-complex. The husband, father of the children, had gone to the front in 1915. Since 1916 there had been no news of him. According to a notification, not completely verified, he had been killed. The uncertainty and the anxiety about the fate of her husband, to whom she was very devoted, had aroused great turmoil and severe depression in the wife. These reactions were also manifested by her two children, with whom she had a particularly tender relationship.

For several months the woman had declared obstinately that her husband was alive and would soon come home. He had, she said, a position in the Swedish Consulate from which she received frequent written communications; moreover, an aristocratic rich family was taking care of her, was preparing a villa for her, and would buy her a car. She had connections with all the state authorities through this family, was plentifully supplied with food, and was about to move into a very elegant apartment prepared for her by the wealthy family in their own house. Her husband was to enjoy all this wealth after his return. A son of the wealthy family was to marry her daughter; a glorious future spread before her own son. The patient's two children shared in every detail their mother's delusions. Her relatives recognized these assertions as delusional, and had the three persons brought to the Clinic.

Here was an exceptionally vivid pseudologia phantastica in triplicate, the elaboration of a *folie à trois* in which each could gratify his own wishes. As soon as one member of the family was ready to correct an error, another introduced his ideas, and perpetuated a cycle. During the treatment of all three I observed that if I succeeded in correcting the ideas of one patient,

[1] Deutsch, Helene: *Kasuistik zum 'induzierten Irresein'.* Wiener klinische Wochenschrift, 1918.

he or she very soon tended to allow himself to be deluded again, but only in certain directions. The son, for example, abandoned the fantasy of a rich marriage for his sister, but not the fantasy in which he was to attain the 'great position' of his father. The same was true of the others who shared the delusion.

II

A seventeen-year-old girl came for psychoanalytic treatment with a diagnosis of incipient schizophrenia. Her father said that the girl had always been peculiar, preoccupied, and unsociable. Her mother had died when the child was ten years old. He had then, without assistance, assumed the task of her upbringing, and was very seldom separated from her. In the course of the last year he had made the acquaintance of a young woman and had revealed to his daughter his intention of marrying. The daughter had welcomed this proposal with great pleasure and had become very much attached to her future stepmother. After the marriage had taken place, the girl began to withdraw more and more from reality and to show changes in her personality. She sat motionless for hours at a time, laughed frequently without ascribable cause, lost contact with other people, and often gave vent to violent outbursts of anger, especially against her father.

The preceding summer the family had spent their vacation in a small Tyrolean village, where they had had a summer house years before. This was the first time the father had gone there since the death of his wife. In the little village there had lived for many years a psychotic man, who asserted that he was the Archduke Rudolph, the former heir to the Austrian throne who had died tragically while still a young man. Among the villagers in Austria there arose from time to time the rumor that the Archduke Rudolph had not died and that he would one day come back. The delusion of the paranoiac was founded on this rumor.

The girl now began to abandon her muteness, allied herself with the mentally sick man, declared that she was completely convinced he was the Archduke Rudolph, and that she would now devote her life to helping him establish his claims. No argument had any effect on her and the doctors consulted, advised that she be committed to an institution.

During a six-months' analysis I brought the patient to the point where she gave up the delusional idea, but I had, nevertheless, the impression that she was schizophrenic. Her father did not agree with this diagnosis, asserted that the patient was cured, and interrupted the treatment. I heard accidentally that the delusional idea did not reappear, but that the patient remained in a stuporous state.

We are interested here only in the psychological basis of her induced delusional idea. The analysis led directly to a 'romance of the family' [2] (*Familienroman*) that the patient had created during her childhood. In the Tyrolean village where she usually spent her vacations as a child, there was an ancient castle belonging to an aristocratic family. In her childhood the patient had created a fantasy, elaborated in the typical manner, that she was the daughter of this family. The analytic interpretation of such a 'family romance' is known to psychoanalysts and need not be discussed here in detail. It was a reaction to her infantile disappointment in her love for her father. On returning to this scene of her childhood some years later, desertion by her father, through his marriage, had become a cruel reality. The patient sought at first to find solace in her stepmother's love, but again disappointed, she

[2] The term 'family romance', as used by Freud, is the name for fantasies of different and manifold content, that are related to one another by their invariable connection with the descent of the person imagining them. The commonest content of the 'family romance' is: 'I am not my parents' child'; sometimes, 'not my father's (or mother's) child'. This negative statement is then followed by a positive one, in answer to the question: 'Whose child am I, then?' There are two typical, repeatedly recurring versions. The commoner is: 'I am of higher birth.' The other: 'I am of lower birth', is rarer.

The 'family romance' is an extremely common fantasy, and scarcely a single child does not experience it in one form or another. The motives for such fantasies are many and various. The provocation is always a disappointment, and the fantasy serves to compensate the child for deprivations it has suffered. *Cf.* Freud: *Familienroman der Neurotiker*, Ges. Schr., Vol. XII. Deutsch, Helene: *Ueber den Familienroman*, Int. Ztschr. f. Psa., XVI.

withdrew entirely into introversion and was already in a completely autistic state when she came to the summer place. The memories associated with the place revived the old fantasy of the 'family romance'. The earlier fantasy of childhood had been warm with object-relationships, although in an introverted form. Later, this fantasy had also perished in the *Weltuntergang* of her emotional life. Under the circumstances, and in the familiar setting, traces of the childhood fantasy were repetitively revived, but now in a psychotic manner. What had formerly been fantasy and had perished, was now rebuilt in the outer world as a delusion. The mechanism was not the suggestive influence exerted by the mentally sick man, nor an identification with him. The identification related merely to the delusional creation and lay in the fact that the content of his delusion was so close to her original fantasy. The analytic interpretation of the adopted delusion reads 'If it is true, that one can be the disowned child of high-born parents and have a justifiable claim to a throne, then it is also true that I am unjustly disowned and have a right to the old castle of my former day-dreams'.

This case shows a particular mechanism of the induction of a delusional idea which is completely independent of the inducing object, and has as a foundation an already existing psychic situation.

III

The third case is a *folie à deux* between a mother and daughter. There was no psychoanalytic treatment in this case. The material is taken from a case history in this country which was kept over a period of twelve years by a very conscientious social worker. This social worker was a particularly clever, intuitive, warm-hearted person, fortunately untouched by any knowledge of psychoanalysis or psychological terminology. This lack of knowledge makes the case history especially objective and valuable.

The social worker took charge of the child when she was ten, after the death of the child's father in an accident. The mother obviously had paranoia, but dissimulated so cleverly that she was never institutionalized. Since she took excellent care of the child, there was never any necessity during the twelve years for separating the mother from her daughter.

The mother's delusion was that enemies wanted to separate her from her daughter; she had to save the child from danger and return to the home of her own childhood, to her mother in Holland. Her entire life was built around this plan to return to Holland with her daughter. Enemies prevented her from accomplishing this, the scheme of her enemies being worked out in a typically paranoid way. She·gave lack of money as the reason for the postponement of her trip. Whenever she did collect the necessary amount, she made the excuse that she could not leave until she had made some arrangements about her husband's grave and provided for its future care. She obviously had an additional delusion which did not permit her to leave America—that is to say, her husband.

She lived in perpetual worry that people, men and women, would take her child away and prevent her daughter from going with her to Holland. *De facto* this meant: destroy the erotic bond between her and her daughter. The two-fold course of her homosexuality is interesting. The enemies were women, above all, social workers. The actual danger to the daughter, however, lay in men. Her chief anxiety centered upon a married man with many children, with whom her daughter was having a love affair. But it was his *mother* who was using the love affair to take her daughter away from her. The daughter had had in fact a love affair with this man but she soon broke the relationship for the sake of her mother and morality.

The daughter might be seen at times—especially after a quarrel with her mother—in a half-dazed condition, introverted, wandering around the streets of the city, searching for the married, tabooed man. She always returned to her mother in deep remorse, to resume the delusional plan for the journey and to try everything to make their departure possible, but also to prevent it, following the pattern of her mother's delusional idea. Finally she became engaged to a younger man, but put off her marriage for four years because she could not bring herself to frustrate by her marriage her mother's delusional obsession. At times she gave the impression that she was only making concessions to her mother's delusion under the pressure of a severe feeling of guilt towards her. Again she would accept her mother's delusion as reality—especially after any particularly strong impulse towards freeing herself from her mother.

The case history showed that the mother had left her husband in America when the child was two, and had lived in Holland with the child for four years. Obviously, she had the wish even then to separate the child from its father in order to possess it completely—probably as a repetition of an earlier bond with her own mother. One observes that she returned to her husband, and that after his death she elaborated an ambivalent conflict in a delusional manner, gave her homosexual bond with her daughter the *content* of a persecutory delusion, and then, in an endless split, sought to separate the child from its dead father, represented specifically in this case by his grave in America and by the married man with whom the daughter was in love.

I am acquainted with the mother only from the case history. The daughter I know personally. She told me that she spent her childhood very happily with her mother in Holland. She could not remember whether she ever thought about her father, but recollected well that when she came to America as a six-year-old girl, she was the first to recognize him at the dock, 'as if he had always been with me'.

She had often seen her mother vex her father with her notions. He frequently took up his hat to leave, and the patient was afraid that he would desert her mother, but he remained with her, 'just as I do now'. This identification with her father in relation to her mother was expressed by her at other times. Particularly clear was her assertion that she knew, if she left the man to whom she was engaged and went away with her mother, that she would always sit and fantasy how lovely it would be to go to him, to have his child. She already had the feeling that she preferred fantasy to reality. 'I must not reproach myself with having deserted my mother.'

There is a certain similarity between the psychological processes in this case and the one preceding it, namely: the delusional creation of the mother and the fantasy life of the daughter go in the same direction. In this case, however, over a period of twelve years, the mother did not succeed in drawing her daughter completely into the sphere of her delusion. The daughter's object-relationships were not destroyed, as they were in the preceding case. On the one hand, the sublimation of her positive homosexual strivings through her relationship with the social worker, on the other, a continual attempt to realize a heterosexual relationship, saved her from the psychotic induction. What still bound her to her mother, however, and did not permit her any release from the influence of her mother's delusion, was the fact that her mother's delusion and her own repressed fantasy life, her hysteria, had a similar content. The fact that the mother's delusion corresponded to the œdipus fantasies of the girl resulted in a morbid bond, with the danger that in time, because of the girl's neurotic dependence, a psychotic *folie à deux* might arise.

IV

Two sisters attracted psychiatric attention after an attempt at double suicide by gas. The elder died soon afterwards; the younger, who lived, was able to undergo a thorough psychoanalytic exploration.

The two sisters lived together after the death of their parents. The elder by fifteen years took the place of a mother with the younger; both were tenderly devoted to one another. The elder was always 'peculiar', unsociable, suspicious, seclusive. For financial reasons the younger had to take a position as housekeeper for a widower in another city and she married her employer. She was 'contented' in her marriage and had two children but never felt any real warmth of emotion for her husband or the children. Her connection with her sister was strikingly loose; she did not visit her for years and wrote her seldom.

It was only when she received news of her sister's severe illness that she decided to visit her. She asserted that as she was on the staircase to her sister's home, she heard voices calling: 'There comes the second one.' 'Now they will sleep together again.' 'She will help her.' She thought to herself, 'My poor sister, how she must suffer here!' When her sister related to her her old persecutory system, the younger sister never doubted its truth for a moment. They spent a couple of miserable weeks together and then decided to die together.

It is possible that the assertion of the rescued sister that she had perceived the persecutions *first,* before she saw her sister, was a falsification of memory and that the process of projection took place only after it was induced by the elder. This seems to me to make very little difference.

She had come to her sister's home full of timid feelings of anxious tension. The old homosexual, very ambivalent bond to her sister expressed itself in these feelings. It is possible that the hate, which she attempted to discharge on the staircase, was already projected at this point, like the fear of homosexuality, which betrayed itself in the content of the 'voices'. It is probable, however, that only later did she take over from her sister the paranoid process which she could use well in the service of her own defense.

The epilogue—joint suicide—confirms our suspicion as to the genesis of 'induced madness'. Since the hate they felt for one another could not be absorbed by projection into the persecutors outside themselves, they murdered one another under the guise of committing joint suicide.

Such paranoid pairs of siblings of the same sex are the most frequently encountered phenomena in *folie à deux.* As etiology, one thinks of constitutional predisposition in two individuals, separated from the rest of the world, living closely together, in which the more active infects the more passive with his ideas.

I believe, on the contrary, that this close living together, apart from others, is from the beginning *expression* of those unconscious bonds which later bring *both* parties to similar delusional ideas. That the one who is more active in the delusion eventually imposes it on the other is probable.

In these cases we have described various forms of *folie à deux;* in the first case, a common pseudologia phantastica in the sense of joint, conscious and unconscious wish fulfilment in three members of a family. The basis of the shared illness was the libidinal relationship of the three persons to one another and their joint reaction to the loss of a person to whom all three stood in an affect-relationship. In the second case, we saw a schizophrenic process of identification, free from any object-relationship to the inducing object. It was possible, however, to discover behind the delusional idea the remnants of old libidinal bonds. In the third case there was a parallel process between the delusional ideas of one psychotic person and the fantasy life of a neurotic person, and we found in this identity the link to the induction. In the fourth case we have a true paranoid *folie à deux,* in which the psychotic distortion of reality of two individuals did not arise from one sister's influencing the other, but from the fact that both already possessed in common, repressed psychic contents which broke out earlier in one and later in the other.

A little theoretical discussion of these clinical observations still remains. I do not want to enter into a discussion of the problem of projection and the meaning of delusional ideas as a 'process of restitution' in Freud's sense.[3] I want only, in connection with the problem of *folie à deux,* to indicate the presence of a deeper psychological process, which certainly functions in *folie à deux* in psychotic form.

The tendency to consider an inner psychic process as per-

[3] Freud: *Der Realitätsverlust bei Neurose und Psychose.* Ges. Schr., Vol. VI.

ception operates regularly within us. A typical example of
this in normal life is the dream. During the process of dreaming the happenings of the dream have the character of perceptions, and often retain this character, without modification,
for a time after awakening.

It is a complicated developmental process, to be able to distinguish inner content from perception. The simplest criterion is: perception is that which others accept as perception.
A contact with the surrounding world is indispensable in
applying this criterion. A psychotic individual has not only
given up the differentiation of the inner world from the world
of reality, but he has given up the need for confirmation from
the latter by destroying the bridge between himself and other
objects. The ego then takes its delusion for reality and
professes it as truth.

It can also happen, however, that a slight adaptation to
reality prevents the outbreak of the delusion. In this process
the ego only gradually frees itself from the cathexes, and makes
a boundary autistically between itself and the surrounding
world, without the ability to achieve the psychotic 'restitution
process' in the delusional creation. In this case, however, an
affirmative gesture from the surrounding world, a confirmation,
an encouragement, is enough to induce the development of the
delusion. What then appears to us as suggestion or induction
is only the making active of an inner content already there, an
encouragement to a projection already latent.

Freud considers the delusional ideas of the psychically ill
person a 'rebuilding of the vanished object world'.[4] I believe
that induction plays an important role in this process. In *folie
à deux* in psychotics, the *common delusion appears to be an
important part of an attempt to rescue the object* through
identification with it, or its delusional system. This was shown
particularly clearly in the example of the two paranoid sisters.

I am not attempting here to explain the difference between
hysterical suggestion and schizophrenic induction. Common to

---

[4] Freud: *Psychoanalytische Bemerkungen über einen autobiographisch
beschriebenen Fall von Paranoia.* Ges. Schr., Vol. VIII.

both, however, is: first, that neither in suggestion nor in induction is anything adopted by the subject which is alien to his ego; and second, that the person affected by the suggestion, as well as the person affected by the induction, attempts through identification to come closer to the object, or to find again a lost object. The phenomena of *folie à deux* described above can also be found in a psychic state so universally human that its character of 'normality' cannot be denied 'being in love'. I shall leave this problem to a paper devoted to it alone.

In conclusion, I should like to return to the starting point of my remarks: that processes such as we have seen here in individuals can also affect large groups of men, entire nations and generations. We must, however, distinguish here as with individuals between hysterical, libidinally determined mass influences, and schizophrenic ideas held in common; likewise between mass liberations of instincts under the guise of ideals, and paranoid projections, etc. Many things have their place in these *folies en masse* and the approval or disapproval of the surrounding world is often the sole criterion as to whether a particular action is deemed a heroic deed or an act of madness.

5

SOME
OBSERVATIONS
ON REALITY
TESTING AS A
CLINICAL
CONCEPT

SOME OBSERVATIONS ON REALITY TESTING AS A CLINICAL CONCEPT

BY SANDER M. ABEND, M.D.

This paper asserts that reality testing is a complex ego activity which cannot be characterized globally as either intact or defective. In normals, neurotics, and "borderlines" it is actually a highly variable function. Some problems of nomenclature are addressed. Among many analysts there is an implicit tendency to concretize the means by which reality testing is performed. This may lead to certain conceptual problems and clinical inaccuracies. The relationship of reality testing to unconscious conflicts from all phases of development is emphasized and illustrated. Issues in the technical handling in analysis of manifestations of disturbed reality testing are discussed.

Several years ago while I was participating in a Kris Study Group on "borderline cases" in psychoanalytic treatment,[1] my attention was drawn to certain problems in the clinical evaluation of patients' capacities to test reality. In the course of discussions, colleagues tended to speak of reality testing as though it could be characterized globally as either intact or defective, and as if the criteria for reaching that judgment in respect to any given patient are well established and generally understood by all analysts. In fact, the term was applied to different kinds of data. Sometimes it referred to what the analyst thought of how the patient acted in various life situations as described in

---

[1] The Kris Study Group of the New York Psychoanalytic Institute, under the chairmanship of Dr. Charles Brenner, met from 1973 to 1977. A preliminary summary of its findings was presented to the New York Psychoanalytic Society on April 25, 1978. A monograph based on this material is currently in press (see, Abend, Porder, and Willick, 1982).

analytic sessions; at other times it was applied to behavior in the sessions themselves. At still other times it reflected an evaluation of their patients' reported thoughts, judgments, perceptions, and/or interpretations of themselves, their analysts, or other people and situations they had encountered. It also became apparent, as examples accumulated, that the extent and degree of failure or defect in reality testing was quite variable, as was its tendency to persist or recur.

The literature on the topic is extensive but rather confusing. A review of a number of essential contributions, in conjunction with an examination of the clinical material brought forward in the Study Group, suggests that some clarifications and simplifications concerning reality testing are warranted. I believe that insofar as analytic data shed light on the problem, the aberrations of reality testing which afflicted the sicker patients we studied are not demonstrably different in nature from those milder fluctuations inherent in all neurotic symptomatology or, for that matter, from those evident in so-called normal mental functioning when it is subject to very close scrutiny as well. They are, to be sure, far more blatant and disruptive, both in the analytic situation and in the lives of those more disturbed patients. However, the assumption that their increased severity is attributable to a unique underlying defect of some kind, or to essentially different mental mechanisms, has not been convincingly documented, in my view, while similarities to lesser degrees of difficulty are, on the other hand, clinically verifiable.

Our collaborative work on "borderlines" led me to become interested in certain implications of reality testing as a clinical concept which apply to all patients, not just to the sickest ones. To my knowledge, the literature does not contain a generally comprehensive formulation of the problem along lines which are supported by the clinical findings of psychoanalysis. Detailed illustrations of the data in respect to reality testing in "borderline cases" can be found in the Kris Study Group monograph (Abend, Porder, and Willick, 1982). For the purposes of this presentation I will confine myself to the following: 1) summarizing certain key contributions to the sizable literature on reality testing; 2) underlining the disadvantageous tendency to concretize the means of testing reality; 3) highlighting the potential confusion inherent in certain aspects of nomenclature; 4) formulating, in a general way, what can be said about all degrees of disturbance of reality testing from the standpoint of metapsychology; 5) raising questions about the kinds of conflicts which contribute to these problems; 6) offering a suggestion that subjective disturbances in the feeling of reality are more accurately regarded as independent symptoms, unrelated to those other disturbances of perception, thought, judgment, and behavior subsumed under the heading of faulty reality testing; and, finally, 7) calling attention to certain problems of technique in respect to the analysis of these disturbances, in the milder as well as the more blatant forms in which they are regularly encountered in the analytic situation.

Although the essence of Freud's ideas about reality testing was already implicit in Chapter VII of *The Interpretation of Dreams* (1900), he actually introduced the term in his 1911 paper, *Formulations on the Two Principles of Mental Functioning*. His interest was in formulating the development of the mental apparatus, especially in respect to the evolution of the secondary process. In a key passage he stated, "A new principle of mental functioning was thus introduced; what was presented in the mind was no longer what was agreeable, but what was real, even if it happened to be disagreeable" (p. 219). The operation of the reality principle, which only partly supplanted the (newly renamed) pleasure principle, assumed, among other things, acquisition of the means to distinguish what is real from what is merely imagined. Freud's description of the factors involved in this developing capacity was, in essence, a preliminary formulation of the ego functions which facilitate reality testing, although, as Hartmann (1956) pointed out, this paper antedated the beginnings of ego psychology by a dozen years. Freud (1911) included heightened importance of the sense organs and of *consciousness* and *attention*; *memory* and *objective judgment* were added to complete the picture. These are contrasted in operation to *repression*, which Freud said merely follows the dictates of the pleasure-unpleasure principle. Reality testing, unlike repression, may lead to decisions about the truth or falsity of ideas.

In *A Metapsychological Supplement to the Theory of Dreams* Freud (1917) addressed the problem of how hallucinatory images are sometimes able to overpower reality testing. He began with an idea, first expressed in *Instincts and Their Vicissitudes* (1915), that perceptions of external events can be distinguished from perceptions from inside the organism according to whether or not they can be made to disappear by muscular action. He then reasoned that the system *Cs (pcpt)* "must have at its disposal a motor innervation which determines whether the perception can be made to disappear or whether it proves resistant. Reality-testing need be nothing more than this contrivance" (1917, p. 233). He went on to suggest that unacceptable reality might, by influencing the withdrawal of cathexis from the system *Cs (pcpt)*, abolish the possibility of reality testing, thus already clearly stating the case for a defensive interference with reality testing. The essential point was to emphasize the distinguishing of perceptions from ideas, or, in other words, the crucial decision was whether a given mental stimulus originated inside or outside the mind.

Freud restated his ideas in the paper, *Negation* (1925), with additional refinements. The question became "whether something which is in the ego as a presentation can be rediscovered in perception (reality) as well. It is, we see, once more a question of *external* and *internal*. What is unreal, merely a presentation and subjective, is only internal; what is real is also there *outside*" (p. 237). He added that presentations of perceptions are not always faithful; they "may be modified by omissions, or changed by the merging of various elements. In that case, reality-testing has to ascertain how far such distortions go" (p. 238). Once again he had emphasized that perceptions are vulnerable to defensive alteration, and he laid the burden of assessing that possibility upon reality testing.

Although these contributions unmistakably reveal the stamp of clinical experience, they are expressed in the form of theoretical expositions of mental development, to which Freud was devoted throughout his career. A recent extensive review article by Hurvich (1970) indicated that much of the subsequent literature on the subject follows this model, addressing itself to presumptive explanations of the psychological factors involved in gaining and exercising a knowledge and understanding of reality in mental life. Clinical studies of the circumstances under which reality testing fails are fewer in number. Ferenczi's classic "Stages in the Development of the Sense of Reality" (1913) is a case in point. Its sole clinical base is the observation that obsessional patients believe in the omnipotence of their thoughts, feelings, and wishes. His description of the antecedent stages of magical thinking, which has become so widely accepted, is a hypothetical construct of compelling intuition. The theoretical and developmental speculations of other writers have given rise to some less convincing theories.

For instance, in Federn's (1952) work, an explanatory model different from Freud's was utilized. He suggested that what he called the "sense of reality" becomes the means of distinguishing internal from external stimuli. This qualitative experiential distinction is a function of the "boundaries of the ego" acting analogously to organs of perception. He applied his theory to clinical problems, explaining symptoms of estrangement (Federn, 1927) by means of a postulated mechanism of variability in the energic investment of the ego boundaries. Although Federn's ideas no longer appear to command much attention from contemporary analysts, they do illustrate very well several problems which have continued to complicate the clinical study of reality testing in subsequent years.

The first of these is the problem of nomenclature. E. Weiss (1952), in his introduction to Federn's *Ego Psychology and the Psychoses*, indicated that *reality testing* is a term to be applied only to the process of obtaining knowledge of reality, while *sense of reality* refers to the more important discrimination of what is real and what is unreal. Modell (1968) pointed out the efforts of analytic observers to break down the reality testing concept into separate parts, noting the lack of uniformity which resulted. Unfortunately, he then inadvertently illustrated the problem when, after stating his agreement with Frosch's (1964) attempt to distinguish the *relationship with reality* from *reality testing*, he went on (pp. 90-91) to use both terms somewhat differently from the way Frosch did.

Frosch (1964) actually proposed differentiating three areas, the *relationship with reality*, the *feeling of reality*, and the capacity to *test reality*, although he acknowledged that they are functionally interwoven (p. 84). He said that the relationship with reality "involves a person's capacity to perceive the external and internal world and the appropriateness of his relationship with them" (p. 84). Feelings of reality refer to subjective sensations of the reality (or alteration of it) of what is perceived, while testing of reality means the capacity to "evaluate appropriately the reality of phenomena going on around and within . . ." (p. 86). On the other hand, Modell (1968) apparently thought of the relationship to reality as referring to the degree of psychological interest an individual is able to maintain in external reality, while all evaluative functions were subsumed under the heading of reality testing, in his interpretation.

Still further confusion may attend the distinction between *reality principle* and *reality testing*. While it is clear that Freud meant the reality principle as an abstract conception, its ramifications in respect to describable mental functioning include aspects attributed by others to reality testing. In "Notes on the Reality Principle" Hartmann (1956) pointed out that the reality principle is used in two different ways: (1) the idea of taking into account, from the standpoint of adaptation, the "real" features (i.e., according to the observer) of an object or situation, and (2) the tendency to shift activities away from immediate needs for discharge. Difficulties in the first area clearly manifest themselves as misreadings or misjudgments of features of reality, while problems in the second area may appear as impulsivity or, generally speaking, as difficulties in control of libidinal and/or aggressive tensions. The behavior which expresses these latter tendencies is often described as unrealistic or inappropriate by clinicians. Careful examination of the mental content of analysands who have control problems of this sort may indeed reveal that they are able to assess reality quite well, including the possible consequences of their activities, but disregard such assessments in favor of immediate gratification of certain of their instinctual urges. Hartmann (1956) also stated that "the reality principle includes both knowledge of reality and acting in regard to it" (p. 252). It seems to me, however, that analysts, in evaluating reality testing problems, do not seem especially concerned with distinguishing such patients from others who appear actually to misperceive or misjudge features of reality.

In point of fact, all these niceties of nomenclature seem to be ignored in actual practice. The analysts in the Study Group and those in clinical conferences, discussion groups, and seminars I have attended, by and large disregard these attempted distinctions which have entered the literature and speak only of patients' reality testing when they discuss clinical material. In the broadest sense, *they use the term defective reality testing to express a clinical judgment that certain of a patient's views of the world, that is to say, of people and situations, are, or appear to be, quite unrealistic.* Those who are dedicated to greater precision of thought and definition may disagree with or criticize such usage, but I believe it is the rule and not the exception among contemporary analysts.

A second problem which persists in complicating the understanding of reality testing, sometimes in subtle ways, stems from an implicit concretization of the means by which reality is assessed. Freud himself was fond of mechanical analogies, and Federn's (1952) notion of the ego boundaries as a sort of organ of perception, although expressed impressionistically, is also a mechanistic model. It is as though reality testing is a function performed by a piece of psychic apparatus—a complicated measuring and recording device of sorts. Its components, to be sure, are sense organs, consciousness, attention, memory, and judgment, as Freud said in 1911, all arranged in some contraption like a scientific instrument, as it were. This "instrument," then, may be imagined to be working properly or not as an entity; or perhaps instead it may be regarded as having a certain inherent degree of accuracy, less in sicker patients, greater in those who are healthier.

The implication of this concrete model of how reality testing is performed is that individuals have some sort of baseline capacity in this regard, albeit one which can be altered by special circumstances, such as psychotic decompensation or drug intoxication, to choose obvious examples. Furthermore, this baseline reading, whatever it may be, affords a fundamental measurement of the severity of the pathology which afflicts a given patient. Thus, "intact reality testing," included in a clinical assessment, may be offered as a reassurance of analyzability while, conversely, "defective reality testing" immediately suggests more grave pathology and reservations about analyzability.

Perhaps a more sophisticated version of this theoretical assumption is that the variations in reality testing observed in healthier patients are attributable to the impact of neurotic conflicts, but that other, sicker patients' psychic apparatuses include some more global "weakness" or "defect" in the sphere of reality testing. This latter condition may be presumed to be derived from constitutional sources or from early traumatization, or both, but whether the origin is specified or not, it is regarded as comprising a sort of deficiency state, i.e., "defective reality testing," with implications for pathology and analyzability as noted.

Modell (1968), who explicitly disagrees with the notion that reality testing works in an all-or-nothing way, nevertheless sug-

gests a more complex, but fundamentally analogous explanation of how it works, based upon "two organs for the structuring
of reality." One is represented by genetically determined
autonomous ego structures, which are impaired only if there has
been an absence of the maternal environment in the course of
development. The second is a structure formed by each individual that requires "good enough mothering" for healthy
development. Even in psychotics, he believes, the autonomous
structures can provide accurate data of reality, although it is
likely to be masked by the effect of the pathological functioning
of the second organization. According to Modell, the central
theme of this second structure is related to the capacity for
acceptance of (painful) separateness of objects.

All such schemata suffer from the disadvantage that they tend
to favor categorical distinctions which may interfere with accurate observations of the specific and highly individual variability of reality testing. They also seem to favor the belief that
reality testing is a capacity which, from a developmental standpoint, is primarily derived from and influenced by the earliest
interactions with the environment.

Hartmann's (1956) contribution to the subject was a complex
and sophisticated analysis of the issues involved, and it defies
ready synopsis. He elaborated on Freud's point that the reality
principle is a modification of the pleasure principle, showing
that ego development leads to a reassessment of pleasure values.
While the id does not change, the interactions of the systems
can and do become modified. What are altered, then, are not
the characteristics of pleasure-unpleasure, but the conditions
which determine each of them. For instance, for a child, instinctual renunciation may be compensated for and thus facilitated
by the anticipation of parental approval as a substitute kind of
pleasure. Instinctual renunciation, originally merely unpleasur-
able, can actually become pleasurable as the ego develops.

Hartmann also noted that there is not a simple correlation
between the degree of objective insight and the degree of
adaptiveness of the corresponding action which follows upon

it. He observed that what may be adaptive in one respect may well interfere with adaptation in another.

He moved to the heart of the question of reality testing when he showed that even knowledge of reality is subject to inevitable distortion. As a consequence of the child's great dependence on objects, these relationships influence his or her mind in respect to such fundamentals as concept formation, language, habits of thought and emotion, and even perception. The pleasures to be gained from conforming often lead to "the acceptance by the child of erroneous and biased views which the parents hold of reality" (p. 256). In short, tensions will develop between a knowledge of, in Hartmann's language, "objective" or "scientific" reality and a knowledge of *social* reality. The concept of objective reality as used by Freud, Hartmann said, is opposed both by what we refer to as magical thinking and also by a view of reality "in which not validation but intersubjective acceptance is used as a criterion . . ." (p. 259).

Certainly our studies of "borderline" patients (Abend, Porder, and Willick, 1982) confirmed the correctness and importance of Hartmann's observations on social versus scientific reality. Moreover, the influence that parental reality pathology has on a child's development is neither confined to the earliest months of life nor limited to the mother's relationship with the child. One patient, for example, had totally internalized her father's propensity for frightening and bizarre catastrophic hypochondriacal beliefs and preoccupations. Another had taken in and taken over her mother's pathological denials of and distortions regarding the circumstances surrounding her father's repeated abandonments of them, which began during the latter part of the second year of her life and recurred until his final departure when she was twelve. To these we may add that when one or both parents are very sick themselves, children not infrequently develop powerful needs to deny the painful reality they observe—i.e., the manifestations of the illness of their parent(s)—and also to deny what they themselves really wish in respect to that reality.

Another major contribution to the understanding of reality testing was Arlow's (1969a) paper, "Fantasy, Memory, and Reality Testing." His essential point was that there is a continuous and inescapable interaction between what he called "fantasy thinking" and the perceptual input registering aspects of external reality. He referred to a striking visual analogy of two motion picture projectors simultaneously flashing images on opposite sides of a translucent screen. Continuous ego activity must go on, evaluating and attempting to integrate these different factors in reaching judgments about what is real. However, fantasy thinking is largely unconscious and is inevitably centered around the crucial instinctual concerns of childhood mental life and their associated conflicts and derivatives. It is therefore likely to be a source of wishful and defensive distortions in the amalgamated final products of the ego's perpetual integrative activities, which can never be completely discounted. Although Arlow stopped short of saying so categorically in this paper, we can see that Freud's concept that reality testing must discriminate between inner and outer sources of stimuli describes a task which is impossible to accomplish in any absolute sense.

No individual is without an unconscious fantasy life, and no individual completely and permanently abolishes the influence of instinctual conflicts on it, even with the aid of analysis. Even with optimal results, one cannot maintain continuous conscious awareness of all these conflictual elements. Therefore, no individual can always take into account their impact on the perception and evaluation of external stimuli. Thus it follows that reality testing is always potentially subject to some limitations. It is not so much a question of defective reality testing as opposed to intact reality testing, but of assaying the nature and degree of the defect, a far more relative and variable distinction. The clinical issue becomes one of evaluating how significant is its effect and of ascertaining the circumstances in which the extent and impact of deficiencies in reality testing are most likely to be evident. Implicit in this task is the assessment of the role of various factors, such as unconscious fantasies and the effect of social forces, both familial and cultural, to which Arlow and Hartmann have called attention. The possible impact of special features, such as physical limitations and handicaps and their psychological elaborations, may also be added to the list of influences to be considered.

Viewing the problem from another perspective, *all degrees of disturbance of reality testing may be understood as manifestations of the impingement of unconscious conflict and its consequences on the capacity to perceive, remember, think, and judge with "realistic" objectivity.* This constitutes the "final common pathway" in which biological, psychological, and social forces become confluent and achieve their pattern of expression. It follows from this restatement that conflicts from *all* stages of development, not just the very earliest ones, may bring about such disturbances, and this can be readily confirmed by clinical observation. On the other hand, as tempting as the search for broadly and uniformly applicable explanations for the so-called more serious degrees of disturbed reality testing may be, analytic data do not support across-the-board distinctions and explanations very well at all. What the Kris Study Group observed was that material from *many* conflicts at *all* levels seemed involved in the reality testing deficiencies of "borderlines."

Hartmann (1956) pointed out that highly charged areas such as sexuality are particularly vulnerable to subjective deformation, and the material considered by the Kris Study Group confirmed that many manifestations of problems with reality testing appeared in the context of the complications of sexual wishes and their attendant conflicts and fantasies. This is hardly a new observation; Freud, Ferenczi, and others have noted that special conditions in respect to reality apply to sexual wishes in the mental life of humans. In present-day psychoanalysis we place emphasis on the role of anxiety, which is invariably associated with the child's observations of the anatomical differences between the sexes and of the primal scene, and which also accompanies infantile theories of sex and childbirth and the wishes connected with them. In the clinical setting of analytic therapy, it is precisely these anxiety-laden wishes, fantasies, thoughts, and experiences which frequently appear to be associated with perceptual distortions, persistent irrational beliefs, and alterations of memory. In fact, late in his life when Freud departed from his schematic dichotomy regarding patients' relation to reality and described the split in the ego in respect to reality (1927, 1940), it was clinical material of precisely this nature that he cited as evidence for his revised postulate. Modell (1968) has, quite correctly in my opinion, related these later observations of Freud's to the theoretical problem of reality testing.

Arlow (1969a), with reference to an observation made by Lewin (1948), noted and described patients who, because they unconsciously equate reality with the female genital, treat it in a manner analogous to the way fetishists treat the genital itself: "They refuse to face it. They cannot take a really good look at anything. This tendency influences them in the direction of impracticality and propels them into unrealistic behavior in many areas of their lives" (Arlow, 1969a, p. 44).

The small group of patients studied most thoroughly by the Kris Study Group on "borderlines" demonstrated without exception that sexual conflicts interfered with reality testing, sometimes in dramatic fashion. Other conflicts, of course, also did so. For example, murderous rivalry with a sibling, completely concealed from consciousness by strong reaction formations, so pervaded the mental life of one patient that she regularly misinterpreted social and professional situations and was convinced that others, who represented sibling substitutes, were hostile toward her. She selectively exaggerated minor incidents and ascribed motivation to others' behavior in accordance with her projected aggression and guilt. *What was clear in the clinical material we studied was that any and all conflicts, not just early ones, could bring about unconscious interference with reality testing.* Furthermore, even with these very ill patients, whose reality distortions were more blatant and more persistent than those we usually encounter with neurotic analysands, analytic progress was regularly accompanied by notable improvement in their reality testing. This served to support the impression that the amelioration of sexual and aggressive unconscious conflicts from all levels of development leads to improved ego functioning in those areas which subserve reality testing.

I should now like to take up a third problem, already in evidence in Federn's work, that even today continues to complicate the study of reality testing: the assumption that alterations in subjective feelings about reality, such as the sense of estrangement or derealization, as we usually call it, are inherently linked to the other manifestations of faulty reality testing we have been considering. Since Federn's explanation of this symptom was essentially an economic one, derived from the model of a sense organ of reality perception whose functioning was affected by changes in cathexis, this kinship seemed an entirely plausible one. Frosch treated them as correlated, as do, I believe, most contemporary analysts. Yet, unless one subscribes to the notion that an organ of reality perception exists and that alterations in its mode of functioning are perceived as subjective variations in the feeling of reality, why should a structural correlation be assumed?

In fact, explanations of derealization which are independent of content, i.e., of its unconscious meaning, are derived from theoretical assumptions about the functioning of the mental apparatus which necessitate subscribing to a belief in endopsychic perception. A quite different approach is advocated by Arlow (1966, 1969b), who suggests instead that the report of such subjective experiences should be treated the same as any other analytic data—subjected to scrutiny, with the aid of free association, to determine its exact meaning in the mental life of the patient. My own preference is for the latter course. An analogous critique concerning subjective reports of identity disturbances was put forth by Spiegel (1959) and elaborated on by Abend (1974).

In the small study population of "borderline" patients to

which I have referred, symptoms of estrangement and the like were, in fact, not a notable feature of *any* of the cases, contrary to expectation. In contrast, a recent clinical instance which occurred in a patient whom I did not consider to be severely ill serves to illustrate the relation of derealization to conflict, and so-called "higher-level," phallic-oedipal conflict at that. This young woman had been struggling in her analysis against acceptance of the importance in her mental life of unconscious fantasies of having been castrated. She was knowledgeable about analysis and psychodynamics and recognized and understood the implications of her own associations very well, but an important transference manifestation of her wish for phallic equality was expressed through her stubborn, argumentative, although generally good-humored resistance to my interpretive efforts. In one session, which centered on memories of a serious childhood injury, its interconnection with the theme of castration was unmistakable, but she continued to make fun of these connections and of my "Freudian orthodoxy" to the end of the hour. The next day she reported that on leaving the office she had been overcome by a powerful and distressing feeling that everything around her had changed and felt strange and unreal. She was so upset that she had to sit down on the steps which lead to my office suite for quite some time before she had felt able to go home. She had wept uncontrollably, not knowing quite why. The feelings of derealization persisted all that night and were still present on this, the following day, although to a milder degree. So distressed was she, and distracted by these uncomfortable feelings, that she could not recall what we had been talking about in the session before she became upset.

Other material reintroduced the theme of sexual differences, which reminded her of the content of the previous hour. Her subsequent associations focused on this material until she spontaneously brought up the recollection that in her childhood one of the ways she had of distinguishing between males and females was that the latter have to sit down to urinate! Suddenly the connection to her need to sit down the previous day was clear.

Her weeping (see Greenacre, 1945), the accompanying feeling
of sadness, and the need to think that what she saw and felt were
strange and unreal (referring to perceptions of her own and
others' anatomy and to fantasies of damage to her genitalia)
became progressively clarified as well. Confirmatory material
continued to "pour out," so to speak, and toward the end of
the hour she observed that the feelings of unreality were gone.

The proposition that a greater propensity to experience
symptoms of derealization is derived from problems at the very
earliest stages of development is difficult to document with
analytic data, as are analogous theories about the vulnerability
of reality testing. An uncritical adherence to this theoretical
position may, as in the Federn example, reduce the analyst's
interest in seeking out the specific unconscious content connected with these symptoms. Certainly, such an assumption
might have handicapped the analysis of the incident just
recounted. To concentrate both on disturbances of reality testing and on alterations of feelings of reality (even if, as I believe,
the two are unrelated) as symptoms, rather than as manifestations of deficiency states or developmental defects, can facilitate
our understanding of them in yet another way. To so identify
them—that is, as symptoms—calls attention to the fact that they
are the product of compromise formation. Accordingly, the role
of the superego in their genesis is more likely to be appreciated
than it would be otherwise. This point was elaborated and
convincingly documented by Stein (1966) in his paper, "Self
Observation, Reality, and the Superego." One of the patients
in the Kris Group "borderline" study was so agitated by guilt
following her first gratifying coital experience that she would
not answer her telephone afterward, convinced that her parents
were calling to berate her.

Stein (1966) also addressed the important question of how
analysis attempts to deal with patients' faulty reality testing in
the following passage:

> Our approach differs from other psychotherapies in that we
> explicitly *avoid* reality testing—at least in the usual sense. We

need not tell our patients that they have misjudged a life situation, nor do we as a rule give in to the temptation to correct a misapprehension of some analytic event. Instead, we attempt to correct, by analysis, those distortions of self observation which become evident in the analytic situation. By attaining a clearer vision of his own mental processes, by unsparing honesty with himself, we hope that our patients' distortions of perception of the outer world will be reduced to a minimum (p. 276).

This theoretically sound technical prescription is one which is frequently ignored, to judge from clinical discussions. Two chief rationales for explicit educative or confrontational comments are often presented. One is simply that "sicker" patients require such help as part of an adequate therapeutic program to enable them to manage their lives. This appears to be based on an assumption that their problems with reality testing derive from, or at any rate constitute, a deficiency state rather than represent a potentially reversible symptom. The latter view is a more accurate assessment, and it yields a more fruitful analytic benefit, as I have tried to indicate.

The second justification for correcting patients' misinterpretations and misjudgments is that this step facilitates analytic scrutiny of the sources of the distortion. Here, an adequate discussion would necessitate the detailed examination of a number of specific clinical instances, but this would be beyond the scope of this presentation. Obviously, the range of possible technical approaches is broad. For instance: supplying correct information; indicating directly that a misperception or misinterpretation exists; implying that that is the case by virtue of questioning the patient's basis for a statement or a judgment, calling attention to the manner in which such material has been presented, or offering interpretive commentary as to the source and nature of the distortion without any of the above intervening steps; all these constitute a variety of technical maneuvers which may be applied in different situations.

On the whole, analysts are probably more alert to the advan-

tages of the stance advocated by Stein (1966) when distortions
arise in respect to the analyst, since the possibility that correc-
tion may serve to blunt or discourage the expression of transference fantasies and their accompanying affects is widely recognized and generally regarded as undesirable. The handling of
situations in which events and relationships outside of the
analysis are being described is less uniformly agreed upon,
according to my observations. These pose interesting questions
for discussion, among which is the sometimes overlooked one
of the possible unconscious dynamic significance of the patient's
presenting such distortions to the analyst. What transference
fantasy or fantasies may be expressed in such behavior on the
part of the analysand?

To illustrate the point, the following brief clinical example,
commonplace rather than unusual, will serve. A married
woman, in analysis for a number of years, from time to time
reported incidents in which she experienced her husband as
contemptuous, critical, and belittling, if not outright abusive.
Although throughout the analysis her accounts of his behavior
had consistently given the impression of a rigid, angry, and per-
fectionistic man, the incidents in question appeared to the
analyst to be distorted, exaggerated, and misinterpreted. Furthermore, at other times the patient had given indication of an
awareness that she tended toward a selective skewing of the
picture in her describing of her husband. Attention to the
disturbance in reality testing had been focused for a long time
on establishing its exact nature and then elucidating the unconscious sadomasochistic fantasies which contributed to its genesis.
This conventional approach perhaps delayed an appreciation
that the patient was subtly issuing an appeal to the analyst to
intervene and rescue her, which corresponded to some aspects
of important family romance fantasies. However, the distortions
of reality testing had still another, more specific meaning. They
proclaimed that the patient was merely a small, frightened,
confused, and innocent child, who wished from the analyst only
a parent's sympathy and protection, not the response of a

romantic hero. In this defensive transference fantasy she also repeated the wish for her mother's aid and comfort against an older brother, who was at times haughty and ridiculing.

In sum, it seems fair to say that the technical handling of faulty reality testing is not a simple matter, but that it poses many problems. Implicit theoretical assumptions about the origin of the difficulty are likely to exert an influence on analysts' technique. A more explicit consideration of the basis for one's approaches to the varied spectrum of manifestations of faulty reality testing may prove illuminating and useful in clinical practice.

SUMMARY

In clinical discussions, reality testing is spoken of as though it can be characterized globally as either intact or defective; it is, in fact, invoked in respect to different kinds of clinical data and is both varied and variable in its manifestations.

Freud's ideas on the subject are summarized. He emphasized the distinction between internal and external sources of mental stimuli and noted the potential for defensive and wishful alterations of perception.

The problem of inconsistent and confusing nomenclature is addressed. Attempts to define different aspects of reality testing have not produced uniformity of usage and seem to be ignored in actual practice by most analysts. Analysts apparently use the idea of defective reality testing to express their clinical judgment that certain of a patient's views of the world, that is to say, of people and situations, are or appear to be quite unrealistic. An implicit concretization of the means by which reality testing is assessed seems rather widespread. This concretization leads to certain incorrect assumptions tending to favor categorical distinctions which may interfere with accurate observation of the specific and highly individual variability of reality testing.

All degrees of disturbance of reality testing may be understood as manifestations of the impingement of unconscious conflict and its consequences on the capacity to perceive, remember, think, and judge with realistic objectivity. Conflicts from all stages of development, not just the very earliest ones, may bring about such disturbances. The assumption that alterations of subjective feelings of reality, such as derealization, are closely linked to the other manifestations of faulty reality testing is questioned. Although unrelated, both kinds of disturbance are most usefully regarded as symptoms, that is, as products of compromise formation, and the superego, like the other components of instinctual conflict, plays a role in their genesis.

Analysis of the important conflicts that interfere with the ego functions which comprise reality testing regularly leads to improvement in its manifestations, even in "borderline" patients. Certain problems in the technical handling of manifestations of disturbed reality testing are noted.

REFERENCES

ABEND, S. M. (1974). Problems of identity. Theoretical and clinical applications. *Psychoanal. Q.*, 43:606-637.

——, PORDER, M. S. & WILLICK, M. S. (1982). *Borderline Patients: Psychoanalytic Perspectives.* New York: Int. Univ. Press. (In press.)

ARLOW, J. A. (1966). Depersonalization and derealization. In *Psychoanalysis—A General Psychology: Essays in Honor of Heinz Hartmann*, ed. R. M. Loewenstein, et al. New York: Int. Univ. Press, pp. 456-478.

—— (1969a). Fantasy, memory, and reality testing. *Psychoanal. Q.*, 38:28-51.

—— (1969b). Unconscious fantasy and disturbances of conscious experience. *Psychoanal. Q.*, 38:1-27.

FEDERN, P. (1927). Narcissism in the structure of the ego. In *Ego Psychology and the Psychoses*, ed. E. Weiss. New York: Basic Books, 1952, pp. 38-59.

—— (1952). *Ego Psychology and the Psychoses*, ed. E. Weiss. New York: Basic Books.

FERENCZI, S. (1913). Stages in the development of the sense of reality. In *Sex in Psychoanalysis*. New York: Basic Books, 1950, pp. 213-239.

FREUD, S. (1900). The interpretation of dreams. *S.E.*, 4/5.

—— (1911). Formulations on the two principles of mental functioning. *S.E.*, 12.

—— (1915). Instincts and their vicissitudes. *S.E.*, 14.

—— (1917). A metapsychological supplement to the theory of dreams. *S.E.*, 14.

—— (1925). Negation. *S.E.*, 19.

—— (1927). Fetishism. *S.E.*, 21.

—— (1940). Splitting of the ego in the process of defence. *S.E.*, 23.

FROSCH, J. (1964). The psychotic character: clinical psychiatric considerations. *Psychiat. Q.*, 38:81-96.

———— (1970). Psychoanalytic considerations of the psychotic character. *J. Amer. Psychoanal. Assn.*, 18:24-50.

GREENACRE, P. (1945). Pathological weeping. *Psychoanal. Q.*, 14:62-75.

HARTMANN, H. (1956). Notes on the reality principle. In *Essays on Ego Psychology: Selected Problems in Psychoanalytic Theory.* New York: Int. Univ. Press, 1964, pp. 241-267.

HURVICH, M. (1970). On the concept of reality testing. *Int. J. Psychoanal.*, 51:299-312.

LEWIN, B. D. (1948). The nature of reality, the meaning of nothing, with an addendum on concentration. In *Selected Writings of Bertram D. Lewin,* ed. J. A. Arlow. New York: The Psychoanalytic Quarterly, Inc., 1973, pp. 320-322.

MODELL, A. H. (1968). *Object Love and Reality. An Introduction to a Psychoanalytic Theory of Object Relations.* New York: Int. Univ. Press.

SPIEGEL, L. A. (1959). The self, the sense of self, and perception. *Psychoanal. Study Child,* 14:81-109.

STEIN, M. H. (1966). Self observation, reality, and the superego. In *Psychoanalysis—A General Psychology: Essays in Honor of Heinz Hartmann,* ed. R. M. Loewenstein, et al. New York: Int. Univ. Press, pp. 275-297.

WEISS, E. (1952). Introduction to *Ego Psychology and the Psychoses* by P. Federn. New York: Basic Books.

6

Unconscious Fantasy and Disturbances of Conscious Experience

UNCONSCIOUS FANTASY AND DISTURBANCES OF CONSCIOUS EXPERIENCE

BY JACOB A. ARLOW, M.D. (NEW YORK)

The role of unconscious fantasy in mental life has been recognized as of primary importance in psychoanalytic theory and clinical practice from the very beginning. Expressing the fulfilment of unconscious wishes, such fantasies were recognized by Freud as the common basis of dreams and the symptoms of hysteria (25, 28). He showed how hysterical attacks proved to be involuntary daydreams breaking in upon ordinary life. He had no doubt that such fantasies could be unconscious as well as conscious. Under favorable circumstances, it was possible to account for otherwise inexplicable disturbances of conscious experience in terms of the intrusion of an unconscious fantasy. The example he gave involved an upsurge of affect. He reported how a patient burst into tears, without apparent cause, while walking on the street. Thinking quickly, she came to realize that she had been involved in an elaborate, sad, and romantic daydream. Except for the psychotherapeutic experience in which she was involved at the time, the awareness of the fantasy and of its connection to her otherwise unaccountable outburst of emotion might have eluded her completely. Observations of this kind have since formed part of the experience of every practicing psychoanalyst.

Freud went on to demonstrate other ways in which the drives may find discharge by way of the intrusion of unconscious fantasies upon ordinary conscious experience (31). These may not only influence daily activity, as part of the psychopathology of everyday life, but they may also become part of the character. Certain hysterical persons may express their fantasies not as symptoms; they may instead consciously realize them in ac-

Abraham A. Brill Memorial Lecture presented before the New York Psychoanalytic Society, November 24, 1963.

tion and by doing so bring about assault, attacks, and sexual aggressions. The masochistic character, Freud noted, may represent the repetitive translation into action of a persistent, unconscious fantasy with a relatively fixed mental content, namely, the fantasy of being beaten. He said, 'People who harbour phantasies of this kind develop a special sensitiveness and irritability toward anyone whom they can include in the class of fathers. They are easily offended by a person of this kind, and in that way (to their own sorrow and cost) bring about the realization of the imagined situation of being beaten by their father' (*31*, p. 195). In the situation just described, the patient may be seen as operating on two levels of mental activity, i.e., he responds inappropriately to realistic events because he misconstrues them in terms of an unconscious fantasy.

Many authors have written of the intrusion of unconscious fantasy into conscious experience, apart from symptom-formation, dreams, and the psychopathology of everyday life. Anna Freud, for example, demonstrated the connection between social maladjustment, delinquency, and distorted ego functioning, on the one hand, and the effects of repressed masturbation fantasies on the other. She described cases in which the struggle against masturbation is abnormally successful and in which masturbation is totally suppressed. 'As a result, the masturbation phantasy is deprived of all bodily outlet, the libidinal and aggressive energy attached to it is completely blocked and dammed up and eventually is displaced with full force from the realm of sex life into the realm of ego activity. Masturbation phantasies are then acted out in dealing with the external world, which becomes, thereby, sexualized, distorted and maladjusted' (*23*). In a clinical communication (*5*), I described how such a process resulted in a transient change of identity and social role in a hysterical patient during adolescence. This transformation took place shortly after she had voluntarily suppressed all masturbatory activity. Her fantasies, until that time, were masochistic in nature. They were fantasies in which she imagined herself working for a harsh employer who subjected her to many indignities, culminating in humiliating sexual relations. After she abruptly stopped masturbating, she left home, wandered through a public park, avoided being picked up by a seedy-looking man, and finally accepted a job as a domestic, assuming the name of the Negro servant who had recently been employed by her parents.

In what has been said so far, we can see how Freud first delineated the role of unconscious fantasies in symptoms, dreams, and parapraxes. There are other ways, however, in which unconscious fantasies affect mental life. My purpose in this communication is to focus on other less familiar manifestations of the influence of the unconscious fantasy.

It would seem that a concept so well founded clinically and so much a part of the body of our theory would long since have ceased to be a problem for psychoanalysts. This is not the case however. Freud called attention to some of the difficulties involved in the idea of unconscious fantasies. Methodologically, the difficulty arises from the fact that such fantasies, although unconscious, are composed of elements with fixed verbal concepts. In addition, these fantasies have an inner consistency, i.e., they are highly organized. According to the topographic theory such attributes are alien to unconscious processes. They are associated with preconscious derivatives which operate according to the laws of the secondary process. Freud stated this succinctly. 'Among the derivatives of the *Ucs.* instinctual impulses . . . there are some which unite in themselves characters of an opposite kind. On the one hand, they are highly organized, free from self-contradiction, have made use of every acquisition of the system *Cs.* and would hardly be distinguished in our judgement from the formations of that system. On the other hand, they are unconscious and are incapable of becoming conscious. Thus *qualitatively* they belong to the system *Pcs.*, but *factually* to the *Ucs.* . . . Of such a nature are those phantasies of normal people as well as of neurotics which we have recognized as preliminary stages in the formation both of dreams and of symptoms and which, in spite of their high degree of organization, remain repressed and therefore cannot become conscious' *(30,* pp. 190-191). These were among the considerations which led Freud to the conclusion that accessibility to consciousness is not a reliable criterion on which to erect psychic systems. The passage cited above was indeed an adumbration of the structural hypothesis.

Within the structural hypothesis, however, many questions remain to be resolved concerning unconscious fantasies. This was brought out by Beres who wrote the most recent review of the problem. He states: 'In clinical work psychoanalysts have found the concept of unconscious fantasy to be a working tool of great value, if not indispensable. When we attempt to understand it theoretically, we are faced with difficult questions, some at present unanswerable. Paradoxically, the state of consciousness appears to be of secondary importance in the understanding of fantasy, its formation, and structure. Of greater significance are the cathectic shifts, the structure of mental content, the relation to verbalization and imagery, and the role of other ego functions—especially the synthetic or organizing function' *(15,* pp. 326-327). He states it is difficult to conceptualize unconscious mental content but that the unconscious fantasy is devoid of imagery or verbal concepts and that verbalization enters only during the process of making the fantasy conscious.

Thus it would appear that unconscious fantasies embarrass our methodology. The evidence is clear that such fantasies do exist but precisely where is one to place them in our conceptual frame of reference? What is their nature and in what form do they exist? Are they merely vehicles for the instinctual energies of the id or do the other components of the psyche, the ego and the superego, play a role in their formation? How high a degree of organization can we ascribe to unconscious fantasy?

A further purpose of this communication is to attempt to answer these questions from an examination of pertinent clinical material. It is my impression that a clearer understanding of the functioning of the mind may be achieved from examining the role that certain aspects of unconscious fantasy play in mental life.

Before we proceed let me make clear how the term fantasy is used in this paper. It is used in the sense of the daydream. Our understanding of the role of the unconscious fantasy has been hindered greatly by drawing too sharply the line of distinction between unconscious and conscious. It would be more useful, in my opinion, to speak in Brenner's terms of different mental contents which are fended off with a greater or lesser measure of countercathectic force *(17)*. In other words, ease of accessibility of a particular mental representation to consciousness may vary. The appearance in consciousness of a fantasy or of a derivative expression of a fantasy is governed by the same rules that apply to the emergence of any repressed material, i.e., it depends upon the balance between the cathectic potential and the opposing, repressing forces. The specific way in which unconscious fantasies influence conscious experience depends on several factors: the nature of the data of perception, the level of cathectic potential, and the state of the ego's functioning. Of the ego's functioning, reality testing, defense, adaptation, and integration are most significant. How the interplay of these factors determines the mental products which finally emerge will be considered in the light of clinical examples.

Some general comments on the phenomena under consideration are in order. Instead of unconscious fantasies, it would be more appropriate to speak of unconscious fantasy function. The purpose of this variation in terminology is to emphasize a very important point, namely that fantasy activity, conscious or unconscious, is a constant feature of mental life. In one part of our minds we are daydreaming all the time, or at least all the time we are awake and a good deal of the time we are asleep.

The private world of daydreams is characteristic for each individual, representing his secret rebellion against reality and against the need to renounce instinctual gratification *(27)*. Fantasy reflects and contains the persistent pressure emanating from the drives *(5, 10)*. In earlier communications *(4, 5, 9, 10, 11)*, I have described the hierarchy of fantasy formations in the mental life of each individual. Fantasies are grouped around certain basic instinctual wishes. Each group is composed of different versions or editions of the fantasy, each version indicating how at different stages of development the ego attempted to integrate the instinctual wishes with moral considerations and with reality. The same wish may find expression in various fantasies of which some may be pathogenic by virtue of the intrapsychic conflict which they engender, while others may occasion no conflict whatsoever. Under ordinary circumstances, the more recently organized fantasy expressions are usually readily accessible to consciousness without provoking anxiety reactions. The most primitive fantasy expressions may be barred from consciousness by the defense function of the ego. Every instinctual fixation is represented at some level of mental life by a group of unconscious fantasies. The specific expressions in conscious mental life of a fixation or of a repetitive trauma may be traced to the ever-present, dynamic potentiality of the specific details of that individual's unconscious fantasy activity to intrude upon his ordinary experience and behavior.

While it is true that the world of daydreams is individual and largely idiosyncratic, there is nonetheless a certain communality of elements in the fantasy life from one individual to another. Communality is the result of similarities of biological endowment and developmental experiences. The communality of the fantasy life is more pronounced in members of the same cultural or social group or of any group of individuals whose early childhood experiences are patterned more or less in the same way and who share a common tradition. The element of communality establishes the empathic base which makes possible communication and empathy, and at a higher level of mental organization it is an indispensable aspect of such group phenomena as religious experience and the enjoyment of artistic creations *(12, 13)*.

The concept of persistent unconscious fantasy activity may be used to elucidate certain elements of language, with regard to both general and individual usage. Sharpe wrote as follows: 'Metaphor fuses sense experience and thought in language. The artist fuses them in a material medium or in sounds with or without words. . . . When dynamic thought and emotional experiences of the forgotten past find the appropriate verbal image in the preconscious, language is as predetermined as a slip of the tongue or trick of behavior. Metaphor, then, is personal and individual even though the words and phrases are not of the speaker's coinage. The verbal imagery corresponding to the repressed ideas and emotions, sometimes found even in a single word, will yield to the investigator a wealth of knowledge' (47). In my own experience, and in some of the examples to be given, I have found the examination of metaphor to lead directly to concrete representations of an unconscious fantasy. Metaphor constitutes an outcropping into conscious expression of a fragment of an unconscious fantasy. The æsthetic effectiveness of metaphor in literature is derived, in large measure, from the ability of metaphorical expression to stimulate the affects associated with widely entertained, communally shared unconscious fantasies (40, 46).

The fact that the analysis of metaphorical expressions may lead associatively to repressed fantasy material comes as no surprise to the analyst, versed as he is in dream interpretation. It is a well-known technical rule that the words and adjectival phrases which the patient uses to describe a dream are to be considered part of the dream proper and may be used as a point of departure for eliciting associations. When patients characterize their dreams as 'vivid', 'eerie', 'consisting of X number of parts', etc., we customarily treat these elements as part of the manifest dream. The insight which we gain thereby enables us to infer unconscious mental content. Thus in metaphor, as in dreams, a single phrase or expression may be the conscious representative of unconscious fantasy activity. Later in this paper, I hope to demonstrate how the same principle may be

applied to the analysis of alterations of how one experiences
the external world and even how one experiences the self. Very
often the words which the patient uses to characterize such states
represent, in the same way as does metaphor, a derivative of
unconscious fantasy activity.

There is a mutual and reciprocal effect of the pressure of
unconscious fantasy formations and sensory stimuli, especially
stimuli emanating from the external world. Unconscious fantasy activity provides the 'mental set' in which sensory stimuli
are perceived and integrated. External events, on the other
hand, stimulate and organize the re-emergence of unconscious
fantasies. In keeping with its primitive nature, the basic fantasy is cathected with a highly mobile energy, and presses for
gratification of the sort which Freud characterized as tending
toward an identity of perception. The pressure may affect many
of the functions of the ego. Derivatives of fantasies may influence ego functions, interfering, for example, with the neutral
processes of registering, apperceiving, and checking the raw
data of perception. Under the pressure of these influences, the
ego is oriented to scan the data of perception and to select dis-
criminatively from the data of perception those elements that
demonstrate some consonance or correspondence with the latent, preformed fantasies (42).

Situations of perceptual ambiguity facilitate the foisting of
elements of the life of fantasy upon data of perception. This
plays a very important role in such experimental situations as
the Rorschach test and subliminal sensory stimulation (21).
Kris noted the importance of ambiguity in the æsthetic experience (40). This feature is related to the fact that the lack
of specificity of elements in a work of art makes it possible to
stimulate a wider range of unconscious fantasy activity. In this
context, sensory stimuli become significant, but not because of
their indifferent or inconsequential nature, as is supposed to be
the case in the day residue and the dream. On the contrary, the
perceptual data which facilitate the emergence of unconscious

fantasies are effective precisely because they are not indifferent, because they contain elements which correspond to features already present in the preformed unconscious fantasies. This interplay between the inner mental set, which is determined by the fantasy life and the stimuli afforded by experience, is a complex of interactions that can be expressed at another level of conceptualization in the language of electronics, in terms of reciprocity of signal and feed-back.[1]

When the cathectic potential of the fantasy activity is high, under appropriate circumstances the pressure for discharge may organize and structure the data of perception into illusions, misconceptions, and parapraxes. Thus, for example, a patient in a very angry mood, occasioned by an altercation with an authority figure and entertaining fantasies of revenge, reported the following illusion. While crossing the street on the way to the session, out of the corner of his eye he saw a sign in bold red letters which read, 'murder'. When he looked again he saw that the sign actually read, 'Maeder', the name of the proprietor of the shop. He had seen the sign many times before.

The intrusion of fantasy upon conscious experience may at times be so overpowering as to seem relatively independent of the influence of perceptual data. Hallucinations, fugue states, and certain transient confusional episodes may eventuate under these conditions, depending upon the degree of intactness of the function of reality testing. Let me cite an example which is common enough in analytic practice. This material was taken from the analysis of a patient whose transference relationship was dominated by an unconscious wish to castrate the analyst. Among the specific manifestations of this wish were attempts to deprive the therapist of time and money. On occasion, when these impulses were frustrated, the pa-

[1] A closer examination of the relationship of the day residue to the manifest dream would probably demonstrate also that the elements of daytime experience enter into the structure of the dream precisely because they are characterized by a high degree of consonance with the unconscious fantasy activity.

tient would act out by means of some drinking episode or homosexual activity, an unconscious fantasy of castrating the analyst. After a short but stormy period of protest over being charged for a session which he could not attend, the patient paid his bill. Two days later, as he entered the consultation room, entertaining a fantasy of recouping his money, the patient was overcome by a sense of confusion. Suddenly he was convinced that he had not paid the bill. This vengeful undoing of the payment in fantasy was so vivid that for the moment he could not tell whether his fantasy was real or whether his memory was fantastic. The momentary inability to distinguish which of the two sets of experiences, fantasy or memory, was the real one resulted in the state of confusion.[2] The confusion experienced by the patient, upon being presented the task of distinguishing between two sets of data, is comparable to the confusion which is experienced by patients with fugue states and hallucinatory hysteria. As the patients emerge from their daydreaming experience, there is a momentary, confusing inability to distinguish between fantasy and perception.

The function of reality testing may be interfered with by the fantasy life, even when the fantasy does not become conscious. Only a fragment of the unconscious fantasy may find representation in conscious experience and this fragment need not necessarily be only a derivative of an instinctual wish of the id. It may represent the effects of the defense function or other functions of the ego and of the activity of the superego. The example which follows is a temporary disturbance of the sense of reality, namely an attack of *déjà vu*. In this example, it will be possible to illustrate what has just been mentioned and to indicate, at the same time, that unconscious fantasies are highly structured and contain verbal concepts and imagery. The attack of *déjà vu* was unusual in the following respect. It occurred in surroundings with which the patient was thoroughly familiar. He had, in fact, seen the sight many times before. Thus the

---

[2] I am indebted to Dr. Peter Manjos for this example.

false judgment of *déjà vu* which seems so strange when one is in unfamiliar surroundings was all the more mystifying in this case. Clearly, the sense of unwarranted familiarity had nothing to do with the physical location in which the attack occurred.

Since I have presented this material in another communication *(8)*, only a condensed account will be given here. Among the patient's symptoms were claustrophobia, specifically anxiety about tunnels. The anxiety was not associated with entering tunnels; it began to appear only after the patient had been in a claustrum for a while. The analytic work demonstrated that these symptoms were based upon an unconscious fantasy of a murderous encounter, inside the mother's body, with the father and/or his phallus.

The attack of *déjà vu* took place under the following circumstances: the patient had an interview with the financial officer of the institution for which he was working. This interview was in response to a letter of complaint the patient had written regarding a delay in receiving his salary. He went to the treasurer's office, where the attractive secretary told him that the treasurer was busy at the moment. She invited him to sit down and talk for a while. Her manner was reassuring. It was at this moment that the patient looked out of the window at the fields and the surrounding landscape, with which he was thoroughly familiar and felt, 'I've seen all of this before. I've been through this before.' This experience was accompanied by an unpleasant affective state, a mixture of anxiety and feelings of uncanniness.

Let us compare the objective situation with the patient's unconscious fantasy. In reality, the patient found himself with a sexually tempting woman while waiting to enter the inner office. In the office was an authority figure, an adversary, with whom he might quarrel over money. This configuration corresponded to the elements of his unconscious fantasy—namely, an encounter with the father and/or his phallus within the body of the mother. The anxiety which he experienced was appropriate to the concomitant fantasy which he was unconsciously entertaining at the time. The feeling of *déjà vu*, of having been through all this before, was connected with defense against castration anxiety and was stimulated by the reassuring presence of the secretary. He felt she was on his side and in his fantasy imagined that she would side with him against her employer, even as his mother had taken his part against his father. In fantasy he had often identified himself with Jacob in the Bible story in which Rebecca helps her son deceive his father and steal the blessing. In his old Hebrew schoolbook, which he resurrected from his library at this point in the analysis, was a picture of Rebecca at the entrance of the tent reassuring Jacob as he is about to enter. When the patient was a child, his mother used to help him overcome his fears of the barber and the doctor (his father was a doctor) by telling him, 'Don't be afraid. You have been through all of this before and everything came out all right. The same will happen now.'

Thus we see that both danger and defense were part of the unconscious fantasy activity. The danger contributed to the consciously experienced feeling of anxiety and the defense became evident in the feeling of *déjà vu*, to wit, 'You have been through all of this before and you came out all right because mother was at your side. The same will happen now.' The transposition of affect in the *déjà vu* experience is similar to the transposition of affect in the typical dream of missing trains or failing an examination. The disturbing, manifest content of the dream contains the reassurance against anxiety connected with a currently experienced danger. So too, the disturbing, conscious experience of *déjà vu*, in this case, arises in response to the emerging danger of retaliation and punishment. Not all attacks of *déjà vu* necessarily convey this specific form of reassurance in fantasy. Other forms of defense connected with unconscious fantasies may be involved. This has been demonstrated by Marcovitz (43). In the *déjà vu* experience cited above, unconscious fantasy activity, in the service of defense against anxiety, intruded momentarily upon the function of reality testing.

Is it possible to demonstrate other ways in which unconscious fantasy contributes to the function of defense? Clinical practice indicates that the answer to this question is affirmative. It is not possible, however, to say that all defense mechanisms are mediated through unconscious fantasy. The use of fantasy in defense was described by Anna Freud in connection with the mechanism of denial in fantasy (22). Defensive uses of identification, undoing, and denial are readily incorporated into unconscious fantasies. One of the best known of fantasies, a fantasy which is oriented almost exclusively toward the ego function of fending off anxiety, is the unconscious conceptualization of the woman with a phallus. Although this fantasy serves as the essential condition for sexual gratification of the fetishist, the fantasy itself is primarily defensive in nature. The function of this particular fantasy is to reassure the subject against castration anxiety. It was in discussing this phenomenon that Freud described the split of the ego in the defensive process (33). He was referring to the contradiction between the accurate conscious conceptualization of the female anatomy as opposed to the unconscious concept which in fantasy endows the woman with a phallus. What the fetishist perceives in reality, he denies in fantasy. Certainly this demonstrates that unconscious fantasy may involve definite visual and verbal concepts. The fantasy of the phallic woman is a specific example of denial in unconscious fantasy and it is a common feature of many clinical entities, e.g., voyeurism, exhibitionism, transvestitism, some forms of homosexuality, and some special types of object choice in men.

A defensive use of identification with the aggressor, a mechanism described by Aichhorn (2) and Anna Freud (22), may be incorporated into an unconscious fantasy and be utilized at different times to fend off feelings of humiliation, anxiety, or reproach from the superego. In a case of depersonalization, which I have described (11, 14), the patient had grown accustomed during childhood to master feelings of humiliation by identifying herself in fantasy with her tormentors. As a child, whenever she felt humiliated, she would fantasy that she was one of the group who were laughing at her, the unfortunate victim from whom she felt alienated. In her adult neurosis, in which the principal presenting symptom was depersonalization, the patient would unconsciously resort to this for purposes of defense: under circumstances which ordinarily would have aroused anxiety or humiliation, the patient would become depersonalized. The analysis of these attacks demonstrated the influence of a fantasy in which the patient once again defensively split her self-representation into two parts. One self-representation was an observer and retained the quality of selfness; the other self-representation was the object of observation and was seen as involved in some painful situation. From this second self-representation, the patient felt detached and alienated.

How the external situation in which a person finds himself, or how the activity in which he is engaging at the moment, may facilitate the contribution that unconscious fantasy makes to conscious experience can be observed in everyday analytic practice. From the technical point of view, the analysis of this interplay constitutes the immediate tactical approach of the therapist. In this regard, it is advantageous to note the introductory statements patients make in transmitting a communication, especially if it is the opening statement of the session or if something in the way the patient says it impresses the analyst that the statement is superfluous. One should be alert on such occasions to the possibility that superfluous comments of this nature point to the influence of unconscious fantasy. Thus when a patient states, 'While riding in a bus, I had the following thoughts . . .', what usually follows in the patient's associations is some derivative of a fantasy of being in an enclosure. Or if the patient begins with, 'On my way to the session . . .', the ensuing associations almost invariably lead to some fantasy concerning the analyst.

Let me cite a particularly illuminating example at greater

length. 'While squeezing some oranges this morning for juice',
a patient began, 'I had the following thoughts'. The associations that emerged may be summarized as follows. He was
thinking of nourishment, liquid in bottles, and poison. Suddenly he recalled that this was his sister's birthday. He thought
of presenting her with a bottle of 3-Star Scotch, when the
thought flashed through his mind of presenting her instead
with 3X poison. At this moment he became aware of the hem-
ispherical shape of the sections of the oranges which he had
cut and which he had been squeezing with unusual violence.
Parenthetically, this patient had been abandoned twice by his
mother. The first time was when he was less than a year old;
she weaned him abruptly and turned him over to the care of
his grandmother so that she herself could go back to school to
finish her professional training. The second time was when his
younger sister was born. The sister had a congenital defect
which caused the mother to be occupied with her almost
exclusively.

The patient's thoughts continued. He was concerned about
his mother. The doctor had reported that the cancer of the
breast from which she was suffering was now in an advanced
stage. Some years earlier, the patient, a physician, had given
his mother injections of estrogenic hormones to control meno-
pausal symptoms. Had these injections caused her illness? He
had never forgiven his mother for abandoning him. He thought
of his previous treatment with a woman analyst. He felt it had
not been successful. She had a child while he was in treatment
and sometimes she would sew during the analytic sessions. He
was sure that she was sewing for her newborn child. The patient then began to think of the time when his grandmother
used to care for him. He had been told that when his mother
left him to go to professional school, he refused to take the
bottle. He was so importunate in his demands for the breast
that his grandmother gave him her dry breast to suckle. He
grew up to become an inconsolable pessimist. Another memory
came back at this point. He recalled watching his grandmother

grind meat for hamburger. The patient would stand by and eat the raw meat as it came out of the machine.

This material may be formulated in terms of the interaction of unconscious fantasy and conscious experience. Against the background of his lifelong hostility toward his mother and sister, the patient's mental set is intensified by his sister's birthday and his mother's illness. In this setting, the ordinarily routine activity of squeezing oranges becomes the activity which facilitates the emergence of derivatives of an unconscious fantasy, cannibalistic in nature, i.e., of destroying and devouring his mother's ungiving, frustrating breasts. This fantasy in turn influences the manner in which the patient perceives the shape of the oranges and the violence with which he extracts the juice. While squeezing oranges in reality, he is destroying breasts in fantasy.

To this point we have been discussing unconscious fantasies that emerge in the course of psychoanalytic treatment, but an even broader problem is involved, namely the precipitation of neurotic illness in general. In his early studies of neurosogenesis, Freud (29) traced the onset of illness primarily to a disturbance in the quantitative relationship between drive and defense. He emphasized especially those features which tended to intensify the pressure of the drives upon the mental apparatus. Later, Freud (32) demonstrated the existence of what is perhaps a more common mode of onset of neurotic illness. A neurosis may be precipitated when the individual finds himself in a realistic situation which corresponds to some earlier traumatic experience. The new experience contains in it elements that are unconsciously interpreted as a repetition of the original trauma. An addition to, or perhaps an elaboration of, the concept of how neurotic illness may be precipitated in adult life may be found in the consonance between the realistic situation and the specific, unconscious fantasy which it reactivates. That may be illustrated with material from the analysis of a patient who suffered from claustrophobia, especially while riding in subway trains. Ten years before the onset of his illness, his twin brother, whom the patient had momentarily abandoned, collapsed in a train and subsequently died. The patient held himself responsible for his brother's death. Years later, a week before the onset of his illness, the patient was in the unhappy position of having to decide whether to take his uncle to the hospital or to risk having him treated at home. The patient decided to take the uncle to the hospital, but the latter died in the ambulance before they reached their destination. The patient grieved, but did not develop claustrophic symptoms until several days later *when he was traveling in a subway in the company of a group of sibling figures.* The analysis demonstrated that this symptom was connected with unconscious fantasies concerning his twin brother and the interior of the body. In these fantasies, the patient would imagine himself inside the mother's body with or without his twin. On other occasions, the fantasy concerned the activities of the brother within the patient's body. The specific details of the symptoms were directly related to the behavior which he unconsciously fantasied the introject to be carrying on within the claustrum.

Returning to the point of this discussion, we can see that the uncle's death reactivated the earlier trauma of the brother's death. However, it was the precise experience of traveling in the subway with sibling figures which precipitated the neurotic symptoms. This experience corresponded to elements from a set of unconscious childhood fantasies. In these fantasies, he imagined himself and his twin engaged in various activities inside the mother's body, e.g., struggling with his twin for food, fighting over who should emerge first, and above all, destroying his sibling within the womb so that he could be born as an individual and not as one of a set of twins. It was indeed the conflicts over these childhood fantasies that had caused him, at eighteen, to respond traumatically to his brother's death. The actual death of his brother constituted an actualization of his fantasy wish to have been born without a twin. The uncle's death confirmed his guilt and finally the experience in the train—claustrum—triggered the onset of his symptoms.

Writing about neurotic reactions to the symptoms of neurological disease, Beres and Brenner *(16)* stated that such symptoms become traumatic psychologically because of the existence of an antecedent, unconscious conflict. What is pathogenic, they add, depends upon a fixation. To extend these ideas and the concept which I have been developing, I would add the following. Since fixation is specifically expressed in a set of unconscious fantasies, the precipitation of mental illness under such circumstances is determined by how the symptoms of organic disturbance affect the fantasy life of the patient and how they facilitate the emergence of pathogenic fantasies.

Even in highly organized symptom-formations, the specific details of the symptomatology may vary from time to time. A careful examination of these variations will demonstrate how the details of the symptoms are exquisitely related to the different versions of the unconscious fantasy. In the case of the twin patient cited above, he experienced various intra-abdominal sensations, depending upon what his daydreams were at the moment about the behavior of the introject within the body. In his studies of claustrophobia, Lewin *(41)* showed how a patient's symptomatology reflected the patient's immature grasp of reality and of the physiology of the foetus at the time when the conflict was given expression in the form of an organized fantasy. Whenever he found himself within a claustrum, the patient could breathe only intermittently. This detail of the symptom corresponded to the patient's childhood concept of intrauterine physiology. He knew that there was fluid within the maternal enclosure and as a child became apprehensive as to how the foetus, with whom he had identified, could breathe. He solved the problem by utilizing what he knew of the operation of the flushing mechanism of a toilet. When the water level receded it left the chamber with air. The bobbing ball of the flush mechanism resembled the head of the foetus. Based on this model, the patient, as a child, had an idea which he incorporated into an unconscious fantasy that the water level within the womb receded intermittently whenever the mother urinated and that only during this interval could the fœtus get air to breathe. This material demonstrates how an unconscious fantasy may be studied to gain insight not only into infantile sexual theories, but also into forgotten primitive concepts of reality and of the self. The fantasy which is regressively revived in neurotic illness reflects the immature state of the ego at the time of the origin of the fantasy. Unconscious fantasy represents an area which remains to be explored for the purpose of furnishing data concerning the early phases of ego development.

The quick and facile interaction between external events and the appearance of derivatives of unconscious fantasies furnishes ample proof of the hypothesis that fantasy activity is a persistent and constant function. It suggests that what Freud (25) said about the formation of dreams may be applied with equal validity to many disturbances of conscious function. Commenting on the rapid organization of a dream in response to an external stimulus experienced during sleep, Freud said that there must be preformed, readily available unconscious fantasies which can be woven instantaneously into the structure of the dream. The clinical material presented shows how the same holds true for experiences in waking life. This concept contributes to the understanding of such diverse phenomena as wit, illusion, misperception, *pseudologia phantastica (20)*, imposture *(1, 18, 34)*, and transient disturbances of identity *(37)*.

For purposes of presentation, till now, it has been necessary to isolate the specific functions that unconscious daydreams may serve. It must be remembered, however, that in common with all other mental products, the effects of unconscious fantasy are governed by the principle of multiple function *(49)*. Id, ego, and superego derivatives may all become manifest in a conscious experience that is determined by unconscious fantasy even though the conscious disturbance is only of minor significance.[3] This may be illustrated in the following example

[3] See also, Eidelberg *(19)*.

demonstrating a disturbance of the sense of time. A woman patient entered the consultation room on a Monday and said that she felt very strange because she felt as if she had not seen me for one hundred years. She spoke at some length about this feeling of an extraordinarily extended lapse of time since the last meeting of the previous Friday. This session took place on the Monday following Father's Day. Her father was dead. The patient blamed herself for his death. For certain reasons, during adolescence, she had wilfully and stubbornly insisted that the family return home from a relative's house, although it was snowing. This house was many miles from the patient's home and the family had expected to spend the night there. Because the patient was adamant, the family reluctantly acquiesced and undertook the hazardous drive back. The car skidded and the father sustained injuries from which he died one week later.

I was struck by the patient's introductory phrase which reflected her subjective sensation of having been away from the analysis for one hundred years. Her associations to this statement ultimately led to the legend of the Sleeping Beauty. This fairy tale appealed to her as the fulfilment in fantasy of a wish to be reunited with her father, either in life or in death. For her, the Sleeping Beauty story made it possible to undo the finality of her father's death and her guilt. In the story, when Sleeping Beauty is awakened after a sleep of one hundred years, the redeeming lover represents a member of another generation. Through this magical suspension of the barrier which time interposes, it becomes possible to breach the barrier of the incest taboo. Œdipal wishes may be fulfilled and the dead father re-emerges as the resurrecting prince. Thus the subjective sensation of an unnaturally extended period of time represented in a condensed way the unconscious fantasy of Sleeping Beauty. The distortion of the sense of time expressed at the same moment the fulfilment of œdipal wishes and the warding off of superego reproaches, in a fantasy which made it possible to undo the death of her father.

Unconscious fantasy activity has a special relationship to clinical phenomena involving the psychology of the self. This is an area of psychoanalysis that deserves a much more extensive discussion than is possible at this time and in this communication. Alterations in the experience of the self are very common, especially as transient phenomena in the psychoanalytic setting. These disturbances usually fall under one or more of the following three headings: problems of identity, disturbances of the body image, and disturbances of the sense of self. Difficulties pertaining to the first two of these categories may be conscious or unconscious. The manifest dream often contains a concrete visual representation of the self. From the study of dreams, we observe how wide is the range of possible self-representations.

Let us apply what has been stated earlier about the function of fantasy to the realm of self-representation. The multiplicity of self-representations is organized into many different fantasies and fantasy systems. Self-representations in unconscious fantasy, persistently and selectively reactivated and fused with each other, help make up the individual's identity. There is a similarity between these ideas and the concept of 'pooled self-representations' (48).

From time to time, under the impact of conflict, the organized identity, built up from many different self-representations, may begin to disintegrate into its component parts. One or another self-representation comes to the foreground of consciousness, mediated by way of an unconscious fantasy in which the self-representation is expressed in concrete terms. Identical considerations apply to the self-representations involved in the body image and the concept of self. The impingement of such fantasies upon consciousness contributes to the clinically observable alterations of the experience of the self. The structure and meaning of many alterations of self-experience can be determined by reconstituting and analyzing the concomitant, unconscious fantasy.

Language furnishes many clues to the nature of the unconscious daydreaming which accompanies altered experiences of
the self. Several examples have already been given; a few relatively uncomplicated ones follow. For example, unless they
are unusually sophisticated, patients rarely complain that they
suffer from depersonalization. Instead they describe their sensations in some form of imagery, ofttimes quite dramatic. One
patient who was suffering from depersonalization, expressed
her discomfiture in the statement, 'I feel like a Zombie'. The
analysis subsequently revealed that she had indeed identified
herself with a dead relative and that when she was depersonalized she was under the influence of an unconscious fantasy of
suspended animation. Other patients say they feel empty inside, or like a passively manipulated puppet, wrapped in cot-
ton, etc. Rangell (45) described a patient who had transient
alterations of the sense of self while on the couch. The patient
described this experience in terms of disappearing into the
background or becoming fused with the couch. These sensations
were based upon an unconscious fantasy of merging into the
body of the mother. Joseph (38) reported a case in which the
emergence of an unconscious self-representation intruded into
conscious experience and took the form of what was, for all
intents and purposes, a hallucination. This patient was one of
a set of twins. In his unconscious fantasy life, he often represented himself and his brother as a sexual couple, with himself in the role of the woman. During the treatment of this
borderline patient, a series of events culminated in the two
brothers separating. In this state of longing for his twin, the
patient experienced an upsurge of homosexual feeling. While
passing a highly polished store window, the patient saw himself as a woman, reflected in the glass. Similarly, in the seminar
of the Kris Study Group, Milton Horowitz presented material
from a patient whose behavior constituted exquisite acting out
of a very detailed unconscious fantasy of identification with
his dead mother. In addition, Jacobson (37) has written of
conflicts of identity within the ego as the basis of certain dis-

turbances of the self. Such conflicts between different identities are probably mediated through unconscious fantasies derived from specific experiences in the patient's life and tend to influence conscious experience simultaneously or alternately *(11)*. Finally, disturbances of the body image during analytic sessions are perhaps the most common of the phenomena under discussion. The wish-fulfilling aspect of the intrusion of unconscious fantasy in such situations is too well known to require comment. The defensive and self-punitive aspects could be investigated with profit.

To summarize the main points of this paper: Unconscious daydreaming is a constant feature of mental life. It is an ever-present accompaniment of conscious experience. What is consciously apperceived and experienced is the result of the interaction between the data of experience and unconscious fantasying as mediated by various functions of the ego. Fantasies are grouped together around certain basic childhood wishes and experiences. In these systems of fantasies, one edition of the fantasy wish may represent a later version or defensive distortion of an earlier fantasy. Which fantasy version of the unconscious wish will contribute to conscious experience depends upon a number of factors that have been discussed. Unconscious daydreaming is closely allied to instinctual fixations. It is this activity that supplies the mental set in which the data of perception are organized, judged, and interpreted.

The contribution that unconscious fantasy makes to conscious experience may be expressed illustratively through the use of a visual model. The idea for such a model occurred to me several years ago. It was after Thanksgiving dinner and a friend had brought a movie projector to show the children some animated cartoons. Since we did not have a regulation type movie screen, we used a translucent white window shade instead. During the showing of the cartoons, I had occasion to go outdoors. To my amusement, I noted that I could watch the animated cartoons through the window on the obverse side of

the window shade. It occurred to me that an interesting effect
could be obtained if another movie projector were used to flash
another set of images from the opposite side of the screen. If
the second set of images were of equal intensity to the first and
had a totally unrelated content, the effect of fusing the two images would, of course, be chaotic. On the other hand, however,
if the material and the essential characters which were being
projected from the outside and the inside were appropriately
synchronized according to time and content, all sorts of final
effects could be achieved, depending upon the relative intensity
of the contribution from the two sources.

The concept of unconscious fantasy activity has two implications of general import for psychoanalytic theory. One concerns the theory of technique, the other methodology. One may
describe .the psychoanalytic situation as structured in a way
that is most favorable for obtaining data indicating the influence of unconscious fantasies. One immediate technical goal of
the therapist is to help the patient learn to distinguish between
reality and the effects of unconscious fantasies. In order to do
this, the analyst maintains a neutral position and avoids getting
involved in his patient's life. Transference analysis becomes the
proving ground in which one can demonstrate to the patient
how he confuses the past with the present, the daydream with
reality. This is how I understand Nunberg's *(44)* view that the
transference is a projection; it represents a foisting upon the
analyst of the patient's preformed, latent, unconscious fantasies.
Thus analysts who minimize the role of unconscious fantasy
in mental life *(3)* are also ready to play roles in therapy.

The point about methodology is simple but fundamental.
If we are cognizant of the tendency of unconscious fantasies to
influence conscious experience and behavior, then we must be
very careful in evaluating data from a superficial, i.e., from a
strictly phenomenological, point of view. Unless one knows the
patient's unconscious fantasy, one can easily be led into a confusing dilemma as to whether a certain action represents activity or passivity, masculinity or femininity, self-punishment or

masochism, etc. Anna Freud *(24)* pointed this out in analyzing different types of male homosexuality. She showed how a patient, whose actual role in homosexual relations could be described as passive, receptive, masochistic, and feminine, was in fantasy unconsciously identifying himself with the so-called active, sadistic, masculine partner. His behavior was one thing, his fantasy another.

In the introduction to this paper, a number of questions were posed concerning the nature of unconscious fantasy. In the light of the material presented, we can formulate our answers to these questions. No sharp line of distinction can be made between conscious and unconscious fantasies. In the framework of the structural hypothesis, it seems more appropriate to speak of fantasies which are fended off to a greater or lesser extent, bearing in mind that the role of defense may change radically with circumstances. A very high degree of organization may be attributed to unconscious fantasy, though this need not always be the case. Fantasies are not exclusively vehicles for discharge of the instinctual energies of the id. The ego and superego play a part in their formation. The contribution which unconscious fantasy makes to conscious experience may be dominated by defensive, adaptive, and self-punitive trends as well.

REFERENCES

1. ABRAHAM, KARL: *History of an Impostor in the Light of Psychoanalytical Knowledge.* This QUARTERLY, IV, 1935, pp. 570-587.
2. AICHHORN, AUGUST: *Wayward Youth.* New York: Viking Press, Inc., 1925.
3. ALEXANDER, FRANZ: *Analysis of the Therapeutic Factors in Psychoanalytic Treatment.* This QUARTERLY, XIX, 1950, pp. 482-500.
4. ARLOW, JACOB A.: *A Creative Spell Simulating Orgasm.* Paper Delivered before the New York Psychoanalytic Society, 1952.
5. ———: *Masturbation and Symptom Formation.* J. Amer. Psa. Assn., I, 1953, pp. 45-58.
6. ———: *A Contribution to the Psychology of Time.* Paper First Presented at the Los Angeles Psychoanalytic Society, 1957.
7. ———: *On Smugness.* Int. J. Psa., XXXVII, 1957, pp. 1-8.
8. ———: *The Structure of the Déjà Vu Experience.* J. Amer. Psa. Assn., VII, 1959, pp. 611-631.
9. ———: *Fantasy Systems in Twins.* This QUARTERLY, XXIX, 1960, pp. 175-199.

10. ———: *Ego Psychology and the Study of Mythology.* J. Amer. Psa. Assn., IX, 1961, pp. 371-393.

11. ———: *Conflict, Regression, and Symptom Formation.* Int. J. Psa., XLIV, 1963, 12-22.

12. ———: *The Madonna's Conception Through the Eyes.* Psa. Study of Society, III, 1964, pp. 13-25.

13. ———: *The Reaches of Intrapsychic Conflict.* Amer. J. Psychiatry, CXXII, 1965, pp. 425-431.

14. ———: Depersonalization and Derealization. In: *Psychoanalysis—A General Psychology. Essays in Honor of Heinz Hartmann.* Edited by Rudolph Loewenstein, Lottie M. Newman, Max Schur, and Albert J. Solnit. New York: International Universities Press, Inc., 1966.

15. BERES, DAVID: *The Unconscious Fantasy.* This QUARTERLY, XXXI, 1962, pp. 309-328.

16. BERES, DAVID and BRENNER, CHARLES: *Mental Reactions in Patients with Neurological Disease.* This QUARTERLY, XIX, 1950, pp. 170-191.

17. BRENNER, CHARLES: *An Elementary Textbook of Psychoanalysis.* New York: International Universities Press, Inc., 1955.

18. DEUTSCH, HELENE: *The Impostor.* This QUARTERLY, XXIV, 1955, pp. 483-505.

19. EIDELBERG, LUDWIG: *A Contribution to the Study of the Masturbation Phantasy.* Int. J. Psa., XXVI, 1945, pp. 127-137.

20. FENICHEL, OTTO: *The Economics of Pseudologia Phantastica.* Int. Ztschr. f. Psa., XXIV, 1939, pp. 21-32.

21. FISHER, CHARLES: *Dreams and Perceptions: The Role of Preconscious and Primary Modes of Perception in Dream Formation.* J. Amer. Psa. Assn., II, 1954, pp. 389-445.

22. FREUD, ANNA: *The Ego and the Mechanisms of Defense.* New York: International Universities Press, Inc., 1946.

23. ———: Certain Types and Stages of Social Maladjustment. Searchlights on Delinquency. In: *Yearbook of Psychoanalysis, Vol. IV,* Edited by Sandor Lorand. New York: International Universities Press, Inc., 1949.

24. ———: *Some Clinical Remarks Concerning the Treatment of Cases of Male Homosexuality.* Abstr. in Bull. Amer. Psa. Assn., VII, 1951, pp. 117-118.

25. FREUD: *The Interpretation of Dreams* (1900 [1901]). Standard Edition, V.

26. ———: *The Psychopathology of Everyday Life* (1901). Standard Edition, VI.

27. ———: *Creative Writers and Day-Dreaming* (1908). Standard Edition, IX.

28. ———: *Hysterical Phantasies and Their Relation to Bisexuality* (1908). Standard Edition, IX.

29. ———: *Types of Onset of Neurosis* (1912). Standard Edition, XII.

30. ———: *The Unconscious* (1915). Standard Edition, XIV.

31. ———: *'A Child is Being Beaten': A Contribution to the Study of the Origin of Sexual Perversions* (1919). Standard Edition, XVII.

32. ———: *Moses and Monotheism: Three Essays* (1939 [1934-38]). Standard Edition, XXIII.

33. ———: *Splitting of the Ego in the Process of Defence* (1940 [1938]). Standard Edition, XXIII.

34. GREENACRE, PHYLLIS: *The Impostor.* This QUARTERLY, XXVII, 1958, pp. 359-382.

35. HARTMANN, HEINZ: *Ego Psychology and the Problem of Adaptation.* New York: International Universities Press, Inc., 1958.

36. JACOBSON, EDITH: The Self and the Object World. In: *The Psychoanalytic Study of the Child, Vol. IX.* New York: International Universities Press, Inc., 1954, pp. 75-127.

37. ———: *Depersonalization.* J. Amer. Psa. Assn., VII, 1959, pp. 581-610.

38. JOSEPH, EDWARD D.: *An Unusual Fantasy in a Twin with an Inquiry into the Nature of Fantasy.* This QUARTERLY, XXVIII, 1959, pp. 189-206.

39. JOSEPH, EDWARD D. and TABOR, JACK H.: The Simultaneous Analysis of a Pair of Identical Twins and the Twinning Reaction. In: *The Psychoanalytic Study of the Child, Vol. XVI.* New York: International Universities Press, Inc., 1961, pp. 275-299.

40. KRIS, ERNST and KAPLAN, ABRAHAM: Æsthetic Ambiguity. In: *Psychoanalytic Explorations in Art.* New York: International Universities Press, Inc., 1952, pp. 243-264.

41. LEWIN, BERTRAM D.: *Claustrophobia.* This QUARTERLY, IV, 1935, pp. 227-233.

42. LINN, LOUIS: *The Discriminating Function of the Ego.* This QUARTERLY, XXIII, 1954, pp. 38-47.

43. MARCOVITZ, ELI: *The Meaning of Déjà Vu.* This QUARTERLY, XXI, 1952, pp. 481-489.

44. NUNBERG, HERMAN: *Transference and Reality.* Int. J. Psa., XXXII, 1951, pp. 1-9.

45. RANGELL, LEO: Personal Communication, 1955.

46. SACHS, HANNS: The Community of Day Dreams. In: *The Creative Unconscious.* Cambridge: Sci-Art Publishers, 1942.

47. SHARPE, ELLA FREEMAN: Psychophysical Problems Revealed in Language: An Examination of Metaphor. In: *Collected Papers on Psycho-Analysis.* London: The Hogarth Press, Ltd., 1950.

48. SPIEGEL, LEO A.: The Self, the Sense of Self, and Perception. In: *The Psychoanalytic Study of the Child, Vol. XIV.* New York: International Universities Press, Inc., 1959, pp. 81-109.

49. WAELDER, ROBERT: *The Principle of Multiple Function.* This QUARTERLY, V, 1936, pp. 45-62.

7

COGNITIVE DIFFICULTIES IN PSYCHOANALYSIS

COGNITIVE DIFFICULTIES IN PSYCHOANALYSIS

BY ERNEST KAFKA, M.D.

The author raises a number of questions about cognitive diffi-culties in relation to psychoanalysis. He presents the case of an adult patient in whom previously unrecognized childhood cogni-tive difficulties were discovered during the course of analysis. Their relationship to the patient's problems in adulthood is dis-cussed. Some suggestions and speculations about the questions raised are presented with the hope of stimulating further explo-ration of what the author considers to be an interesting and im-portant subject for psychoanalysis.

Certain individuals manifest unusual cognitive characteristics in childhood. These include exceptional abilities in one or another area—in musical or mathematical talent, for example—as well as special disabilities. Often they occur in mixtures. Dyslexia, minimal brain dysfunction, learning disorder, and hyperactivity are among the terms that workers in fields other than psycho-analysis have applied to childhood conditions in which partic-ular cognitive difficulties or combinations of them are promi-nent. In recent times, psychologists, educators, neurophysiolo-gists, and workers in other disciplines have become increasingly interested in aspects of the general subject. Formerly, the cog-nitive difficulties of individuals went unrecognized more often than they now do. My clinical experience has been that people with such idiosyncrasies appear fairly frequently as patients. Their cognitive difficulties, whether they had been recognized in childhood or not, play a significant part in adult analyses and therapy, both through their effects on development and, if they persist, through their continuing effects in adulthood. With the exception of some work of Victor Rosen (1955, 1961) and Annemarie Weil (1978), however, little else dealing with the subject has appeared in the psychoanalytic literature.

This paper is presented with the hope of encouraging greater psychoanalytic interest in and discussion of this subject. I wish to raise a number of questions that have occurred to me in the course of working with such patients. For some of these questions I can suggest partial answers, based on my experiences, and for some, I cannot, but I hope that others may become interested in reporting their findings and ideas.

1. What traces of cognitive difficulties that appear in childhood but go unrecognized may persist into adult life, and how can they be discovered in analyses? How can cognitive difficulties that first occurred in childhood and may have persisted into adult life be detected in analyses when the patient is unaware of their presence?

2. What can we learn about the effects of such problems on the development of individuals?

3. How do these problems influence patients as analysands?

4. Do such problems require modifications of analytic technique, or alterations of emphasis or modes of communication, in adult analyses?

5. Can analytic data increase our understanding of the sources of such cognitive idiosyncrasies, or are we limited to achieving understanding of their specific psychological meanings in the childhood conflicts and psychological development of affected persons?

6. Why has the question received so little attention in the psychoanalytic literature?

By way of orientation, I will summarize what the common manifestations of cognitive "deficits" are thought to be by non-analysts. I will briefly interpolate one view of some characteristic dysfunctions; this is taken from the extensive review of the subject by a child psychiatrist, Paul Wender. In his book, *Minimal Brain Dysfunction in Children*, Wender (1971) writes, "The principal abnormalities of motor function are . . . a high activity level and impaired coordination" (p. 13). "A few children are hyperactive and listless." A typical history is of a "clumsy, inept child" (p. 14), perhaps with "poor fine motor coordination," and "difficulty in learning to throw and catch a ball. . . . Shortness of attention span and poor concentration ability are common" (p. 14). There is often "an inability to organize hierarchically so that all aspects of a percept or an idea are of equal importance," which may lead to "an obsessive quality." There are associated learning difficulties. The most serious learning difficulty is "learning to read (although problems in writing, generally sloppiness, and problems in comprehension and arithmetic may be present as well)" (p. 16). Wender writes that, "working with Swedish teenage dyslexics of normal intelligence, Frisk [and co-workers] found that approximately one-third to one-half showed current distractibility and restlessness, sleep disturbance, or impaired motor abilities, and that as children they had had an increased prevalence of speech difficulties, clumsiness and enuresis" (pp. 16-17). Such children often have "low frustration tolerance" and "impulsivity, poor planning and judgment," "defective control." They are often "obstinate" and "controlling." Wender does not note that right-left confusion is a frequent concomitant phenomenon.

I will continue by presenting a case report of an analysis of a patient who manifested a number of these characteristics as a child and as an adult, and who did not become aware of some of them or of their consequence until they were described in his treatment.

Mr. R.'s internist referred him to a consultant, a psychoanalyst colleague, for evaluation of a potency disturbance that the internist could not explain. He came thence to me. He had been married three years to a woman five years younger. His sexual symptom, he told me, was an exaggerated version of a life-long difficulty. It consisted of a lack of interest in intercourse and frequent loss of erection or premature ejaculation on those approximately monthly occasions when he and his wife attempted intercourse. This situation had become increasingly severe over the year preceding his coming to treatment. He had had a life-long anxiety about performing sexually before meeting his wife. His earlier sexual activity had consisted mainly of masturbation. He had had two affairs of several months each and many "one-night stands," more or less successful, before meeting his wife. During the year of courtship and the first year of his marriage, he felt he "performed"—his word—successfully enough to sat-isfy himself and, by and large, his wife as well, although she informed him that he was inhibited and less pleasing than any of her previous lovers.

The patient connected his idea that he "performed," when I asked him what he meant in using this term, to a notion he often had that he was a "faker," that there was something "not genuine" about him, as if he "pretended" that he had abilities he really lacked in the sexual sphere and in other areas, but he could not be more specific about what he meant. Despite a certain feeling of anxiety and humiliation, things went fairly well until his wife developed pneumonia. He was fearful about approaching her sexually during and for some months after her recovery and felt somewhat less aroused by her after they resumed more frequent intimacy.

More recently, probably when Mrs. R. began to indicate a wish to have a child, Mr. R. noticed that he had less sexual interest in her than before and that he also began to experience periods of irritability, an increased difficulty in getting his work done, and embarrassing mental lapses. He came late to work appointments, misfiled papers, "forgot" names, and neglected to pay bills. His work situation was at that time a cause of con-siderable anxiety to Mr. R. He was an executive in a large pa-ternalistic advertising corporation with the responsibility for evaluating future directions in which his company might go, as well as for planning administrative structures. The company was doing badly, his advice was not followed, and he felt he was not well regarded. His "Guru," the man who had hired him, had lost influence and seemed on the verge of being let go. If he lost his "Guru," he would risk being exposed as a "faker";

he would feel "lost" himself because he would be "found out" as one who could not "find his way" by himself. Mr. R. felt fearful about his future prospects, especially so since he had distinguished himself neither in selecting his three previous jobs—two of the companies had gone out of business—nor in his own work accomplishment. He had the tendency to begin jobs with energy and enthusiasm and then to become bored, inefficient, and unproductive. He lost interest. Sometimes, he had "superior" ideas and insights he could not clearly communicate to others. Difficulty organizing his ideas in logical sequence impaired his ability to write, slowed him, and added to his work problems. In addition, he felt guilty about his superiority, but mortified when it was unappreciated.

The past history was as follows. The patient was the elder of two children, with a sister four years younger. The mother had been the youngest of three sisters. Mr. R.'s maternal grandfather had become reasonably successful as an engineer, and his mother admired him greatly. This grandmother died when Mr. R.'s mother was in her early twenties. Her older sisters were married, and she cared for her father, keeping house for him until he died suddenly when she was in her mid-thirties. She received a modest inheritance, and shortly after her father's death, married the patient's father, a man eight years younger, who had separated from his family when he emigrated from Europe. After a period of infatuation, she quickly became disappointed in her husband. His defects, she thought, were that he was uncultured and uninterested in becoming more cultured, and that he was a drinker who preferred to spend his evenings in the local bars with cronies rather than working hard to advance himself intellectually or financially. Mr. R. was born in the second year of this marriage, and by the time his sister was born, he felt he was superior to his father, was destined for great things, was charming and brilliant, and was much like the revered, dead grandfather—or would soon become so. Unlike his father, he could already appreciate and understand poetry, novels, and political and economic problems which he heard about on the radio, from his mother's readings to him, and in discussions with adults. His sister's birth, he thought, had led to only a minor and transient deflation. He continued to feel preferred and superior and treated her with contempt and condescension, as he thought his mother did.

When he was sent to a local school under religious auspices at age six, he suffered a great blow. Though he thought he was more intelligent than the other children, academically more gifted and generally superior, he was disliked and excluded by them, felt physically large and inept, and was unable to make friends. He had to make do with being a teacher's pet. Throughout his childhood and adolescence, he felt deprived, lonely, and angry because he seemed unable to make friends and felt he was not one of the group. Partly, these feelings were the result of his view of himself as special and imaginative, but unappreciated. He described his behavior at this time as ingratiating and passive with peers, sparkling and brilliant with adults—for example, with teachers with whom he discussed subtle theological points. He was extremely fearful, avoided fights and arguments, and could not stand up for himself. He was a "sissy" and a "mama's boy." However, he did well enough academically to be transferred to a special school for gifted children and later to win a scholarship to a prestigious university. Nevertheless, in adolescence, as in childhood, he lacked self-confidence. He could not approach girls, came to feel he was under the thumb of his mother and the clergy, and began to resent his father for his lack of involvement with him, as well as for the other flaws that he and his mother agreed his father had. He resented the college he attended because he felt it was too strict and too much his mother's choice, but he could not bring himself to transfer. Instead, he cut classes, stayed out at night later than the rules allowed, and was almost expelled. This experience frightened and cowed him. He attended graduate school in New York, lived with his parents, and continued to bask in his mother's approval—which was withdrawn when he showed signs of independent interest, especially in women. He did not move out of his parents' home until he reached his mid-thirties.

At this time he began to form a more affectionate and understanding relation with his father and to conceive a new view of his mother. Gradually, he came to regard her as manipulative and exploitative and a millstone around his neck. When he moved out of the convenient and comfortable parental home into his own apartment, he began to date more seriously, met his wife to be, and married.

Having given something of an overview of the manner of Mr. R.'s presentation and of his history, I will now proceed to a description of the course of his analysis. Mr. R. was a tall man, six feet three inches in height, but not of impressive appearance. His frame was not broad, his appearance pudgy and soft, and he was perhaps thirty pounds overweight. He was very involved with his dress and owned many clothes, including some dozens of suits. He favored large patterns in expensive and conservative materials but in odd, bright colors. His manner matched his appearance. It was correct, yet incorrect, acquiescent, yet assertive. He would come into the office, lie down on the couch, and speak in a professorial, somewhat arrogant, lecturing manner. For several weeks he spoke in meticulous detail of his history, as though he were reciting a book. He seemed hardly to pay any attention to me, except for polite hellos or goodbyes. There was little hint of the state of his feelings or of more than a scholarly interest in the story he was unfolding.

In the second month I began to make comments to Mr. R. to the effect that there was something official in his manner, that he revealed few feelings, that he seemed to concentrate on historical matters. He was annoyed and responded by telling me that he had thought psychoanalysts were particularly interested in the histories of their patients and that he would be pleased to discuss whatever I might think best. He wished to cooperate as best he could. Perhaps he should talk more about current problems. And so he began to tell me about the office politics and the difficulties of the projects he was working on. Gradually, I told him he wished to think of me as a guide or as a "Guru," as the boss who had hired him was, someone to please and satisfy in the hope of being led. He agreed with me, noting that he was aware that I was an expert in my field, that he had come to me for help, that he hoped I would be able to explain his problems to him. Again, gradually, repeatedly, I pointed out that he seemed to act as though his observations or ideas about himself were of little account, that he wanted to leave most of the thinking about him to me, and that this seemed inconsistent with the common aim we both had to understand him and his difficulties in being more active. It also seemed inconsistent with his attitude of intellectual superiority.

Slowly, the work became somewhat more spontaneous and immediate. Mr. R. expressed some angry feelings about his years of religious indoctrination. He complained about the narrowness of his mother's and his teachers' views and concluded that his inhibitions had resulted from his "brainwashing" upbringing. He rarely spoke of his own impulses, wishes, or intentions, or indicated that he had any, other than to satisfy the desires of his employer, wife, analyst, and others, and he felt guilty and resentful about being imperfectly able to do so. I was able to convey to him that he had nevertheless told me of his opinions and attitudes about business, of disagreements with others throughout his life, of feelings of disdain for colleagues and superiors, of fears of fighting and of punishment.

Again, over a period of time, and with numerous such interchanges, Mr. R.'s manner gradually changed. He spoke of his anger with his mother and his feelings of ineptness and inadequacy. He never could live up to her expectations and thus felt incompetent or helpless in many instances. He revealed that he masturbated frequently and compulsively even now, two or three times a day, and that he had done so since adolescence. Later, with much shame, he described fantasies of being shown how to do it by an older man, then of arousing himself by fantasies of watching two women arousing each other orally, then having intercourse with dildos. I pointed out to him his tendency to make himself aloof, distant, an observer, even in his fantasies. Fears of losing control began to come up. Mr. R. remembered having frightening dreams in childhood—dreams of gory automobile crashes related to fear of his drunken father, dreams of robbers and murderers against whom he had to defend his family, especially his mother and sister. I suggested to Mr. R. that in the preceding period of his analysis, he seemed to have behaved toward me as he described his behavior toward adults in his early childhood. That is, he adopted a seemingly ingratiating manner, acting like a "goody-goody," a compliant student. Probably he hid his feelings of rivalry and contempt for the feared rival. His attitude toward superiors at work appeared to parallel his behavior toward me. His repeated infatuation with bosses and jobs, followed invariably by feelings of disappointment and disillusionment, reflected, besides fear over rivalrous wishes, an emulation of his mother's attitude of disappointment with his father and superiority to him, thus revealing his close tie to his mother.

Gradually, the patient became more querulous with me. He responded more and more to my comments with associations that took the form of "yes, but." At the same time he more frequently felt anger toward his work superiors and even openly questioned and opposed them. Rare dreams, dimly remembered, concerned battles and revolutions. His potency problem became worse. He became overtly angry with his mother, refused to see her over long periods of time or even to speak with her on the telephone. He recalled adolescent feelings of resentment toward women in general. Mr. R. came to see his rebellion against religion during his teens, his unproductivity at work, and his sexual negativism toward his wife as expressions and defenses against his underlying hostility toward his mother, whom he wished to torture by depriving her of the satisfaction of her wish to dominate him while living vicariously through him. He also thought he had "seen through" the members of the clergy who deluded themselves, thinking they were pious, when actually they craved power and domination. His method for concealing arrogance derived from identification with clergy rivals as well as with mother. Mr. R. came to understand that he had a belief that he was dependent on his mother, later on his father, teachers, the "Gurus," on his wife and on the analyst, and that criticisms by them led to the fear of being "lost," unable to fend for himself, and to feelings of extreme anger. He talked about how angry he felt when interpretations indicated that he could not "orient" himself; he then felt like withdrawing and withholding. His submissive attitude and his passive posture toward superiors diminished. He quit his job and began to search for a better position.

During this period of career transition, Mr. R. felt an uncomfortable, variable anxiety, which he blamed on me. I had deprived him of his hope that he would achieve success by attaching himself to a powerful male. I had frustrated him in his wishes to outdo his mother at her own game, to succeed where she had failed. I had caused his potency symptom to worsen. I had pointed out to him his envy of his sister, who had married a wealthy and successful businessman and had thus succeeded where he could not. I was able to expand on earlier interpretations. I explained these angry feelings as reflecting resentment at the messenger who told unwelcome truths. We were able to enlarge Mr. R.'s understanding of his adoption of a feminine attitude in terms of earlier relations within his family, as well as to clarify his fears about his competitive and hostile strivings, especially in relation to feelings of guilt over his superiority. The sexual disturbance continued. Mr. R.'s anxiety and anger focused more on his wife's wish to have a child. He would then be replaced as a favorite by the child as he had been with his father when his sister was born. He would become a "meal ticket" as his father had been. I remained puzzled about the reason for the intensity of his need to conceal his ambitiousness, the intensity of his feelings of vulnerability, the intensity of his anxiety.

In the fourth year of analysis symptomatic acts he had earlier experienced in other contexts now appeared in relation to me. He arrived late for our appointments, neglected my bills, and misremembered what had been said in preceding sessions. Investigation of his mental lapses proceeded in response to my requests for further details, requests which were influenced by my puzzlement about the intensity of the feelings of mortification and humiliation Mr. R. had when parapraxes occurred. He was unable to give any reasons why he felt so humiliated over his "mistakes" or so reluctant to investigate them. His parapraxes seemed motivated in part by transference fear of me. He wished to appear a harmless, incompetent, childish person. The reasons for the intense anxiety remained obscure. I now became more curious about the form the parapraxes took.

A pattern became evident over a period of months. Mr. R. misfiled my bills. On describing the geography of his home office, he said he had put my bill in the file on the left, not in the appropriate one on the right. After a lateness, he explained that he had turned in the wrong direction in the subway and gotten on a train leading away from my office. The following night he reported remembering a dream. In it, he was interviewing an applicant for a job (he had just recently found one for himself) and rejected him. When he awoke, it was some time before he realized this had been a dream, not a reality. In the interim, he wondered whether he had been "right" in rejecting the applicant. In the session, he suggested that his sense of humiliation with me had to do with the feeling that "I am never right. I want to reverse our relationship and be right." On another occasion, as he was discussing a political office problem in which he was arguing a point with the head of his company, he explained that the "head" had been on his right, and he gestured with his left hand. I pointed out a transference connection I thought was related—Mr. R. had recently seen me driving and envied me my car—as a partial explanation of his underlying anxiety: perhaps he wished to be the "head." Was the gesture with the left hand a gesture toward the driver's seat? He had gestured with his left hand while describing the "head" who sat on his right. I was also dimly aware that the emphasis on geography—location—might have some significance.

Mr. R. responded with much embarrassment. Again he had made a slip. He felt humiliated, incompetent, like a child. He could not tell right from left. I suggested that the right-left question might be important. I pointed out the spatial confusion in the episodes of the misfiled bills, his taking the wrong direction, the dream question, "who was right?" Mr. R. became angry; I wanted to make him feel small. I had no "right" to suggest that he had a defect. I had not made this suggestion, I replied. Why did he think he had become so angry? He replied that I was mocking him for his left-handedness. His father had mocked him when he had difficulty learning to write. That he was left-handed was news to me, I indicated, as was the fact that he had had difficulty learning to write. It had never occurred to him to mention these two facts, he said. He recalled a painful memory, from the age of about four, of having gone shopping with his mother and having lost her. He had been terrified about being lost, unable to find his way to her.

This new element in the patient's life was explored and defined and its ramifications revealed to some degree. Again, feelings of guilt and fear consequent to his wish to defeat his father, and me, played a part in motivating his inhibitions. In addition, his anxiety was related to his fear that criticism indicated to him that he could not find his own way, lacked an independent ability to orient himself, and had to depend on others. He was a "faker" because he pretended that he did not have to depend on others. His writing problem and his difficulty in orienting himself in childhood had been the source of deeply humiliating feelings to him and had aggravated his anger when he felt neglected by those on whom he depended. He had also had great difficulty in spelling correctly as a child. He had never learned to spell letter by letter as other children did, but had overcome this problem by memorizing how words looked. This was a secret he had never told, because it indicated to him that he had a defect that he had to conceal to avoid being laughed at, and it contributed to his idea that he was a "faker" who concealed an embarrassing flaw.

A certain characteristic lack of humor, particularly about himself, came to seem connected to his early responses to and persisting tendency toward spatial confusion. He felt he had a defect. Something was missing that others had. Mr. R. soon thought that this "defect" played a part in his feminine identification. He had equated his spatial problem with a lack of masculinity. His physical clumsiness added to his sense of inadequate masculinity and to his sense of dependence and enforced passivity. Childhood fears and memories of being lost continued to come up, as did the relation of these experiences to later interests and characteristics. He had early become extremely interested in travel and maps. He had developed his visual capacity, his preferred visual imagery, and had come to emphasize sexual looking, as, for example, in his peeping masturbatory fantasies. He recalled a persisting difficulty in remembering which was the "x" and which was the "y" axis in high school math. His interest in organizing companies, in ordering administrative structures, in market identification, in futurology, came to seem related partly (there were various determinants) to a need to locate himself spatially, to know where he was in relation to others. His clumsiness in childhood was more closely described, and Mr. R. theorized that his tendency "to find the banana peel in life and slip on it," and the mirth it provoked in others, had added to his angry, defensive negativism, his fear of competition, and his lack of humor and spontaneity. After all, he believed he had a "defect." The banana peel image was unusual for Mr. R., who, as noted, had rarely permitted himself to be comical.

Another aspect of his childhood cognitive difficulty emerged through further memories Mr. R. recovered, relating to how he learned to read in the second and third grades, with the help of a special personage in his life, a teacher who took a special interest in him. As noted, he could not manage the abstraction of letters signifying sounds, but instead learned how words look

and how to reproduce their appearance. In a way he felt a
cheat, an impostor who pretended to read and write but could
not really do so. He was afraid of being found out and felt
guilty about being a pretender. Clearly, this "defect," so stren-
uously denied, concealed, and compensated for, also served as
a defense against phallic aggressive strivings. The defect also
made the satisfaction of these strivings seem unlikely to the
patient. At the same time, his capacity to visualize supported
his sense of being special and superior. He used his defect as a
defense—it helped him to appear innocuous—and he de-
fended himself against his profound feelings of defectiveness
by emphasizing his superior qualities. At the same time, his
pride over his capacity to visualize contributed to his anxious
fantasies about impending punishment.

In his new capacity for greater ambition and aggressiveness
Mr. R. now determined to have a child but discovered he was
sterile. He attempted various medical treatments to remedy his
new defect but was unsuccessful. Six months later, he arranged
to adopt a baby, was pleased with good success at his new job,
and had only a moderate fear mixed with his enjoyment of the
political wars at work. Sexual ennui persisted and so did his
masturbatory fantasies. He was able to recognize and understand feelings of anger and depression related to the recent
blow of discovering his sterility, but claimed adoption would be
a satisfactory solution. At this point, he said he was satisfied
with the analytic results and was determined to end his treatment. As reasons for a more abrupt termination than I would
have regarded as optimal, he cited questions of time and money
related to job and child, and an unwillingness to enter into a
struggle with his insurance company, which was demanding
lengthy reports on his condition. The insurance question was
unfortunate, but significant, because it played into his continuing anxiety about his defects and his persisting tendency to
defend against feelings of anxiety and depression related to
them. It also influenced his decision to take his life "into his
own hands" at this time.

I have presented a case report of the treatment of a middle-aged man who came to treatment because of work problems and sexual dysfunction. In the course of the analysis, we came upon what seemed to be hints of a cognitive difficulty. Memories appeared that confirmed the presence of difficulties and of special childhood abilities that had contributed to his problems in adult life and to his character development. In childhood, this left-handed patient had suffered from right-left confusion, impulsiveness, lexical problems respecting the written word, clumsiness, and some difficulty involving abstraction, or perhaps the capacity to categorize the significant and less significant. He also thought he had a special ability to visualize and to remember. In adulthood, he was inhibited, controlled, passive, humorless, fearful about competing, passively aggressive, and sexually dysfunctional. He was also methodical, rigorous, interested in structure, visually gifted, and felt guiltily and fearfully superior. The treatment had clear, positive, but limited results. Mr. R. became more successful at work and in his relationships. He will probably enjoy fatherhood, but he remained relatively constricted and somewhat anxious. He learned a great deal but was unable to work analytically in a termination phase. His departure seemed to reflect a newfound ability to be more active, but it also seemed to suppress his only partly analyzed aggression and his transference fears of punishment, now in relation to fantasies about fatherhood. Certain characteristics were relatively unaffected by the analysis. His responsiveness to interventions in general remained less spontaneous and original than that of many other patients. His dream reports remained rare, and his associations unimaginative, perhaps vaguely concrete. At the same time, he maintained an arrogant sense of superiority which compensated him to some extent for his continuing feelings of defectiveness, but his guilt and fear of retaliation, which he was able to analyze to some degree, persisted and contributed to his decision to terminate.

I return to the original Question 1 about how one can detect previously unrecognized cognitive difficulties in analysis. In this case, a number of the patient's adult characteristics led to my suspicion that such difficulties might have been present in childhood. These included certain characterologic qualities. They were general qualities: an underlying level of anxiety and a corresponding defensiveness, a narcissistic vulnerability and rigidity of character, a distance and humorlessness, and a constriction of dream and fantasy life that seemed out of keeping, in my clinical judgment, with the historic factors that I knew and with his general competence. The severity of Mr. R.'s separation problems and the intensity of his bisexual conflicts were more specific factors that led me to wonder. Still more specific keys involved his propensity to feel humiliation, almost mortification, in response to seemingly minor parapraxes and, finally, his repeated use of imagery involving location, particularly in relation to right and left in his associations, as well as in many parapraxes. Ultimately, these cues led to the discovery of Mr. R.'s childhood lexical difficulties, writing problems, clumsiness, and spatial uncertainties. This grouping corresponds to Wender's (1971) description of minimal brain dysfunction: Mr. R. had "impaired coordination," "clumsiness," "problems in arithmetic" (including the x-y axis confusion), "short attention span" (which seemed to persist and to influence Mr. R.'s work performance), "impulsivity," and an "obsessive quality."

As to Questions 2 and 3 regarding the effect of these difficulties on development and on the patient as analysand, the effects—e.g., heightened anxiety and defensiveness, and their developmental vicissitudes—became obvious during the course of the work. Mr. R.'s sense of defect had supported his vulnerability to separation at first and his susceptibility to castration fears later. The sense of defect added to his sense of loss at his sister's birth, and later, when he went to school, it contributed to his tendency toward depressive ideas of incompetence and dependence, to his susceptibility to ridicule, to his humorlessness, and to his tendency toward sulking and withholding. It also spurred him to compensatory development of his visual capacities and to efforts at finding alternative ways of orienting himself spatially and temporally.

Regarding Question 4, about the possibility of needing to modify technique with such patients, I do not believe that this case required technical modification, although it was necessary to repeat interpretations in various words, using a variety of examples, more patiently and tactfully than usual. This seems to be similar to tutorial methods used to aid children with cognitive difficulties, which depend on presenting concepts in alternate forms and using a variety of sensory modalities to aid the child in finding alternative routes around his difficulties. It might be that in a more seriously impaired patient than Mr. R. was, more literal and concrete examples and analogies would have to be given, to convey the meaning intended in an intervention. In some instances, a supportive, encouraging, more psychotherapeutic approach may be required.

As to Question 5, having to do with the issue of etiology, I do not personally think that psychoanalytic data can be used as definitive evidence regarding the question of immanent versus developmental factors. In Mr. R.'s case there is perhaps a piece of negative evidence: none of his cognitive idiosyncrasies could be explained to my satisfaction, in the way that symptoms, dreams, and other psychological phenomena can, simply as the consequence of compromise formation. Nor did his tendency toward right-left confusion or his difficulty in organizing his ideas and in sometimes translating images into words significantly change with analysis. It is possible that Mr. R.'s functioning deteriorated more readily under stress than one might expect on dynamic and developmental grounds. Perhaps, under stress, characteristic forms appeared because of an underlying physiological organization which became mobilized for psychologic reasons. It is clear that Mr. R. used the forms for defensive and wish-gratifying aims, both consciously and automatically.

Finally, I would like to speculate briefly about why this subject has received little attention from psychoanalysts. First, until recent years, it has received little attention from anyone. The likelihood is that had Mr. R. had his reading difficulty as a child today, a diagnosis of dyslexia would have been made, and remedial efforts would have been instituted. He might have been referred for psychotherapy or analysis as well. Second, such difficulties have received attention in recent years, but mainly as a problem of children, not as a problem of adults. It must occur often that such difficulties in childhood have, as they did for Mr. R., important effects on the development of later pathologic and characterologic formations, just as physical infirmities, illnesses, or such defects as color blindness do. That they may persist and continue to affect cognition may also be so. But this has not been generally recognized. Thus if the difficulty is subtle, it may not be recognized. If severe, such patients may not be considered candidates for analysis.

REFERENCES

ROSEN, V. H. (1955). Strephosymbolia: an intrasystemic disturbance of the synthetic function of the ego. *Psychoanal. Study Child,* 10:83-99.
―――― (1961). The relevance of 'style' to certain aspects of defence and the synthetic function of the ego. *Int. J. Psychoanal.,* 42:447–457.
WEIL, A. P. (1978). Maturational variations and genetic-dynamic issues. *J. Amer. Psychoanal. Assn.,* 26:461-491.
WENDER, P. H. (1971). *Minimal Brain Dysfunction in Children.* New York: Wiley & Sons.

8

THE
NEUROTIC'S
INDIVIDUAL
MYTH

THE NEUROTIC'S INDIVIDUAL MYTH

BY JACQUES LACAN

FOREWORD

"The Neurotic's Individual Myth" was given as a lecture at the Philosophical College of Paris, organized by Jean Wahl, late Professor at the Sorbonne. The text was distributed in 1953 without the approval of Dr. Lacan and without his corrections.

The desire of The Psychoanalytic Quarterly to publish a translation of this lecture led me to make the necessary corrections. The present version, which has been reviewed by the author, will take the place, then, of the revision which he announced in 1966 in his *Écrits* (French edition, p. 72, n.1) and which was never carried out.

I ought to emphasize to the American reader that this presentation, which is more than twenty-five years old, should be regarded as the rudiments of later developments in the thought of Dr. Lacan: these are the first trials of a concept of structure in keeping with analytic discourse.

JACQUES-ALAIN MILLER

I am going to discuss a subject which I must characterize as new and which, as such, is difficult.

The difficulty of this lecture is not especially intrinsic to it. It comes from the fact that it deals with something new which I became aware of both through my analytic experience and through my effort, in the course of teaching what is styled a seminar, to investigate the fundamental reality of analysis. To abstract this new element from that teaching and from that experience so that you can appreciate its implications involves quite special difficulties in a lecture.

That is why I ask your indulgence in advance if perhaps there seems to be some difficulty in your grasping, at least on first contact, the matter under discussion.

Translated by Martha Noel Evans, Ph.D.

Text edited by Jacques-Alain Miller. The French text appeared in Issue No. 17 of *Ornicar? Periodical Bulletin of the Champ Freudien.*

I

Psychoanalysis, I must recall by way of preface, is a discipline which, among the sciences, appears to us in a truly singular position. It is often said that psychoanalysis is not, strictly speaking, a science, which seems to imply by contrast that it is quite simply an art. That is erroneous if one takes it to mean that psychoanalysis is only a technique, an operational method, an aggregate of formulas. But it is not erroneous if you use this word *art* in the sense in which it was used in the Middle Ages to speak of the liberal arts—that series going from astronomy to dialectic by way of arithmetic, geometry, music, and grammar.

It is most assuredly difficult for us to comprehend today the function and implications of these so-called liberal arts in the lives and thought of the medieval masters. Nevertheless, it is certain that what characterizes these arts and distinguishes them from the sciences that are supposed to have emerged from them is the fact that they maintain in the foreground what might be called a fundamental relation to human proportion. At the present time, psychoanalysis is perhaps the only discipline comparable to those liberal arts, inasmuch as it preserves something of this proportional relation of man to himself—an internal relation, closed on itself, inexhaustible, cyclical, and implied pre-eminently in the use of speech.

It is in this respect that analytic experience is not definitively objectifiable. It always implies within itself the emergence of a truth that cannot be said, since what constitutes truth is speech, and then you would have in some way to say speech itself which is exactly what cannot be said in its function as speech.

Moreover, we see emerging from psychoanalysis certain methods which in themselves tend to objectify ways of acting on man, the human object. But these are only techniques derived from that fundamental art of psychoanalysis, inasmuch as it is constituted by that intersubjective relationship which, as I said, is inexhaustible since it is what makes us human. That, nevertheless, is what we are led to try to express in a form that conveys its essence, and that is why there exists at the heart of the analytic experience something that is properly called a myth.

Myth is what provides a discursive form for something that cannot be transmitted through the definition of truth, since the definition of truth must be self-referential and since it is only insofar as speech remains in process that it establishes truth. Speech cannot contain itself nor can it contain the movement toward truth as an objective truth. It can only express truth— and this, in a mythic mode. It is in this sense that one can say that the concretization in analytic theory of intersubjective relationship, that is, the oedipus complex, has the value of a myth.

I bring you a series of experiential facts which I will present as examples of those formations we observe in the living experience of the subjects we accept for analysis, neurotic subjects, for instance, and which are familiar to all those for whom the analytic experience is not entirely alien. These formations require us to make certain structural modifications in the oedipal myth, inasmuch as it is at the heart of the analytic experience, which correlates with the progress we ourselves are making in understanding the analytic experience. These changes permit us, on a second level, to grasp the fact that underlying all analytic theory is the fundamental conflict which, through the mediation of rivalry with the father, binds the subject to an essential, symbolic value. But this binding always occurs, as you will see, in conjunction with an actual debasement, perhaps as a result of particular social circumstances, of the father figure. [Analytic] experience itself extends between this consistently debased image of the father and an image our practice enables us more and more to take into account and to judge when it occurs in the analyst himself: although it is veiled and almost denied by analytic theory, the analyst nevertheless assumes almost surreptitiously, in the symbolic relationship with the subject, the position of this figure dimmed in the course of history, that of the master—the moral master, the master who initiates the one still in ignorance into the dimension of fundamental human relationships and who opens for him what one might call the way to moral consciousness, even to wisdom, in assuming the human condition.

If we proceed from the definition of myth as a certain objectified representation of an epos or as a chronicle expressing in an imaginary way the fundamental relationships characteristic of a certain mode of being human at a specific period, if we understand it as the social manifestation—latent or patent, virtual or actual, full or void of meaning—of this mode of being, then it is certain that we can trace its function in the actual experience of a neurotic. Experience reveals to us, in fact, all sorts of instantiations which fit this pattern and which, strictly speaking, one may call myths; and I am going to demonstrate this to you in an example I think will be familiar to all of you who are interested in these questions, one which I will borrow from one of Freud's great case histories.

These case histories periodically enjoy a renewal of interest in academia, but that did not prevent one of our eminent colleagues from revealing recently—I heard it from his own mouth—something like contempt for them. Their technique, he said, is as clumsy as it is antiquated. One could, after all, maintain that position if one considers the progress we have made in our awareness of the intersubjective relationship and in our limitation of interpretation to the relationships established between us and the subject in the immediacy of the analytic session. But should my interlocutor have gone so far as to say that Freud's cases were ill chosen? To be sure, one may say that they are all incomplete and that many of them are analyses broken off midway, fragments of analysis. But that in itself ought to move us to reflect and to ask ourselves why Freud made this selection. All that, of course, if one has confidence in Freud. And one must have confidence in him.

It is not enough to say, as the person whose remarks I have reported to you continued, that this [incompleteness] certainly has at least one heartening aspect: that of demonstrating that one small grain of truth somewhere suffices to allow it to show through and emerge in spite of the obstacles posed by the presentation. I do not consider that an accurate view of things. In fact, the tree of daily practice hid from my colleague the forest which rises up from Freud's texts.

I have chosen "The Rat Man" to present to you, and I think I am now in a position to justify Freud's interest in this case.

II

The case concerns an obsessional neurosis. All who are concerned with psychoanalysis have heard about what we consider to be the source and structure of this neurosis, specifically the aggressive tensions, the instinctual fixation, etc. Progress in analytic theory has provided as a basis for our understanding of obsessional neurosis an extremely complex genetic elaboration; and it is certain that some element or some phase or other of the phantasmatic or imaginary themes that we habitually meet in the analysis of an obsessional neurosis will also be found in a reading of "The Rat Man." But this reassuring effect that familiar, popular ideas always have for those who read or learn may mask for the reader the originality of this case history and its especially significant and persuasive character.

As you know, this case takes its title from a totally fascinating fantasy which has, in the psychology of the attack that brings the subject to the analyst, an obvious function as precipitating factor. This story of a punishment which has always been strongly spotlighted—indeed, it enjoys real celebrity—includes the thrusting of a rat stimulated by artificial means into the rectum of the victim by means of a more or less ingenious apparatus. His first hearing of this story produces in the subject a state of fascinated horror which does not precipitate his neurosis but rather actualizes its motifs and produces anxiety. There ensues a whole elaboration whose structure we shall examine.

This fantasy is certainly essential to the theory of the determinism of the neurosis, and it can be found in numerous themes throughout the case history. But is that to say that its only interest lies in this fantasy? Not only do I not believe that, but I am sure that, with a careful reading, one will perceive that the principal interest of this case lies in its extreme particularity.

As always, Freud emphasized that each case ought to be studied in its particularity, exactly as if we were completely ignorant of theory. And what constitutes the particularity of this case is the manifest, visible character of the relationships involved. The particular value of this case as a model derives from its simplicity, in the same way one may speak of a particular example in geometry as having a dazzlingly superior clarity when compared with a demonstration where, by reason of its discursive character, the truth remains veiled in the shadows of a long sequence of deductions.

Here is what constitutes the originality of the case, as will appear to any reasonably attentive reader.

The constellation—why not? in the sense astrologers use it— the original constellation that presided over the birth of the subject, over his destiny, and I would almost say his prehistory, specifically the fundamental family relationships which structured his parents' union, happens to have a very precise relation, perhaps definable by a transformational formula, with what appears to be the most contingent, the most phantasmatic, the most paradoxically morbid in his case, that is, the last state of development of his great obsessive fear, the imaginary scenario he arrives at as a resolution of the anxiety associated with the precipitation of the outbreak.

The subject's constellation is made up, within the family tradition, by a narration of a certain number of traits which characterize the parents' union.

It should be noted that the father was a subordinate officer at the beginning of his career and that he remained very "subordinate," with the note of authority, but slightly absurd, that that implies. A kind of belittlement by his contemporaries permanently follows him, and a mixture of bravado and flashiness makes of him a typecast figure that shadows the amiable man described by the subject. This father finds himself in a position to make what is called an advantageous match; his wife occupies a much higher station in the hierarchy of the bourgeoisie and brings to him both their means of livelihood and even the job he holds at the time they are expecting their child. The prestige is, then, on the mother's side. And one of the most frequent forms of teasing between these people who, as a rule, get along very well and who even seem bonded by a real affection, is a kind of game which consists of a dialogue between them: the wife makes a kidding reference to a strong attachment her husband had just before their marriage to a poor but pretty girl, and then the husband protests and affirms each time that it was a passing fancy, long ago and forgotten. But this game, whose very repetition implies perhaps that it includes its share of guile, certainly profoundly impresses the young subject who is later to become our patient.

Another element of the family myth is of no small importance. The father had, in the course of his military career, what one might modestly call *troubles*. He did neither more nor less than gamble away the regimental funds which he held by virtue of his office. And he owed his honor, indeed even his life, at least in respect to his career, the figure he could continue to cut in society, only to the intervention of a friend who lent him the sum he had to refund and who became, then, his savior. This incident is still spoken of as a truly important and significant episode in the father's past.

This is how the subject's family constellation is represented. The story emerges bit by bit during the analysis without the subject's connecting it in any way with anything presently happening. It takes all the intuition of Freud to understand that these are essential elements in the precipitation of the obsessional neurosis. The conflict *rich woman/poor woman* was reproduced exactly in the subject's life when his father urged him to marry a rich woman, and it was then that the neurosis proper had its onset. Reporting this fact, almost at the same time the subject says: *"I'm telling you something that certainly has no connection to all that has happened to me."* Then, Freud immediately perceives the connection.

What, in fact, becomes visible in a panoramic overview of the case history is the strict correspondence between these initial elements of the subjective constellation and the ultimate development of the phantasmatic obsession. What is this ultimate development? In accordance with the mode of thought characteristic of obsessions, the image of the punishment at first engendered all kinds of fears in the subject, in particular that this punishment might one day be inflicted on the people most dear to him, notably either on that idealized figure of the poor woman to whom he devotes a love whose style and particular importance we will examine shortly—the very sort of love which the obsessional subject is capable of—or, yet more paradoxically, on his father who, however, was dead at that time and reduced to a figure he imagines in the other world. But the subject finally found himself drawn into behavior which demonstrates that the neurotic constructs of the obsessional sometimes end by verging on the constructs of insanity.

He is in the position of having to pay the price for an object whose nature is not immaterial, a pair of glasses that he mislaid during the army maneuvers at which time the story of the punishment under discussion was told to him and the present crisis was precipitated. He requests the immediate replacement of his glasses from his optician in Vienna—for all this takes place in the old Austro-Hungarian Empire, before the beginning of the war of 1914—and the latter sends him by express mail a little package containing the object. Now, the same captain who told him the story of the punishment and who impresses him strongly by his display of a taste for cruelty informs him that he must reimburse a Lieutenant A who is in charge of the mail and who is supposed to have paid out the sum for him. It is around this idea of reimbursement that the neurotic occurrence reaches its final development. In fact, the subject makes a neurotic duty of repaying the sum, but under certain, very precise conditions. He imposes this duty on him-

self in the form of an internal command which surges up in the
obsessional psyche in contradiction to its original impulse expressed in the form, *"do not pay."* Instead here he is, bound
to himself by a kind of oath, *"pay A."* But he realizes very
quickly that this absolute imperative is not at all adequate, since
it is not A who is in charge of the mail, but a Lieutenant B.

That is not all. At the very time when all these lucubrations
are taking place in him, the subject knows perfectly well, we
find out later, that in reality he does not owe this sum to
Lieutenant B either, but quite simply to the lady at the post
office who was willing to trust B, an honorable gentleman and
officer who happened to be in the vicinity. Nevertheless, up to
the time when he puts himself in Freud's care, the subject will
be in a state of extreme anxiety, haunted by one of those conflicts so characteristic of the experience of obsessionals and
which centers entirely on the following scenario: since he swore
to himself that he would reimburse A so that the catastrophes
foreseen in the obsession would not happen to those he loves
the most, he must have Lieutenant A reimburse the generous
lady at the post office, and, in his presence, she must pay over
the sum in question to Lieutenant B and then he himself will
reimburse Lieutenant A, thus fulfilling his oath to the letter.
This is where he ends up, through that logicality peculiar to
neurotics, led by the internal necessity controlling him.

You cannot fail to recognize in this scenario—which includes
the passing of a certain sum of money from Lieutenant A to
the generous lady at the post office who met the payment, then
from the lady to another masculine figure—a schema which,
complementary in certain points and supplementary in others,
parallel in one way and inverted in another, is the equivalent
of the original situation, inasmuch as it weighs with an un-
deniable weight on the subject's mind and on everything that
makes of him this figure with a very special way of relating to
others we call a neurotic.

Of course, this scenario is impossible to follow. The subject
knows perfectly well that he owes nothing either to A or to B,

but rather to the lady at the post office and that, if the scenario were fulfilled, she would be the one who, in the long run, would be out her money. In fact, as is always the case in the actual experience of neurotics, the imperative reality of the real takes precedence over everything that torments him so greatly—torments him even on the train that takes him in exactly the opposite direction from the one he ought to have taken in order to accomplish, with respect to the lady at the post office, the expiatory ceremony which seems so necessary to him. Even while saying to himself at each station that he can still get off, change trains, return, he still goes toward Vienna where he will put himself in Freud's hands; and, once the treatment is begun, he is content quite simply to send a money order to the lady at the post office.

This phantasmic scenario resembles a little play, a chronicle, which is precisely the manifestation of what I call the neurotic's individual myth.

Indeed, it reflects, in a mode that is no doubt incomprehensible to the subject—but not absolutely so, far from it—the inaugural relationship between the father, the mother, and the friend, this more or less dim figure in the past. Clearly, this relationship has not been elucidated by the purely factual way I have presented it to you, since its significance derives only from the subjective apprehension that the subject had of it.

What gives a mythic character to this little phantasmatic scenario? It is not only the fact that it re-enacts a ceremony which reproduces almost exactly that inaugural relationship, as it were, hidden there, it also modifies this relationship in accord with a certain propensity. On the one hand, we have originally the father's debt to the friend; I failed to mention that he never found the friend again (this is what remains mysterious in the original story) and that he never succeeded in repaying his debt. On the other hand, there is a substitution in the father's story, substitution of the rich woman for the poor woman. Now, within the fantasy developed by the subject, we observe something like an exchange of the outside terms of each of these functional relations. An investigation of the fundamental facts involved in the obsessional attack shows, in fact, that the object of the subject's tantalizing desire to return to the place where the lady at the post office is, is not at all this lady, but a person who, in the subject's recent history, incarnates the poor woman, a servant girl he met at an inn during maneuvers in the midst of that atmosphere of heroic ardor characteristic of the military fraternity and with whom he indulged in some of those bottom-pinching tactics in which those generous sentiments are wont to overflow. To discharge his debt, he must in some way pay, not the friend, but the poor woman and, through her, the rich woman who is substituted for her in the imagined scenario.

Everything happens as if the impasses inherent in the original situation moved to another point in the mythic network, as if what was not resolved here always turned up over there. In order to understand thoroughly, one must see that in the original situation, as I described it to you, there is a double debt. There is, on the one hand, the frustration, indeed a kind of castration of the father. On the other hand, there is the never resolved social debt implied in the relationship to the figure of the friend in the background. We have here something quite different from the triangular relation considered to be the typical source of neurotic development. The situation presents a kind of ambiguity, of diplopia—the element of the debt is placed on two levels at once, and it is precisely in the light of the impossibility of bringing these two levels together that the drama of the neurotic is played. By trying to make one coincide with the other, he makes a perennially unsatisfying turning maneuver and never succeeds in closing the loop.

And that is indeed how things subsequently turn out. What happens when the Rat Man comes to Freud? In an initial phase, Freud is directly substituted in his affective relations for a friend who had been playing the role of guide, counselor, patron, and reassuring guardian, saying to him regularly after his confession of his obsessions and anxieties: *"You never did the evil you think you did, you're not guilty, don't worry about it.*" Freud, then, is put in the friend's place. And very quickly, aggressive fantasies are unleashed. They are not related uniquely—far from it—to the substitution of Freud for the father, as Freud's own interpretation persistently tends to show, but, as in the fantasy, to the substitution of the figure called the *rich woman* for the friend. Very quickly, in fact, in that kind of momentary madness which constitutes, at least in profoundly neurotic subjects, a veritable phase of passion in the analytic experience itself, the subject begins to imagine that Freud wishes nothing less than to give him his own daughter who becomes in his fantasy a person laden with all earthly riches and whom he imagines in the rather peculiar form of a person with glasses of dung on her eyes. We find, then, substituted for the figure of Freud, an ambiguous figure, at once protective and maleficent, whose masquerading in glasses indicates, moreover, a narcissistic relationship with the subject. Myth and fantasy reunite here, and the experience of passion connected with the actual relationship to the analyst furnishes a springboard, along with the bias of the identifications it includes, for the resolution of a certain number of problems.

I have taken here a quite individualized example. But I would like to emphasize what is a clinical reality that might serve as a guide in analytic experience: there is within the neurotic a quartet situation which is endlessly renewed, but which does not exist all on one level.

To schematize, let us say that when a male subject is involved, his moral and psychic equilibrium requires him to assume his own function—he must gain recognition as such in his virile function and in his work, he must gather their fruits without conflict, without having the feeling that it is someone else who deserves it and that he has it only by fluke, without there being any internal division that makes the subject the alienated witness of the acts of his own self. That is the first requirement. The other is this: an enjoyment one might characterize as tranquil and univocal of the sexual object, once it is chosen, granted to the subject's life.

Now, each time the subject succeeds, or approaches success in assuming his own role, each time he becomes, as it were, identical with himself and confident that his functioning in his specific social context is well-founded, the object, the sexual partner, is split—here in the form *rich woman or poor woman.* What is truly striking in the psychology of the neurotic—all we need do is enter, no longer into the fantasy, but into the subject's real life to put our finger on it—is the aura of abrogation which most commonly surrounds the sexual partner who is the most real to him, the nearest to him, with whom he generally has the most legitimate ties, whether in a love affair or in a marriage. On the other hand, a figure appears who is a double of the first and who is the object of a more or less idealized passion which is pursued in a more or less phantasmatic way, in a style analogous to that of romantic love, and which grows, moreover, into an identification of a fatal kind.

Conversely, if the subject makes an effort in another aspect of his life to find the unity of his feelings again, then it is at the other end of the chain, in the assumption of his own social function and his own virility—since I have chosen the case of a man—that he sees appearing beside him a figure with whom he also has a narcissistic relation insofar as it is a fatal relation. To the latter he delegates the responsibility of representing him in the world and of living in his place. It is not really himself: he feels excluded, outside of his own experience, he cannot assume its particularities and its contingencies, he feels discordant with his existence, and the impasse recurs.

In this very special form of narcissistic splitting lies the drama of the neurotic; and in connection with it, value accrues to the different mythic formations which I have just given you an example of in the form of fantasies, but which can also be found in other forms, in dreams for example. I have numerous examples in the narrations of my patients. It is through these that the subject can really be shown the primordial circumstances of his case in a manner that is much more rigorous and vivid to him than the traditional patterns issuing from the triangular thematization of the oedipus complex.

I would like to quote another example and show you its congruity with the first. To do this, I will take a case very close to the Rat Man case history, but which has to do with a subject of another order—poetry or literary fiction. It concerns an episode from Goethe's youth that he narrates in *Poetry and Truth.* I am not bringing this in arbitrarily—it is in fact one of the most highly valued literary themes in the Rat Man's confessions.

III

Goethe is twenty-two years old, he is living in Strasbourg, and then there is the famous episode of his passion for Frederica Brion which he remembers with nostalgia well into his old age. This passion enabled him to overcome the curse put on him by one of his previous loves, Lucinda by name, against all amorous attachments to other women and, in particular, against kissing on the lips.

The scene is worth describing. This Lucinda has a sister, a little too shrewd to be honest, who is busy convincing Goethe of the devastating effect he is having on the poor girl. She pleads with him both to go away and to give her, the sly little minx, the token of the last kiss. It is then that Lucinda surprises them and says, *"May those lips be cursed forever. May evil befall the first one to receive their tribute."* It is clearly not without good reason that Goethe, absorbed then in the infatuations of swaggering youth, takes this curse as a sanction that will henceforth bar the way to all his amorous undertakings. He tells us then how, elated by the discovery of this charming girl, Frederica Brion, he succeeds for the first time in overcoming the prohibition and feels the ecstasy of triumph following on this fear of something stronger than his own self-imposed, internal prohibitions.

This is one of the most enigmatic episodes in Goethe's life, and no less extraordinary is his abandonment of Frederica. As a result, the *Goethesforscher*—like the Stendhalians and the Bossuetists, that very singular breed of people who attach themselves to one of those authors whose words have given form to our feelings and who spend their time rooting around in papers left in closets in order to analyze what the genius left behind— the *Goethesforscher* have concentrated on this fact. They have given us all kinds of explanations which I will not catalogue here. One thing is certain: that they all smack of that kind of philistinism inseparable from such research when it is pursued in the usual way. It cannot be denied either that there always is, in fact, some obscure concealment of philistinism in the manifestations of neurosis, for it is such a manifestation we are dealing with in Goethe's case, as will be shown by the observations I will now set forth.

There are a number of enigmatic features in the way Goethe approaches this adventure, and I would almost say that the key to the problem can be found in its immediate antecedents.

To be brief, Goethe, living at the time in Strasbourg with one of his friends, has long been aware of the existence in a small village of the open, kind, friendly family of Pastor Brion. But when he goes there, he surrounds himself with precautions whose amusing aspect he relates in his autobiography; actually, when one looks at the details, one cannot help being astonished at the truly contorted structure they reveal.

First of all, he thinks he must go there in disguise. Son of a *grand bourgeois* from Frankfurt, distinguished among his comrades by his smooth manners, his impressive dress, his air of social superiority, Goethe disguises himself as a theology student in an especially seedy and torn cassock. He sets out with his friend, and they are full of laughter on the way. But of course he is very vexed as soon as the reality of the visibly dazzling charm of the young lady against the background of that family setting makes him realize that, if he wants to appear at his handsomest and best, he must change as quickly as possible out of this astonishing costume which does not show him to advantage.

The justifications he gives for this disguise are very odd. He invokes nothing less than the disguises the gods put on to come down among mortals—which, as he himself emphasizes, seems clearly to indicate (even allowing for his adolescent mentality) something more than self-conceit—something bordering on florid megalomania. If we look at the details, Goethe's text shows us what he thinks about it. By this way of disguising themselves, the gods sought above all to avoid vexation, and, to put it bluntly, it was for them a way of not having to take the familiarity of mortals as insulting. What the gods risk most when they come down on a level with humans is losing their immortality; and precisely the only way of avoiding that is to put themselves on their level.

It is indeed something like that we are dealing with here. It is demonstrated even more clearly when Goethe turns back toward Strasbourg to put on his finery again, not without feeling, a little late, how indelicate it was to have presented himself in a form that was not his own and thus to have deceived the trust of those people who welcomed him with charming hospitality; one has a real sense in this narration of a truly *gemütlich* atmosphere.

He comes back, then, toward Strasbourg. But far from following through on his wish to return to the village ceremoniously arrayed, he arrives at nothing better than substituting for the first disguise another that he borrows from a servant boy at an inn. This time he will appear in a disguise that is even stranger, more out of place than the first and, on top of it all, in make-up. To be sure, he treats the whole thing as a game, but this game becomes more and more significant. In fact, he no longer places himself on the level of a theology student, but slightly below. He plays the buffoon. And all of this is deliberately entangled with a series of details which create in all those who collaborate in this farce a sense that what is happening is closely linked to sexual behavior, to the courting display.

There are even certain details that take on importance, if one can put it that way, from their inaccuracy. As the title *Dichtung und Wahrheit* indicates, Goethe was aware that he had the right to organize and harmonize his memories with fictions that filled in the gaps which no doubt he was powerless to fill in otherwise. The ardor of those I mentioned earlier who follow the tracks of great men has demonstrated the inaccuracy of certain details which are all the more revelatory of what one might call the real intentions of the entire scene. When Goethe presented himself made-up and in the clothes of a servant boy, enjoying at length the resultant misunderstanding, he also delivered, he says, a christening cake that he had likewise borrowed from the boy. Now, the *Goethesforscher* have demonstrated that for six months before and for six months after the Frederica episode, there were no baptisms in that locality. The christening cake, traditional gift to the pastor, can only be Goethe's fantasy and, as such, thus assumes in our eyes its entire significance. It implies the paternal function, but precisely inasmuch as Goethe specifies that he is not the father, but only the one who delivers something and who has only an external relation to the ceremony—he makes himself the petty officer, not the principal hero. In the end, the whole ceremony of his concealment actually appears not only as a game but much more profoundly as a precaution which can be placed in the category of what I called before the splitting of the subject's personal function in the mythic constructions of the neurotic.

Why does Goethe act this way? Very obviously because he is afraid—as what follows will show, for this affair will henceforth do nothing but fade. Far from lifting the spell, releasing the original curse by daring to transgress its sanction, Goethe only deepened his fears—one perceives this in all kinds of substitutive forms, the idea of substitution being introduced into the text by Goethe—with respect to the fulfillment of this love. All the reasons one might give for this—desire not to get involved, to protect the poet's sacred destiny, even perhaps the difference in social standing—are only cleverly rationalized forms, the surface of an infinitely deeper current which is, in fact, the flight from the desired object. We see again, when he confronts his goal, this splitting of the subject, his alienation from himself, strategies by which he provides a substitute for himself on whom the deadly threats are to be carried out. The moment he reintegrates this substitute into himself, it is impossible to reach the goal.

Here I can give you only the general thematic analysis of this adventure, but you ought to know that there is also a sister, Frederica's double, who is there to complete the mythic structure of the situation. If you go back to Goethe's text, you will see that what may appear to you in this sketch to be a construction is confirmed by other diverse and striking details, even including the analogy suggested by Goethe with the well-known story of the Vicar of Wakefield, a literary, phantasmatic transposition of his own adventure.

IV

The quaternary system so fundamental to the impasses, the insolubilities in the life situation of neurotics, has a structure quite different from the one traditionally given—the incestuous desire for the mother, the father's prohibition, its obstructive effects, and, around all that, the more or less luxuriant proliferation of symptoms. I think that this difference ought to lead us to question the general anthropology derived from analytic doctrine as it has been taught up to the present. In short, the whole oedipal schema needs to be re-examined. I cannot undertake that now, but I cannot refrain from trying to introduce here the fourth element at issue.

We submit that the most normalizing situation in the early experience of the modern subject, in the condensed form represented by the conjugal family, is linked to the fact that the father is the representative, the incarnation, of a symbolic function which concentrates in itself those things most essential in other cultural structures: namely, the tranquil, or rather, symbolic, enjoyment, culturally determined and established, of the mother's love, that is to say, of the pole to which the subject is linked by a bond that is irrefutably natural. The assumption of the father's function presupposes a single symbolic relation in which the symbolic and the real would fully coincide. The father would have to be not only the *name-of-the-father,* but also the representative, in all its fullness, of the symbolic value crystallized in his function. Now, it is clear that this coincidence of the symbolic and the real is totally elusive. At least in a social structure like ours, the father is always in one way or another in disharmony with regard to his function, a deficient father, a *humiliated* father, as Claudel would say. There is always an extremely obvious discrepancy between the symbolic function and what is perceived by the subject in the sphere of experience. In this divergence lies the source of the effects of the oedipus complex which are not at all normalizing, but rather most often pathogenic.

But saying that does not advance us very far. The following step, which brings us to an understanding of what is at issue in the quaternary structure, is this—and it is the second great discovery of psychoanalysis, no less important than the symbolic function of the oedipus complex—the narcissistic relation.

The narcissistic relation to a fellow being is the fundamental experience in the development of the imaginary sphere in human beings. As an experience of the ego, its function is decisive in the constitution of the subject. What is the ego, if not something that the subject at first experiences as foreign to him but inside him? It is in another, more advanced, more perfect than he, that the subject first sees himself. Specifically, he sees his own image in the mirror at a time when he is capable of perceiving the image as a totality but when he does not feel himself as such but as living rather in that primal incoherence of all his motor and affective functions which lasts for the first six months after birth. Thus the subject always has an anticipatory relationship to his own realization which in turn throws him back onto the level of a profound insufficiency and betokens a rift in him, a primal sundering, a *thrownness,* to use the

Heideggerian term. It is in this sense that what is revealed in all imaginary relationships is an experience of death: an experience doubtless inherent in all manifestations of the human condition, but especially visible in the life of the neurotic.

If the imaginary father and the symbolic father are most often fundamentally differentiated, it is not only for the structural reason I am presently outlining, but also by reason of historic, contingent circumstances peculiar to each subject. In the case of neurotics, one frequently finds that the figure of the father, by some accident of real life, has been split. Either the father has died prematurely and had his place taken by a step-father with whom the subject easily falls into a more fraternal relation, quite naturally established on the level of that jealous virility representing the aggressive dimension of the narcissistic relation. Or the mother has disappeared and the circumstances of life have opened the family group to another mother who is not the real one. Or the fraternal figure introduces the fatal relationship symbolically and, at the same time, incarnates it in reality. Very frequently, as I have indicated, a friend is involved, like the mysterious friend in "The Rat Man" who is never found and who plays such an essential role in the family legend. All of that results in the mythic quartet. It can be reintegrated into the subject's history, and to disregard it is to disregard the most important element in the treatment itself. All we can do here is to underline its importance.

What is this fourth element? Its name is death.

Death is perfectly conceivable as a mediating element. Before Freudian theory stressed in the existence of the father a function which is at once a function of speech and a function of love, Hegel, in his metaphysics, did not hesitate to construct the whole phenomenology of human relationships around death as mediator, the third element essential to the progress by which man becomes humanized in his relationships with his fellow man. And one might say that the theory of narcissism, as I just set it forth, explains certain facts which otherwise remain enigmatic in Hegel. After all, in order for this dialectic of the death struggle, the struggle for pure power, to be initiated, death must not be actualized, since the dialectical movement would cease for lack of combatants; death must be imagined. And, indeed, it is this imagined, imaginary death that appears in the dialectic of the oedipal drama; and it is also this death that is operant in the formation of the neurotic—and perhaps, up to a certain point, in something that goes far beyond the formation of the neurotic, specifically the existential attitude characteristic of modern man.

It would take little pressure to make me say that what functions as mediation in actual analytic experience is something similar to speech, to symbol, called in another language, an act of faith. But certainly, this is neither what analysis requires nor what it implies. What is at issue, rather, is on the order of the last words uttered by Goethe; and you may trust it was not for nothing that I brought him up as an example.

Of Goethe, one can say that, by his inspiration, his living presence, he impregnated and animated Freud's thought to an extraordinary degree. Freud confessed that it was his reading of Goethe's poems that launched him in his medical career and, by the same stroke, decided his destiny; but even that is little enough compared to the influence of Goethe's thought on Freud's work. It is, therefore, with a phrase of Goethe, his last, that I will express the wellspring of analytic experience, with those well-known words he uttered before he plunged open-eyed into the black abyss—*"Mehr Licht"* (*more light*).

9

Assault on a Child's Individuality: A Kind of Soul Murder

ASSAULT ON A CHILD'S INDIVIDUALITY: A KIND OF SOUL MURDER

BY LEONARD SHENGOLD, M.D.

I define soul murder as a deliberate attempt to interfere with another person's separate identity, joy in life, and capacity to love.[1] It usually takes place in childhood: the child's almost absolute dependence upon an adult, most frequently a parent, makes possible a regimen of cruelty and seduction (overstimulation) alternating with indifference and neglect (deprivation) that provides the environmental matrix for soul murder. An identification with and a submission to the tormentor is forced upon the child. The victim needs to be rescued from the overstimulation and to have the deprivation undone. In more fortunate circumstances, the child can turn from the psychotic, narcissistic, or psychopathic parent to another nurturing figure who has enough power and who cares enough to provide another model for identification, a situation described in this communication. Sometimes, however, the child can seek redress only from the very parent who is responsible for the trauma.

Soul murder is maintained by interfering with the child's ability to experience and to register what is happening and has happened. This brainwashing, carried on by the children themselves later in life, is not difficult to achieve under conditions of tyranny, as we know from the political life of our time (see Nadezhda Mandelstam's [1970] memoir showing the cultivation of denial in a whole generation of intellectuals). The need for a good parent, so intense when there is the necessity of alleviating the fear and rage experienced under conditions of trauma and neglect, leads to the delusion of a good parent (a delusion with which the child must then struggle), and a lifelong, symbiotic bond with the tormentor may ensue.

[1] See, Shengold (1975a, 1975b) for a fuller description of my concept of soul murder.

A young woman in analysis told of being handed over after her birth to a nurse whom she remembered as kind and loving. Her mother had a career, which she left when the child was four. The girl's life was suddenly and radically changed. Without warning, the good nurse was dismissed and the devastated child was cared for subsequently by a series of maids who were directed by the mother. Whenever a loving relationship between a maid and the girl appeared likely, the maid would be fired. The old nurse, who had found work nearby, tried to visit her former charge, but was not allowed to speak to her. The patient remembered hating the nurse for her weakness. From the ages of four to six, the girl was brought up according to a strict time schedule which minimized human contact and featured an interminable daily nap. The nap, lasting from mid-afternoon through early evening, was especially objectionable because it prevented the child from seeing her father at dinner. The mother, under pressure from the father, gave up the rigid agenda—except for the nap, which was required up to puberty.

The father did care about his daughter, but he seldom interfered with the mother; he was often away for long periods. Whenever he left, the mother's attitude toward the child would change dramatically. The maid was banished, and the mother would insist upon the child's presence. The daughter was taught to comb her mother's long hair before bedtime, another "interminable" assignment, but one which was full of erotic tension. The daughter would be brought into the bathroom to watch her mother bathe and often to share the bath. She would watch her mother defecate and urinate. The mother took the child into her bed, and physical contact was encouraged. With all of this seductive closeness, there was no expression of love or even of affection. The child was treated as a thing whose presence was required to fulfill needs. She was characteristically hushed when she tried to communicate and deprecated as stupid and ugly. The periods of intimacy would end suddenly, with a peremptory dismissal back to the maid and to the isolatory regimen. (During her analysis, she remembered that the sudden and shocking banishment would sometimes occur after her mother achieved orgasm when masturbating.)

The child was kept back from going to school, and then she had to start directly in the first grade. At first, she was terrified to leave her mother and her home. Gradually, she became fond of school, and she grew to like her kind and understanding teacher. She remembered thinking that her teacher was the smartest and most beautiful person in the world. She adored her and would talk of her at home. During this time her father was at home and her mother was preoccupied with him. There was a happy period for many months during which the girl learned to read and even surpassed her classmates, most of whom had had kindergarten and previous teaching. She no longer felt stupid and ugly. (In Kohut's [1971] terms, she began to mirror her idealized teacher; her father had previously recognized and encouraged the girl's brightness.) Her mother's comparatively benign indifference changed when her father left for a long trip. She began to interfere with her daughter's going to school, insisting that the child was sick. When her mother was called to school for a conference by the teacher, the child became both hopeful and anxious. She recalled to the analyst with tears and bitterness how much she wanted her mother to love her teacher, to be influenced by her teacher, and to become like her. After the conference, she ran up to her mother and asked, "Oh mother, isn't my teacher beautiful?" Her mother responded in a voice full of hatred, "I've never seen such ugliness—she's ugly as sin. What a dog!" The girl was crushed. The precocious achievements at school stopped. A pattern emerged in which she turned away from all authorities as sources of good feelings, and became involved alternately in zombie-like indifference and spiteful, masochistic provocation that often featured pseudostupidity and "ugly" behavior. She both submitted to and identified with her mother.

The story of the spoiling of the "beautiful" relationship with
her teacher obviously screened the feelings involved with the
much more terrible loss of her nurse at age four. By the age of
six, the child had already been damaged enough by the mother
to prevent her from being able to achieve the promise of "starting a new life" (this is how the patient phrased it) with her
teacher or with anyone else. Later on, her father helped the girl
to fight for her health and for her identity, but, unfortunately,
her parents' marriage broke up and she was left with her
mother.

The incident at age six that crushed the child's hope and joy
left her with the feeling that her mother had the power to
get rid of anyone the child cared for and needed. She remembered thinking (her father was away then) that she would always belong to her mother and that it was better not to feel
any longing for anyone else. It was better not to feel anything.
The rage she should have felt toward her mother was suppressed
and displaced, but for the most part was turned against herself.
She saw the world and herself through her mother's eyes. "The
most awful thing," she told the analyst, "was that my teacher
really stopped looking beautiful to me. I couldn't tell if she
was ugly or not. I became indifferent to her and I went back to
not caring about myself." Cognition and affect were both
blocked; the ability to *know* had been interfered with.

Soul murder can be effected in a variety of ways, which
result in crushing the child's individuality and frustrating his
or her need for joy and love. The child is left trapped within
the terrible ambivalence of a hostile, dependent relationship
with the parent (the primary object) responsible for the trauma
that distorts the child's unconscious fantasies and evokes massive, mind-distorting defenses, such as denial and vertical
splitting (see Shengold, 1975b). This mother, cruel, narcissistic,
"crazy" (I am using the word in the popular, descriptive sense
and avoiding diagnosis), and acting out of her own need for
symbiosis, treated her child as a need-fulfilling extension of
herself. A typical remark to her daughter was: "I'm cold, put on

a sweater!" Mahler (1968, p. 148) might call her a "symbiotic parasitic mother."

The mother did her best to interfere with models for identification other than herself. Her hold on the child required her to induce and maintain the delusion of her own goodness and rightness. The child had to share her distorted, narcissistic view of the world. (It was fortunate for the child that her mother's symbiotic parasitic needs were somewhat intermittent so that she made only periodic destructive forays against the child's individuation.) Her mother sensed that the saner and kinder nurse, father, and teacher might give the girl the power to see her mother's disturbance and cruelty, so she tried to isolate and get rid of them. The child could not be allowed a view from outside her mother's dominion. Efficient dictators, such as Hitler, appreciate the importance of propaganda and brainwashing. Physical isolation (especially separating the victim from loving and caring people) is a part of concentration camp brainwashing technique (cf., Orwell's *1984*).

The development by the parent of a closed system for the child is the symbiotic container for soul murder. Entry to another family, sometimes effected by such simple means as frequent visits to a friend's home, has an eye-opening potential for change that is analogous to a visit to another culture by someone brought up in a totalitarian country. And these parents rarely grant visas or visitation rights. (The patient's mother regularly found the child's friends to be "ugly" and "stupid" and "dogs.")

Of course the undoing of brainwashing cannot occur suddenly. To fight denial requires a relationship that can fulfill basic needs and permit the modification of basic identifications. The long and hard analytic work that partially restored my patient's capacity to feel and to know was a continuation of the soul-saving direction initiated for her by the affection and the points of view of her nurse and her father. It was especially (I speculate) the nurse's early loving care and (here I know) the father's intermittent, but eventually reliable approval that helped make the damage done to this patient's soul partly reversible. But for many years before the psychiatric treatment, she lived a life without authenticity or passion—robbed of the sense of identity and the vitality and joy that can lend grace to the human condition.

REFERENCES

KOHUT, H. (1971): *The Analysis of the Self. A Systematic Approach to the Psychoanalytic Treatment of Narcissistic Personality Disorders*. New York: International Universities Press, Inc.

MAHLER, M. (1968): *On Human Symbiosis and the Vicissitudes of Individuation. Vol. I. Infantile Psychosis*. New York: International Universities Press, Inc.

MANDELSTAM, N. (1970): *Hope against Hope. A Memoir*. New York: Atheneum.

ORWELL, G. (1949): *1984*. New York: Harcourt, Brace.

SHENGOLD, L. (1974): *The Metaphor of the Mirror*. J. Amer. Psa. Assn., XXII, pp. 97-115.

——— (1975a): *Soul Murder: A Review*. Int. J. Psa. Psychother., III, pp. 366-373.

——— (1975b): An Attempt at Soul Murder: Rudyard Kipling's Early Life and Work. In: *The Psychoanalytic Study of the Child, Vol. XXX*. New Haven: Yale University Press, pp. 683-724.

10

The Nature of Reality, the Meaning of Nothing with an Addendum on Concentration

THE NATURE OF REALITY, THE MEANING OF NOTHING, WITH AN ADDENDUM ON CONCENTRATION

BY BERTRAM D. LEWIN, M.D. (NEW YORK)

REALITY

Freud states that if a sense of reality accompanies a dream, analysis will show that one or more latent thoughts in it do in fact refer to something real. As an example, he cites a dream accompanied by a sense of reality, in which two pears that the dreamer is given represent the maternal breasts, which the dreamer had once indeed received. The quality of realness in the dream indicates the reality present in the original situation.

One of my patients had a strong castration complex which prevented him from looking at a nude woman. Discussing reality, not in a dream but more abstractly, he lamented that he had never been able to see it starkly. 'I have never faced reality', he said sadly, 'I haven't faced reality since the day I was born'. This equation of reality with the mother's genital differs from the one cited by Freud. However, there are many attitudes to reality, according to whether it is faced optimistically or pessimistically. Proverbially, the optimist sees the doughnut, the pessimist sees the hole.

So far as I have noted, the idea 'reality', as it appears in free associations, stands for the female genitalia. I have been correct in anticipating remarks about the female genital following a patient's expression of thoughts about reality. It occurred to me to check up on some of the literature and see what others have recorded. The Wolf-man's famous dream left him with a strong sense of reality. Among the real things referred to was the real aspect of the vagina. In Ruth Mack Brunswick's paper on paranoid jealousy two pages are devoted to two dreams that had an intense sense of reality. The first dream depicts the patient, a woman, in bed with a woman; the patient is instructed to hold the woman's labia open with one hand and rub the clitoris with the other. The patient has an intense orgasm in the dream and awakes with a feeling of absolute reality; in fact, she examines her own genital with her hand, finds that she is menstruating and wearing a napkin, and only this convinces her that she was dreaming. The second dream, in which reality also appears, is only slightly different: the patient is masturbating her sister, who has an orgasm, and the patient awakes to find her husband's penis in her hand.

As the free association, 'reality', usually refers to the real female genital, so remarks about 'illusion' signify latent ideas about the imaginary one which, as is well known, Rado has called the 'illusory' penis. The words, 'vagueness' and 'confusion' have the same reference; for reasons sufficient to the patient, the female genital is a vagueness, a confusion. 'In my confusion', said one, 'I found something concrete', referring to the clitoris.

I do not know to what extent unconscious associations of this sort have affected philosophers' ideas on the nature of reality. I note in one instance, however, that a philosopher chides authorities he has read for giving him a false impression, as if anatomic charts had led him to false anticipations. He says: 'They have substituted economical and orderly conceptions for the first sensible tangle; and whether they were morally or only intellectually neat, they were at any rate always æsthetically pure and definite, and aimed at ascribing to the world something clean and intellectual in the way of inner structure'. The view he professes 'offers but a sorry appearance'. 'It is a turbid, muddled, Gothic sort of affair, without a sweeping outline, and with little pictorial solidity. Those of you who are accustomed to the classical construction of reality may be excused if your first reaction upon it be absolute contempt. . . . But one must have lived some time with a system to appreciate its merits. Perhaps a little more familiarity may mitigate your first surprise at such a programme as I offer.'

NOTHING

For the association 'I am thinking of nothing', the interpretation is the same. The phrase is soon followed by allusions to the female genital. One of my patients was pleased with this interpretation, which struck his sense of humor. One day he began his analytic hour by telling me, 'Well, doctor, I've been thinking of nothing all day'.

CONCENTRATION

The common remark, 'I cannot concentrate', refers not to the stream of thought, but to the urinary flow, which in women (and in male incontinence) is not concentrated. After numerous instances of this reference in my practice, I ventured to guess at a Technical Seminar that a girl complaining of lack of concentration had a urethral story to tell. The student confirmed this by informing us that she had enuresis.

11

MISRECOGNITIONS AND THE FEAR OF NOT KNOWING

MISRECOGNITIONS AND THE FEAR OF NOT KNOWING

BY THOMAS H. OGDEN, M.D.

A form of pathological internal object relationship is described that timelessly perpetuates the infant's subjective experience of the mother's difficulty in recognizing and responding to her infant's internal state. The individual identifies with both the mother and the infant in this internal object relationship and experiences intense anxiety and despair in relation to his efforts at knowing what he is feeling and therefore of knowing who he is. Substitute formations are utilized to create the illusion that the individual knows what he feels.

The work of a group of British and French psychoanalytic thinkers, including Bion, Lacan, McDougall, Tustin, and Winnicott, has led me to understand certain psychological difficulties in terms of an unconscious fear of not knowing. What the individual is not able to know is what he feels, and therefore who, if anyone, he is. The patient regularly creates the illusion for himself (and secondarily for others) that he is able to generate thoughts and feelings, wishes and fears, that feel like his own. Although this illusion constitutes an effective defense against the terror of not knowing what one feels or who one is, it further alienates the individual from himself. The illusion of knowing is achieved through the creation of a wide range of substitute formations that fill the "potential space" (Winnicott, 1971) in which desire and fear, appetite and fullness, love and hate, might otherwise come into being.

The "misrecognitions" that are used as defenses against the fear of not knowing represent a less extreme form of alienation from affective experience than "alexithymia" (Nemiah, 1977), states of "non-experience" (Ogden, 1980, 1982), and "dis-affected" states (McDougall, 1984) wherein potential feelings and fantasies are foreclosed from the psychological sphere. It is also a less extreme psychological catastrophe than schizophrenic fragmentation wherein there is very little of a self capable of creating, shaping, and organizing the internal and external stimuli that ordinarily constitute experience. The patients I will be focusing upon have the capacity to generate a sense of self sufficiently integrated and sufficiently bounded to be able to know that they do not know. That is, they are able to experience the beginnings of feelings of confusion, emptiness, despair, and panic as well as being able to mobilize defenses against these incipient feelings.

As will be discussed, in the course of development a sense of self evolves in the context of the management of need by the mother-infant pair. When the mother can satisfactorily tolerate the recognition of her own desires and fears, she is less afraid of states of tension generated by her infant that are in the process of becoming feelings. When the mother is capable of tolerating the infant's tension over time, it is possible for her to respond to a given tension state as a quality of the infant's being alive.

A THEORETICAL BACKGROUND

The development of the idea of misrecognitions of one's internal state is in a sense synonymous with the development of psychoanalytic theory. One of the cornerstones upon which Freud constructed his theory of psychological meanings is the idea that one knows more than he thinks he knows. The creation of psychological defenses can be understood as the organization of systematic misrecognitions (e.g., it is not my anger that I fear, it is yours). Freud (1911), in his discussion of the Schreber case, explored the idea that psychosis involves the misrecognition of one's internal state through its attribution to external objects.

It is beyond the scope of this paper to review, or even list, the multitude of contributions to the question of psychological misrecognition and the defenses associated with it. I will, however, briefly discuss a group of concepts developed by French and British psychoanalytic thinkers that have particular relevance to the ideas being developed in the present paper.

Lacan (1948) believed that Freud in his later work "seems suddenly to fail to recognize the existence of everything that the ego neglects, scotomizes, misconstrues in the sensations" (p. 22). Lacan's (1953) understanding of the ego as the psychic agency of *méconnaissance* (misrecognition) derives from his conception of the place of the ego in relation to language and to the imaginary and symbolic orders of experience. The realm of the imaginary is that of vital, unmediated, lived experience. In this realm, there is no space between oneself and one's experience. The acquisition of language provides the individual a means by which to mediate between the self as interpreting subject and one's lived experience. Since language and the chain of signifiers that constitute language predate each of us as individuals, the register of symbols that is made available to us through language has nothing to do with us as individuals. We do not create the symbols we use; we inherit them. As a result, language misrepresents the uniqueness of our own lived experience: "It [language] is susceptible to every alienation or lie, wilful or not, susceptible to all the distortions inscribed in the very principles of the 'symbolic,' conventional dimension of group life" (Lemaire, 1977, p. 57).

In becoming a subject capable of using symbols to interpret our experience rather than simply being trapped in our own lived sensory experience, we exchange one form of imprisonment for another. We acquire human subjectivity at the cost of becoming profoundly alienated from our immediate sensory experience (which is now distorted and misrepresented by the symbols we use to name it). In this way, we unwittingly engage in a form of self-deception, creating for ourselves the illusion that we express our experience in language, while according to Lacan, we are in fact misnaming and becoming alienated from our experience.

Joyce McDougall, an important contributor to the French psychoanalytic dialogue, has discussed her work with patients who seemed "totally unaware (and thus kept the analyst unaware) of the nature of their affective reactions" (1984, p. 388). She understands this phenomenon as a dispersal of potential affect into a variety of addictive actions, including drug abuse, compulsive sexuality, bulimia, "accidental" injuries, and interpersonal crises. Such addictive activities are understood as compulsive ways of defending against psychotic-level anxieties. When the defensive use of the affect-dispersing action becomes overtaxed, the individual regresses to psychosomatic foreclosure of the psychological sphere. Under such circumstances, what might have become psychological strain is relegated to the domain of the physiologic and becomes utterly disconnected from the realm of conscious and unconscious meaning.

Such a conception of the destruction not only of psychological meaning, but of the apparatuses generating psychological meaning, represents an elaboration of the work of Wilfred Bion. Bion (1962) suggests that in schizophrenia (and to lesser degrees in all personality organizations), there is a defensive attack on the psychological processes by which meaning is attached to experience. This represents a superordinate defense in which psychological pain is warded off, not simply through defensive rearrangements of meaning (e.g., projection and displacement) and interpersonal evacuation of endangered and endangering internal objects (projective identification); in addition, there is an attack on the psychological processes by which meaning itself is created. The outcome is a state of "non-experience" (Ogden, 1980, 1982) in which the individual lives in part in a state of psychological deadness, i.e., there are sectors of the personality in which even unconscious meanings and affects cease to be elaborated.

In the course of his writing, Winnicott developed the concept of a "potential space" in which self-experience is created and recognized (Winnicott, 1971; see also Ogden, 1985, 1986). Potential space is the space in which the object is simultaneously created and discovered. That is, in this space, the object is simultaneously a subjective object (an object omnipotently created) and an object objectively perceived (an object experienced as lying outside of the realm of one's omnipotence). The question of which is the case—is the object created or discovered?—never arises (Winnicott, 1953). This question is simply not a part of the emotional vocabulary of this area of experience. We do not move through, or grow out of, this state of mind. It is not a developmental phase; rather, it is a psychological space between reality and fantasy that is maintained throughout one's life. It is the space in which playing occurs; it is the space in which we are creative in the most ordinary sense of the word; it is the space in which we experience ourselves as alive and as the authors of our bodily sensations, thoughts, feelings, and perceptions. In the absence of the capacity to generate potential space, one relies on defensive substitutes for the experience of being alive (e.g., the development of a "false self" personality organization [Winnicott, 1960]).

The "fear of breakdown" described by Winnicott (1974) represents a form of failure to generate experience, in which the patient is terrified of experiencing for the first time a catastrophe that has already occurred. The very early environmental failure that constituted the catastrophe could not be experienced at the time that it occurred because there was not yet a self capable of experiencing it, i.e., capable of elaborating the event psychologically and integrating it. As a result, the patient forever fearfully awaits his own psychological breakdown.

In the present paper, I shall be addressing a specific facet of the phenomenon of the alienation from, and destruction of, experience. My focus will be on the anxiety associated with the dim awareness that one does not know what one feels and therefore one does not know who one is. In this psychological state, the individual has not foreclosed experience psychosomatically or failed to psychologically elaborate early experience, nor has he entered into a state of "non-experience." The patients to be discussed have often attempted, but have not entirely succeeded in, warding off the anxiety of not knowing by means of addictive actions. The form of experience that I am interested in here is one in which the individual is sufficiently capable of generating a space in which to live such that he is capable of knowing that he does not know; he never entirely frees himself of this terror, much as he unconsciously attempts to lure himself and the analyst into mistaking his systematic misrecognitions for genuine self-experience. Such experience is universal and is manifested in a wide variety of forms that reflect the individual's personality organization.

A DEVELOPMENTAL PERSPECTIVE

At the outset, it is the infant's relationship with his mother that is the matrix within which psychological tension is sustained over time sufficiently for meanings to be created and desire and fear to be generated. For example, what will become hunger is initially only a physiologic event (a certain blood sugar level registered by groups of neurons in the brain). This biological event becomes the experience of hunger and desire (appetite) in the context of the mother's conscious and unconscious response to the infant: her holding, touching, nursing, rocking, and engaging in other activities that reflect her understanding of (her conscious and unconscious resonance with) the infant (Winnicott, 1967). Such understandings and attendant activities are the outcome of a crucial psychological function provided by the mother: the psychological process by which the mother attempts to respond to her infant in a way that "correctly names" (or gives shape to) the infant's internal state.

The work of Bick (1968), Meltzer (1975), and Tustin (1981, 1986) has afforded analytic theory a way of conceptualizing the earliest organization of experience into sensation-dominated forms, including autistic shapes ("felt shapes" [Tustin, 1984]) and autistic objects (Tustin, 1980). In the development of "normal autism" (what I have termed the elaboration of the *autistic-contiguous position* [Ogden, 1988a, 1988b]), the infant in the context of the mother-infant relationship achieves the earliest sense of boundedness, the sense of having (being) a place (more specifically, a surface) where one's experience occurs and where a sense of order and containment is generated.

In the earliest mother-infant relationship, the mother must be capable of immersing herself in the infant's sensory world as she allows herself to de-integrate into relative shapelessness. This represents the sensory level of primitive empathy. The mother allows her identity as a person and as a mother to "become liquid" (Seale, 1987) in a way that parallels the internal state of the infant. This "de-integration" (Fordham, 1976) is not experienced by the mother as disintegration when she is able to create for herself a generative dialectical tension between the shapeless and formed, the primitive and mature, the mysterious and the familiar, the act of becoming a mother for the first time and the experience of having "been here before" (in her identification with facets of her experience with her own mother). In this way, the mother helps the infant give shape, boundedness, rhythm, edgedness, hardness, softness, etc., to his experience.

The mother and infant must attempt to sustain the strain of the very inexact, trial-and-error means by which each attempts to "get to know" the other. The mother's efforts at reading, comforting, and in other ways providing for and interacting with her infant are inevitably narcissistically wounding to the mother, since she will often feel at a loss to know what it is her baby needs and whether it is within the power of her personality to provide it even if she somehow could discover what he "wants." Winnicott's (1974) use of the word *agonies* for infantile anxieties applies equally to the pain of the mother's experience of not knowing.

THE STRUCTURALIZATION OF MISRECOGNITION

The early relationship that is of central interest in the analytic setting is not that of mother and infant, but that of the internal-object-mother and the internal-object-infant. This internal object relationship is manifested in the transference-countertransference phenomena that constitute the analytic drama. A mother-infant relationship is never directly observable in the analytic setting even when the patient is a mother describing current experience with her child. Instead, what we observe, and in part experience, in analysis is a reflection of internal object relations (our own and the patient's, and the interplay between the two). Therefore, when I speak of the internal relationship between mother and infant, it must be borne in mind that the patient is both mother and infant. This is so because an internal object relationship consists of a relationship between two unconscious aspects of the patient, one identified with the self and the other identified with the object in the original relationship (Ogden, 1983). Regardless of how fully autonomous an internal object may seem to the patient, the internal object can have no life of its own aside from that deriving from the aspect of the self involved in this identification. In what follows, I will describe a set of pathological internal mother-infant relationships in which the patient is both mother and infant, both the misnamer and the misnamed, both the confused and the confusing.

The (internal object) mother may defend against the feeling of not knowing by utilizing obsessive-compulsive defenses, for example by relying on rigidly scheduled (symbolic) feedings of the (internal object) infant. In this way, the mother (in this internal object relationship) invokes an impersonal external order (the clock) to misname hunger. The infant is responded to as if he were sated every four hours and as if he were not hungry between the scheduled feeds. Such misnaming generates confusion in the infant as well as a sense that hunger is an externally generated event. In the extreme, this mode of defense against not knowing becomes a persecutory authoritarian substitution of the mother's absolute knowledge for the infant's potential to generate his own thoughts, feelings, and sensations.

Mothers enacting this sort of internal object relationship in their actual relationships to their own children are often "psychologically minded" and offer verbal interpretations of their children's unconscious feeling states. For example, a mother being seen in analysis informed her seven-year-old child that even though he claimed to be doing the best job that he could in learning to read, the truth of the matter was that he was angry at her and was doing a poor job of it because he knew precisely how to drive her crazy. Such "interpretations" may be partially accurate (due to the universality of such unconscious feelings as anger, jealousy, and envy in a mother-child relationship), but such comments predominantly have the effect of misnaming the child's internal state. The effect of such interpretation is the creation in the child of a feeling that he has no idea how he "really feels" and that only his mother has the capacity to know this. This patient's behavior in relation to her child represented an enactment of an internal object relationship derived from her own experience with a mother who used fundamentalist religious dogma in the misrecognition of the patient's childhood feeling states. When such a relationship becomes established in the patient's internal object world, the role of this type of internal-object-mother is then projected onto the analyst. As a result, the patient comes to experience the analytic setting as an extremely dangerous, authoritarian one wherein the analyst will certainly tear apart the patient's character structure (including his conscious experience of himself) and "interpret" the shameful truth regarding the patient's unconscious thoughts and feelings.

The analyst may unwittingly be induced (as an unconscious participant in the patient's projective identification) to enact the role of such an authoritarian internal-object-mother (cf. Ogden, 1982). Under such circumstances the analyst may find himself interpreting more "actively" and "deeply" than is his usual practice. He may come to view the analysis as bogged down and feel despairing that the patient will ever arrive at meaningful insight. The analyst may rationalize that the patient needs a more didactic approach in order to demonstrate to him what it means "to think reflectively and in depth." Alternatively, the analyst may feel moved to pursue a line of analytic thinking espoused by his "school of psychoanalysis" or an idea about which he has recently read. Reliance upon analytic ideology represents a common method of warding off the analyst's anxiety of not knowing.

Balint (1968) has suggested that the Kleinian technique of "consistent interpretation" represents a countertransference acting out of the role of an omniscient internal object. From the perspective of the ideas being explored in the present paper, the analyst's unconscious identification with the omniscient internal-object-mother represents a form of defense against the anxiety of not knowing what it is the patient is experiencing. (Obviously, this is so whether or not the analyst is a Kleinian.) The patient's internal version of an early object relationship is in this way being replicated in the analytic setting and, unless analyzed in the countertransference and in the transference, will reinforce the patient's unconscious conviction that it is necessary to utilize omnipotent substitute formations in the face of confusion about what he is experiencing and who he is.

Analytic candidates and other trainees frequently utilize this type of unconscious identification with an omnipotent internal object (e.g., an idealized version of one's own analyst). This identification serves as a defense against the anxiety that the candidate does not feel like an analyst when with his patients.

Searles (1987) has described his own experience during psychiatric residency when he would "prop himself up" while talking with his patients by authoritatively offering them interpretations given to him only hours earlier by his analyst. Decades later, he became aware that he had experienced his own analyst (more accurately, his own internal-object-analyst) as similarly propped up and filled with self-doubt. This deeper level of insight reflects the way in which the omniscient internal object serves as a substitute formation obscuring an underlying confusion about who one is and who the object is.

Patients may also enact the role of the omniscient internal-object-mother, for example, by controllingly interpreting the analyst's shifting in his chair as a reflection of his anxiety, sexual excitement, anger, etc. When consistently subjected to this form of "interpretation" (that is indistinguishable from accusation), the analyst may unconsciously identify with the internal-object-infant (within the patient) who is exposed to continual misnaming of his internal state. Anxiety arising in the analyst under such circumstances may lead him into a form of countertransference acting out in which he attempts to "assist the patient in reality testing" by denying to the patient that he (the analyst) is feeling or acting in accord with the patient's interpretations.

A second form of defense against the fear of not knowing how to make sense of the feeling state of the internal-object-infant is the unconscious effort on the part of the patient to act as if he knows what the internal-object-infant is experiencing. In this way he creates a substitute formation for the feeling of being at a complete loss to make use of his capacities for understanding and responding to the internal-object-infant. Reliance on such a set of defenses may result in a rather stereotypic form of self-knowledge. A mother while in analysis described her attempts at being a mother by imitating the mothers portrayed in books and on television, by imitating her friends who had children, and by imitating the analyst's treatment of her. She later attended every PTA and cub scout function, arranged for swimming, tennis and music lessons, painstakingly prepared home-made pumpkin pies at Thanksgiving and mince pies at Christmas, etc. The schizophrenic child of another such mother told his mother, "You've been just like a mother to me." Such mothers are "just like" mothers, but do not experience themselves (nor are they experienced by their children) as being mothers. The self-esteem of such mothers is brittle, and these women often collapse into depression or schizoid withdrawal as they become emotionally exhausted in their efforts at imitating a psychological state from which they feel utterly alienated.

A thirty-year-old psychologist, Dr. M, in the course of his analysis generated a transference-countertransference externalization of the form of internal object relationship just described. During the first two years of work, I frequently questioned the value of the analysis despite the fact that all seemed to be proceeding well. In the third year, the patient began to wryly refer to me as "the perfect analyst." He described how he was the envy of all his colleagues for his unusual good fortune in having the opportunity to work with me. Only recently had he begun to become aware of his strong belief that he and I were colluding in an effort to hide our awareness of my shallowness and extreme emotional detachment. Dr. M presented a dream in which he had graduated from college but was completely illiterate. In the dream, the patient was unable to work because he could not read and was unable to go back to school for fear of shaming his teachers.

This dream represented Dr. M's emerging feeling (that had been the unconscious context for the entire analysis) that he and I were going through the motions of analysis. Eventually he would have to pretend to be "cured," which would mean that he would live in absolute isolation without hope of ever genuinely feeling a connection with anyone. In this case, the internal object relationship that was recreated in the transference-countertransference involved the defensive use of an illusion of perfection (the reliance on form as a replacement for content) as a substitute for the real work of analyst and patient awkwardly and imprecisely attempting to talk to one another.

A third form of defense against the pain of feeling utterly confused about that which the internal-object-infant is experiencing is pathological projective identification. In this process one "knows" the other by (in fantasy) occupying the other with one's own thoughts, feelings, and sensations and in this way short-circuiting the problem of the externality (and unpredictability) of the other. Under such circumstances, a mother (enacting an internal drama in relation to her own infant) may decide to allow her infant to cry for hours on end because she "knows" that the infant has such tyrannical strivings (the mother's own projected feelings about herself) that it is essential that she not be bullied by this baby Hitler. The mother under such circumstances is not only defending herself against the destructive power of her own tyrannical internal-object-infant by locating these feelings in the actual infant (and at the same time maintaining an unconscious connection with this part of her internal object world); in addition, she is allaying the anxiety of not knowing by experiencing the actual infant as the fully known and predictable internal object for which she has a long-standing, clearly defined plan of defensive action.

In a sense, transference in general can be viewed as serving the function of making known the unknown object. Transference is a name we give to the illusion that the unknown object is already known: each new object relationship is cast in the image of past object relations with which one is already familiar. As a result, no encounter is experienced as entirely new. Transference provides the illusion that one has already been there before. Without this illusion, we would feel intolerably naked and unprepared in the face of experience with a new person.

MISRECOGNITION OF AFFECT: A CLINICAL ILLUSTRATION

Mrs. R, a forty-two-year-old woman who had been seen in analysis for almost three years, punctuated each meeting with ef-

forts to cajole, trick, plead, and in other ways coerce me into
"giving [her] something specific" in the form of advice or insight. She hoped that she would be able to take with her what I
gave her during the meeting and apply it to her life outside the
analysis. When I was silent for an entire session, the meeting
was considered wasted since "nothing had happened." Mrs. R
responded with an intense display of emotion to any disruption
of analytic routine. If I were a few minutes late in beginning the
hour, she would either quietly cry or remain angrily silent for
the first ten to fifteen minutes of the hour. She would then tell
me that my being late could only mean that I did not give a
damn about her. Consistent efforts at analyzing the content and
intensity of Mrs. R's reactions were made. She related the current set of feelings to her childhood experience of waiting for
what seemed like hours for her mother (a college professor)
while her mother spoke with students after class. However,
there reached a point when the material did not become any
richer as the patient repeatedly returned to the image of angrily
waiting for her mother. I found myself becoming increasingly
annoyed and was aware of fantasies of making sadistic comments as the patient cried in response to my informing her of a
vacation break or a rare change of the time of a given appoint-
ment.

In a session at the end of the third year of analysis I was three
or four minutes late in beginning the session. Mrs. R was visibly
upset when I met her in the waiting room. In what had become
her customary pattern, the patient lay down on the couch,
folded her arms across her chest, and was silent for about ten
minutes. She finally said that she did not know why she continued in analysis with me. I must hate her; otherwise I would
not treat her in such a callous manner. I asked her if she were
really feeling at that moment that my lateness had reflected the
fact that I hated her. She reflexively said, "Yes," but it was apparent that the question had taken her by surprise. After a few
minutes, she said that in fact my lateness had not bothered her,
even though she had behaved as if it had. She said that in retro-

spect her recent reactions to me seemed to her to have been a little like play-acting, although she had not had that sense of things until I asked the question that I did today. I suggested that by acting as if she had felt crushed by my lateness, she obscured for herself the feeling that she did not know how she felt about it.

Over the succeeding year, as the analysis took on an increasing feeling of authenticity, it was possible to identify a plethora of forms of defense against the anxiety connected with the feeling of not knowing. The patient recognized that she had been unable to progress in her efforts to become an opera singer because she had from the beginning of her training bypassed various fundamentals of technique. She could create an initial impression of being a very accomplished singer, but this could not be sustained. The inability to "begin at the beginning" and to tolerate the tension of not knowing had severely interfered with Mrs. R's ability to learn. She felt it necessary to create the illusion of being very advanced from the outset. Mrs. R also became aware that it was extremely difficult for her to accurately identify her sensory experience—for example, whether she was anxious or in physical pain, in what part of her body the pain was arising, whether a given sensation reflected sexual excitement or a need to urinate, whether she was hungry or lonely, etc.

The analysis then centered on Mrs. R's fear of the "spaces" in the analytic hour which had formerly been filled by what she referred to as "play-acting" or by pleading with me to give her something that she could take with her from the session. In the period of work during which these matters were being discussed, Mrs. R began a session by saying that since she did not want to overdramatize, nor did she want to throw a temper tantrum, she was having trouble knowing what to say. Later in the same meeting the patient reported the following dream: she was in the office of a dentist who removed two of her molar teeth. She had not known he was going to do this, but had the feeling that she had somehow agreed to have it done. When he showed her the teeth, they looked perfect—they were perfectly shaped and had gleaming white enamel "like something you'd see in a story book." She thought that it was strange that they did not have roots. The extraction had not been painful, and afterwards, instead of pain, there was simply a strange feeling of an empty space in the back of her mouth. The hole that was left in the gums rapidly closed over itself and did not require stitches. In her associations, Mrs. R was able to understand that the two teeth had represented two ways of behaving that she felt she was giving up in the analysis: the overdramatization and the temper tantrums. She said that like the teeth, these ways of being seemed to be losses that left a weird space. Moreover, this loss was a loss of something that did not seem to be quite real— like "storybook teeth without roots." This dream represented the beginnings of a phase of the analysis in which the patient was able to become gradually less reliant on misrecognition as a defense against the experience of not knowing.[1] These misrecognitions had filled the potential space in which inchoate desires and fears might have evolved into feelings that could be felt and named.[2]

MISRECOGNITION AS A DIMENSION OF EATING DISORDERS

Patients with a wide range of eating disorders, including anorexia nervosa and bulimia, regularly report that their overeating or refusal to eat has nothing whatever to do with the

[1] There are, of course, conflicted sexual and aggressive meanings suggested by the manifest content of this dream. However, it was necessary to analyze the patient's experience of not knowing what she was experiencing before it became possible to analyze the conflictual content of that experience.

[2] It is characteristic of the analytic process that each insight (recognition) immediately becomes the next resistance (misrecognition). The patient's awareness of and understanding of the experience of not knowing is no exception to this principle. Invariably, as the analysand recognizes his or her warded off state of not knowing, the feeling of confusion itself is utilized in the service of defending against that which the patient consciously and unconsciously knows, but does not wish to know.

experience of appetite. These patients are rarely able to generate an emotional/physiologic state that they can correctly recognize as an appetite for food. The psychological difficulty underlying the inability of these patients to generate appetite affects their capacity to generate almost every form of desire, including sexual desire, desire to learn, desire to work, desire to be with other people, desire to be alone, etc.

In the course of my work with patients suffering from eating disorders, it has made increasing sense to me to think of many of these patients as suffering from a disorder of recognition of desire. An important aspect of the experience of these patients is an unconscious fear that the patient does not know what he desires. This leads him to ward off the panic associated with such awareness by behaving as if it is food that is desired. The patient may then obsessionally (usually ritualistically) eat and yet never feel full, since what has been taken in is not a response to a desire for food. Rather, the eating represents an attempt to use food *as if* that is what had been desired when in fact the individual does not know what it is to feel desire. In one such case, an adolescent girl, in a state of extreme anxiety bordering on panic, consumed several loaves of bread and two cooked chickens which resulted in gangrenous changes in her stomach secondary to the compromise of blood supply caused by the overdistention of the gastric walls. Surgical removal of two-thirds of her stomach was required. This adolescent had told her mother over the course of the preceding week that everything appeared colorless. The patient's mother had told her that it was natural to feel gray in the autumn; everybody does.

This adolescent, in her frantic eating, was not attempting to meet a need or to fulfill a desire; the problem was that she could not create a psychological space in which either need or desire could be generated. The patient therefore felt, to a large degree, as if she already were psychologically dead, and it was this feeling that had led to her state of panic. Paradoxically, the patient was desperately eating in an attempt to create the feeling of hunger. More accurately, she was eating in order to create the illusion that she could feel hunger which would serve as evidence that she was alive.

The early relationship between this patient and her mother seems to have been characterized by the same fear of recognition of the internal state of the patient that was reflected in the mother's comment about the universality of feelings of melancholy and grayness in the autumn. The bits of meaning that the patient had managed to attach to her own experience (in this case, the experience of colorless, lifeless depression) were stripped of meaning in the interaction with her mother (cf. Bion, 1962). The beginnings of meaning, generated in an internal psychological space, were transformed into a universal and therefore impersonal truth. This had had the effect of obliterating not only the bits of meaning that had been created, but more importantly, the internal psychological space that the patient had tenuously achieved.

PSYCHOLOGICAL CHANGE IN THE AREA OF RECOGNITION AND MISRECOGNITION

The following is an excerpt from the analysis of a forty-six-year-old computer scientist who began treatment not knowing why he had come for therapy (but at the same time did not seem aware of his not knowing). During the initial face-to-face interviews prior to his beginning to use the couch, Dr. L described situations in which he felt anxious, such as while waiting to be assigned a table in a restaurant and before making business phone calls. The explanations the patient offered for his anxiety in these situations were almost verbatim formulae extracted from his extensive reading of popular self-help books.

Dr. L, by the time he turned forty, was internationally known and had amassed a large fortune as a result of his innovations in the area of computer technology. Even though the vast bulk of his money was now invested very conservatively, he experienced both his financial situation and his status in his field as extremely precarious. These fears led him to devote himself with ever-increasing intensity to his work. Only after several months of analysis did he say that he awoke every night in a state of extreme anxiety. He supposed he was anxious about his work, but he was not sure since he was unable to remember his dreams.

It is beyond the scope of this paper to describe the analytic work underlying the psychological changes that ensued. My intention here is simply to illustrate the nature of psychological change in the area of the creation and recognition of desire. I shall use as an illustration of such change a dream presented by Dr. L at the beginning of the third year of analysis.

> I was standing in front of a large house and could see through the windows that the paint on the ceiling was cracking as a result of water that had leaked in from the roof. To my surprise, the old man who owned the house came out and asked me to come in and talk. He asked me if I knew who he was. I didn't, and I told him that. The old man thanked me for being truthful. He told me who he was. . . . I can't remember what his name was. He told me he was going to die in two weeks and would like to give all of his money to me. I said that I didn't want the money. He took me into the next room which was lined with fine old books and very beautiful antique furniture. He offered me the house and everything in it. I again said that I didn't want it. I told him that I could get the water damage fixed. The old man said that the peeling paint was part of the house as he knew it, and he didn't want it changed. I told him it could damage the house. The old man was very calm and explained that he had lived a happy life and that he would be dead in two weeks and so it didn't matter.

Dr. L said that he woke up from this dream feeling a profound sense of contentment that he associated with memories of his maternal grandfather. Dr. L recalled how his grandfather, at the age of eighty-five, had loved his garden, planting seeds for flowers one day, seeds for lettuce the next, seeds for other flowers the next, and so on. One day, when the patient

was about six years old, he said to his grandfather as his grandfather was planting flower seeds, "Grandpa, you planted that
same row with carrot seeds yesterday." The patient's grandfather laughed and said, "Bobby, you don't understand. The
point is the planting, not the growing."

This dream and the associations to it represented a layering
of alteration of what had previously been misrecognitions of affect. Dr. L said that it had been "cleansing" to experience himself in the dream as a person who talked in language that "cut to
the bone," in contrast to the "bullshit" with which he felt he
usually filled his life. "I didn't know who the old man was and I
simply said so. I felt a glimmer of temptation to accept his
money and all of his stuff, but I really didn't want his money.
Ordinarily, I would have thought that what I wanted was his
money. I can see myself acting in a way that would have made
him think that that's what I was after.[3] Actually, I just liked
being with him. The old man and I offered one another things
the other didn't want or have any use for. What meant so much
to me was the way we explained ourselves to each other. I could
feel all the tension in me subside when the old man said that he
lived in the house as it was and didn't want it changed."

Over the course of the meeting, the dream was understood to
be a representation of the way Dr. L wished that he and I could
talk together. In the dream, the patient felt momentarily freed
from his usual isolation that resulted from layer upon layer of
misnamings and misrecognitions of his own internal state and
that of the other.[4] The defensive internal misrecognitions had

___

[3] It had taken me most of the first year of the analysis to become aware of the way
Dr. L unconsciously attempted to lure me into misrecognitions of his internal state
by repeatedly mislabeling them, giving me misleading pictures of himself and of his
relationships, leaving out important details, leading me to believe that he understood what was going on in an interpersonal situation when he did not, etc.

[4] If the individual is unable to know what he feels, he is equally at a loss to know
what it is that the other is experiencing. This is simply another way of stating that in
the internal object relationship under discussion, the individual is both internal-object-mother and internal-object-infant, both misrecognized and misrecognizing.
The outcome is a feeling of alienation from the other experienced by both the self
and the object component of the internal object relationship.

made it impossible for him to feel that he understood anything of what he felt toward other people and what they felt toward him. These misrecognitions had left the patient feeling alone and disconnected from a self (and the other) that he only dimly knew.

In the course of the succeeding months of analysis, Dr. L became increasingly able to understand why he had come to see me in the first place and why he was continuing in analysis. Although he had been unaware of it at the time, the anxiety that he had experienced in going into restaurants and before making business phone calls had, in part, reflected an anticipation of the painful confusion and loneliness that he would feel in talking to people. He unconsciously expected that once again there would be only the illusion of two people talking to one another.

Dr. L gradually related the set of feelings just discussed to a persistent childhood feeling of isolation. He had felt that his parents operated according to a logic that he could not fathom. In the course of analysis, Dr. L. was able to re-experience and articulate this powerful, but heretofore wholly unercognized set of background childhood feelings. The patient, in discussing the events of his current life, would return again and again to such statements as, "What kind of sense does that make?" "That doesn't add up. Why can't anyone see that?" "What kind of bullshit is this?" "Doesn't anyone have any common sense?" Such feelings were increasingly experienced in the transference, for example in relation to my policy of billing the patient for missed appointments. These feelings of outrage served an important defensive function: it was necessary for the patient to feel that he knew better than anyone else "what the story was." This served to obscure the patient's feeling of being utterly confused and disconnected from a firmly grounded sense of what he was feeling, what he wanted or why he wanted it, and most basically, what it meant in a visceral sense to experience (and name) desires and fears that felt like his own.

As the analysis went on, the patient increasingly came to experience me as disturbingly insubstantial and infinitely malleable. Dr. L felt quite alone during the sessions and said that attempting to have a relationship with me was like "trying to build a house on a foundation of Jello." He became preoccupied with the feeling that he had no idea who I was. The patient engendered in me (by means of what I eventually understood as a projective identification) a sense of detachment that I have rarely experienced with a patient. The couch concretely felt as if it were located at a very great distance from my chair. At these times I found it extremely difficult to focus on what Dr. L was saying. This sense of isolation in the relationship with me was gradually understood in terms of the patient's internal relationship with a schizoid mother who "gave the appearance of being there until you realized that she was unable to think."

SUMMARY

In this paper, I have discussed a set of unconscious, pathological internal object relations in which misrecognitions of affect play a central role. These internal object relations timelessly perpetuate the infant's subjective experience of the mother's difficulty in recognizing and responding to the infant's internal state. Internal object relationships are understood to involve a relationship between two unconscious aspects of the ego, one identified with the self and the other identified with the object of the original object relationship. Accordingly, in the kind of internal object relationship under discussion, the patient is both mother and infant, both misrecognized and misrecognizing. In the context of this internal relationship, the patient experiences anxiety, alienation, and despair in connection with the feeling of not knowing what it is that he feels or who, if anyone he is.

Substitute formations are utilized to create the illusion that the individual knows what he feels. Examples of such substitute formations include obsessional, authoritarian, as-if, false self, and projective identificatory forms of control over one's internal and external objects. While these substitute formations help to ward off the feeling of not knowing, they also have the effect of filling the potential space in which feeling states (that are experienced as one's own) might arise.

In the analytic setting, internal object relations are externalized and, through the medium of the transference-countertransference, are given intersubjective life. I have presented clinical illustrations of analytic work addressing the anxiety of not knowing one's internal state and the defenses serving to ward off this anxiety.

REFERENCES

BALINT, M. (1968). *The Basic Fault. Therapeutic Aspects of Regression.* London: Tavistock Publ.

BICK, E. (1968). The experience of the skin in early object-relations. *Int. J. Psychoanal.,* 49:484-486.

BION, W. R. (1962). *Learning from Experience.* New York: Basic Books.

FORDHAM, M. (1976). *The Self and Autism.* London: Heinemann.

FREUD, S. (1911). Psycho-analytic notes on an autobiographical account of a case of paranoia (dementia paranoides). *S.E.,* 12.

LACAN, J. (1948). Aggressivity in psychoanalysis. In *Écrits: A Selection.* New York: Norton, 1977, pp. 8-29.

——— (1953). The function and field of speech and language in psychoanalysis. In *Op. cit.,* pp. 30-113.

LEMAIRE, A. (1977). *Jacques Lacan.* Boston: Routledge & Kegan Paul.

McDOUGALL, J. (1984). The "dis-affected" patient: reflections on affect pathology. *Psychoanal. Q.,* 53:386-409.

MELTZER, D. (1975). Adhesive identification. *Contemp. Psychoanal.,* 11:289-310.

NEMIAH, J. C. (1977). Alexithymia: a theoretical statement. *Psychother. and Psychosomat.,* 28:199-206.

OGDEN, T. H. (1980). On the nature of schizophrenic conflict. *Int. J. Psychoanal.,* 61:513-533.

——— (1982). *Projective Identification and Psychotherapeutic Technique.* New York/London: Aronson.

——— (1983). The concept of internal object relations. *Int. J. Psychoanal.,* 64:227-241.

——— (1985). On potential space. *Int. J. Psychoanal.,* 66:129-141.

——— (1986). *The Matrix of the Mind: Object Relations and the Psychoanalytic Dialogue.* Northvale, NJ/London: Aronson.

——— (1988a). On the concept of an autistic-contiguous position. *Int. J. Psychoanal.* (In press.)

———— (1988b). On the dialectical structure of experience: some clinical and theoretical implications. *Contemp. Psychoanal.*, 24:17-45.

SEALE, A. (1987). Personal communication.

SEARLES, H. F. (1987). Concerning unconscious identifications. Presented at the Boyer House Foundation Conference: The Regressed Patient. San Francisco, March 21.

TUSTIN, F. (1980). Autistic objects. *Int. Rev. Psychoanal.*, 7:27-40.

———— (1981). *Autistic States in Children*. Boston: Routledge & Kegan Paul.

———— (1984). Autistic shapes. *Int. Rev. Psychoanal.*, 11:279-290.

———— (1986). *Autistic Barriers in Neurotic Patients*. New Haven: Yale Univ. Press, 1987.

WINNICOTT, D. W. (1953). Transitional objects and transitional phenomena. A study of the first not-me possession. In *Playing and Reality*. New York: Basic Books, 1971, pp. 1-25.

———— (1960). Ego distortion in terms of true and false self. In *The Maturational Processes and the Facilitating Environment. Studies in the Theory of Emotional Development*. New York: Int. Univ. Press, 1965, pp. 140-152.

———— (1967). Mirror-role of mother and family in child development. In *Playing and Reality*. New York: Basic Books, 1971, pp. 111-118.

———— (1971). The place where we live. In *Op. cit.*, pp. 104-110.

———— (1974). Fear of breakdown. *Int. Rev. Psychoanal.*, 1:103-107.

12

NARRATIVE TRUTH AND THEORETICAL TRUTH

NARRATIVE TRUTH AND THEORETICAL TRUTH

BY DONALD P. SPENCE

Although Freud was inclined to believe that every effective reconstruction contained a "kernel of truth," it is by no means clear how this kernel can be identified and separated from the set of equally likely fabrications which make up a good part of the patient's life story. If we have no sure way of identifying historical truth, we may be seriously handicapped in our attempt to frame theoretical laws. What may be effective in a particular clinical instance (narrative truth) may not automatically generalize to the larger domain of clinical theory.

I

The force of psychoanalytic argument has traditionally relied rather more on rhetorical persuasion than on appeal to the data. This tradition was heavily influenced by Freud who never felt it necessary to reveal *all* the evidence for a particular interpretation. Whatever the reasons for his reluctance, he later rationalized this tendency by stating that if the reader was not inclined to agree with his formulation, then additional data would scarcely change his mind (Freud, 1912, p. 114).

Largely as a result of his initial decision, a custom has grown up which gives contributors to the literature the right to allude to the facts rather than state them in full. Because the evidential basis for any statement is only partly open to public inspection, the criteria for conviction are necessarily softer than they would

---

This paper is an outgrowth of the line of thought developed in a forthcoming book, *Narrative Truth and Historical Truth* (Spence, 1982). More extended presentation of such concepts as the nature of narrative truth, its place in the healing process, and how it compares with the historical truth of what "really happened" can be found in the book.

be in a field where all the evidence must be presented. Precisely because the evidential domain is partly closed, the skeptical reader of the psychoanalytic literature is in no position to challenge any conclusion he may come across. For the same reason, agreement among readers can never be complete or compelling; acceptance of an interpretation or theoretical conclusion always reduces to agreement on faith.

Whether or not this tradition *must* be observed in just this way, the fact that not all the evidence is ever available for public scrutiny must necessarily affect the standards of argument and debate within the field. Just as Freud was unwilling to accept a patient who would not report everything (because, as it happened, he was bound to keep certain professional secrets [see Freud, 1913, p. 136, n.]), so the field cannot function in an ideal manner so long as its reasoning rests on only partial data—and for exactly the same reasons. Just as the reluctant patient would be able to reclassify all his difficult moments as somehow secret and therefore exempt from analysis, so the reluctant author, faced with a piece of fuzzy reasoning or doubtful logic, is able to simply omit the embarrassing details from publication; given the tradition just cited, he does not even need to supply an explanation for the omission.

A further consequence of this tradition bears on the matter of generalizing from clinical particulars to the larger theory. If the full details of a given happening are never cited, then it becomes impossible to challenge the category formed from these details; if a given clinical happening, for example, is used as evidence for the return of repressed oedipal strivings, the assertion can only be taken on faith because the outside reader is never in possession of all the facts. As a result, clinical observations can be rather easily turned into far-reaching generalizations. The generalization, because of its greater visibility and rhetorical appeal, takes on an importance that goes far beyond the merits of its data base. In many cases, the generalization may be completely unwarranted.

To take a homely example from another field—suppose I give you a brief description of a cottage I just bought by saying that it has four walls and a roof. I choose not to provide further details. You hear my description, match it with a description of your own cottage, and conclude that yours is exactly like mine—even though yours is a modern beach house and mine is a made-over garage. In a similar way, incomplete clinical data lend themselves to premature labeling, unwarranted categorization, and give rise to theoretical concepts which are more metaphor than construct because of their largely nonexistent data base. As a result, conceptual agreement is much greater than the data justifies, and the theoretical state of the field seems more advanced than is actually the case.

If all the data for a given formulation are not available for independent examination, there is no possibility for the gradual refinement and clarification of theory. Rather than a particular formulation serving as a tentative and provisional arrangement of the data, subject to subsequent test and cross-validation, the formulation tends to become substituted for the data. Despite Freud's proviso that his theoretical concepts were meant to be taken as only temporary scaffolding subject to subsequent reformulation (Freud, 1914, p. 77), the concepts have proved to be the most enduring parts of the clinical adventure; the relevant data are either incompletely reported or, even when made public, essentially inaccessible to anyone with only normative competence.[1] With the exception of a relatively small number of recorded cases, there is no clinical archive; most utterances exist only in memory, and in a form that is more distorted than veridical.

As a result of this one-sided arrangement, the path from observation to theory can never be retraced. Not only does this fact place a heavy burden on the original discoverer; it also

---

[1] Elsewhere I have discussed the distinction between normative and privileged competence: "Normative competence belongs to all members of the psychoanalytic community. . . . Privileged competence belongs to the analyst at a specific time and place in a particular analysis" (Spence, 1981, p. 114).

makes it difficult to try out other formulations because the data can never be looked at twice. Given the lack of public findings, the theory has necessarily grown in largely individual fashion, with separate investigators each contributing his own set of concepts drawn from his private set of observations (Freud, of course, leads the list). Assuming the usual level of erroneous observation and faulty logic, there would seem, however, to have been surprisingly few conceptual mistakes. How has this high standard of performance been maintained?

Part of the answer lies in what we have identified as the tradition of incomplete data. If the grounds for a general proposition are incomplete, then there is no way for a critic to claim that a particular set of findings did *not* support the concept because the original discoverer can argue that the missing pieces of this set, had they been seen, would suffice to complete the puzzle. On the other hand, it is still possible to support the concept if and when the available findings happen to fit into that particular pattern. Thus the missing data allow occasional support of theory but make falsification impossible. Given this state of affairs, no proposition will ever be disconfirmed. (It should be pointed out, of course, that the apparent confirmation is also suspect because it does not happen in every instance; but since we never have access to the full range of findings, we can never be sure of just what proportion of cases fail to fit.)

A second part of the answer is based on the difference between the *context of discovery* and the *context of justification* (see Reichenbach, 1951). A given theoretical proposition may, in the context of a given clinical encounter (the *context of discovery*), provide necessary and sufficient reasons for a given piece of behavior; because it allows all pieces of the encounter to be fitted into a continuous narrative, it gives a sense of satisfaction and closure and the feeling that now at last a new understanding has taken place. Both patient and analyst may be convinced that an explanation has been found for an anomalous piece of behavior. This kind of "ah-ha" experience seems to be central to the process of therapeutic change; narrative fit permits certain kinds of formulations to "become true" (see Viderman, 1979) and thereby to become an accepted part of the patient's contents of consciousness.

But even though an explanation may be perfectly adequate within the therapeutic hour, it does not instantly qualify for the status of a general law. To reach that level, it must meet other kinds of tests, usually carried out in what is known as the *context of justification*. To become a part of our theoretical system, the proposition must not only suit the individual case, where it was first discovered, but meet the requirements of *all other cases* which share the same characteristics as the target case. When we move from the single case to the larger sample, we need to see all the data—but as already noted, this wish is defeated by the system.

We now begin to recognize the need for two standards of reporting. When the clinician is reporting on a new piece of clinical insight, he has no need to convince his readers; his mission has already been accomplished, so to speak, with the conviction of his patient. He is speaking within a particular context of discovery. Any further reporting is probably after the fact; whether or not his readers agree, the clinical discovery has already taken place. But when he is attempting to justify his concept, the new readers *must* be convinced, and conviction, as we have seen, can only take place when we have access to all the data. This kind of argument requires a different kind of presentation.

Freud never made the distinction between the two kinds of reporting. When describing a new piece of clinical insight, he found it sufficient to present only what he *thought* was sufficient, and he was rather scornful of the need to provide all the evidence; as in telling a joke, if it does not seem funny the first time, telling it in more detail will usually not help. And his aim in his case histories was more to share than to convince; the clinical work had already been accomplished, and he only felt

that others might be interested. For the purpose of initial reports, the tradition of incomplete data is perfectly adequate. But
when he turned to a more general formulation, Freud needed
to present a more complete analysis in order to bring about conviction. He never saw the need to provide a more elaborate
presentation, and the failure to distinguish the two kinds of
reporting has remained with us to the present.

How, exactly, do we go about finding confirmation? In the
context of discovery, we seem to depend heavily on narrative fit
and on the extent to which a given formulation or interpretation lends coherence and continuity to a particular set of happenings. Narrative coherence ranks as one of the four essential
criteria used by Ricoeur (1977) to validate psychoanalytic facts:
to "explain here is to reorganize facts into a meaningful whole
which constitutes a single and continuous history. . ." (p. 861).
Narrative fit has been described by Sherwood (1969) as a critical
feature of the clinical explanation. But while narrative fit can
be highly persuasive in the immediate clinical situation, its compelling quality does not necessarily indicate the presence of
more general truths. And it should be borne in mind that narratives are notoriously accommodating because they are almost
infinitely flexible and because they usually depend on a rather
simple chronological syntax ("and then . . . and then . . .
and then" [see Atkinson, 1978, p. 129]); as a result, they can
almost never be used to *exclude* particular happenings. Thus
a narrative is not well suited to disconfirm a particular hypothesis; I can hardly say, except in a very small set of cases, that
Event A could *not* have happened before Event B.

As a result of its flexibility, a narrative cannot be used to make
a definitive test between two formulations. It therefore follows
that we can hardly ever use narrative fit as a test of historical
truth (and, as we will see later, of theoretical truth). True and
false happenings (in the sense of historical truth) can both be
smoothly fitted into a patient's developing story, and the goodness of fit cannot be used to distinguish the first from the sec-

ond. A good narrative explanation may be useful because it brings together disparate pieces of a patient's life in an appealing way, but what might be called its narrative truth may depend more on its aesthetic properties (which stem from matters of timing and phrasing) than on its historical validity. This state of affairs has an ironical consequence. If we were able to know, by some kind of magic, which pieces of the narrative were historically false and could revise our narrative to leave them out, we might seriously jeopardize its aesthetic appeal, just as a painting might be seriously flawed by turning it into a strict representation of reality.

In what way does narrative truth differ from historical truth? Consider a specific interpretation about how the patient might conceivably have felt at a certain time in his life. Proof that he actually had these feelings is probably out of reach because feelings and attitudes leave few traces—thus the historical truth is always in doubt. But to the extent that the interpretation explains many subsequent aspects of the patient's behavior and to the extent that it completes the unfinished clinical picture in just the right way, it acquires its own truth value and no further checking is necessary. To the extent that an explanation is persuasive and compelling, it acquires features of what might be called narrative truth.

The contrast between the two kinds of truth is highlighted even further when we look at the nature of autobiography. Gusdorf (1980) tells us that

> in autobiography the truth of facts is subordinate to the truth of the man, for it is first of all the man who is in question. . . . The significance of autobiography should therefore be sought beyond truth or falsity, as these are conceived by simple common sense [an apparent reference to historical truth]. It is unquestionably a document about a life, and the historian has a perfect right to check out its testimony and verify its accuracy. But it is also a work of art. . . . The literary, artistic function is thus of greater importance than the historic and objective

function in spite of the claim made by positivist criticism both previously and today (p. 43).

At first glance, the contrast between narrative and historical truth may seem equivalent to the contrast between psychic and external reality. In fact, however, the terms have quite different meanings and should not be confused. External reality, first of all, is not the same as historical truth. We are coming to be skeptical of Freud's far-reaching positivism and are discovering that in many ways external "reality" is very much a construction of the perceiver and thus contains large portions of narrative truth. My account of yesterday's football game is undoubtedly a mixture of what really happened and what I wanted to happen, a mixture of the objective physics of the game and its subjective meaning. Conversely, psychic reality may often be securely grounded in historical fact, and one of our tasks as analysts is to increase the historical truth of the patient's inner world in whatever way we can. At the same time, however, we are also interested in enlarging its narrative base and providing more complete access to fantasy when this seems appropriate. Thus psychic reality may, at any one time, contain elements of both historical and narrative truth, and its power to persuade is apparently independent of which truth is represented. In similar fashion, external reality is usually composed of both fact and fiction, and one consequence of analysis is to make the patient philosophically more sophisticated and less of a naïve realist.

If narrative truth differs from historical truth, how does it compare with theory? We can say that a narrative account derives its appeal from the particular; theory, from the general. Among the elements of the narrative account, some may be true in the sense of having actually happened (historical truth), and others may be true in a narrative sense, but false from the standpoint of history. In a number of places in his writing, Freud admitted that both true and false fragments could be contained within a particular reconstruction, but he claimed (somewhat optimistically it would seem) that this was no problem because it was the "kernel of truth" that made all the difference (Freud, 1937, p. 268). But it is by no means clear how the "kernel of truth" can be identified and separated from the set of equally likely fabrications which make up the patient's life story, and if we have no sure way of identifying historical truth, we are seriously handicapped in our attempt to frame theoretical laws. This is not to say that narrative truth is an unimportant aspect of the true or to deny that it contributes significantly to therapeutic success; it is only to point out that narrative truth is not always equivalent to "the whole truth" and to make clear that we cannot use therapeutic success to validate our general theory (see Hartmann [1964] and Eagle [1980a] for similar cautions). This very success may be an important reason for taking a proposition seriously in the first place, but to rest a general theory on the results of one patient (or even one hour) is to seriously restrict our data base and to ignore the importance of individual differences. Once again, context of discovery should not be confused with context of justification.

But this would seem to be an unfair accusation; confirmation of theoretical constructs always seems to rely on more than one patient, and we can find countless examples in our literature of new clinical findings which seem to support established theory. The trouble lies in the nature of the confirmation, and this problem brings us back to our tradition of incomplete data. As we have seen earlier in this paper, when all the facts are *not* presented, loose confirmation can be rather easily achieved. Precisely for this reason, the fit between theory and findings can never be more than preliminary when not all the facts are available, and particularly good fits are special causes for alarm because of the possibility that the good fit is achieved by judicious selection and arrangement of the findings.

It would seem as if the apparent validation of theory by clinical data, because it is necessarily based on incomplete evidence, must necessarily depend on "soft" pattern-matches. If all the facts were known, many of these matches would not stand up to scrutiny. But because the large store of clinical utterances disappear as soon as they are uttered, there is no going back; thus the validity of a pattern-match can never be tested, and with the authority granted by printer's ink, it comes to take on a status which it probably does not deserve. Soft pattern-matches turn into hard confirmations, without our ever being quite aware that the change is taking place.

Another reason for the general belief in confirmation stems from a second aspect of narrative truth. We have seen that narrative truth can be distinguished from historical truth in the analytic hour and that the former may contribute significantly to the effectiveness of an interpretation. But there is a second kind of narrative truth which lies at the heart of the way each of us thinks about the general theory. We are always constructing a conceptual narrative from a combination of clinical experiences and theoretical exposure, fitting together into a coherent whole our sense of psychoanalytic theory and psychoanalytic process. We bring to this task criteria which are relevant to the problem of narrative fit. As a result, we are more than usually tolerant of soft pattern-matches and incomplete evidence because we aim to construct a coherent theoretical "story," not an ironclad account of the "facts."

This attempt is good enough to provide us with a usable narrative which is always being reinforced by our ongoing clinical experience. Matches between clinical happenings and our developing narrative provide us with the sense that we are privy to a certain part of the truth; what we never stop to examine, of course, is the fact that the matches are often selective and that our theory never accounts for all of the data. We are also inclined to remember the positive and ignore the negative matches because we are searching for coherence and continuity; as a result, we tend to minimize anything which interrupts the "flow" of the narrative. Because we are searching for narrative truth, we are always attempting to write the best possible "story" from all available data; we are not attempting to keep careful track of matches and mismatches.

It could be argued that the very reasons that allow us to construct a usable narrative prevent us from generating a valid theory. As the history of science makes clear, theory-building is discontinuous, episodic, and often marked by critical re-evaluations; at certain points along the way, old paradigms must be dismantled and replaced by substantially different world views. To build good theory, we must be prepared to give up a familiar formulation and return to the data of observation until a new explanation is discovered. But such a step not only requires access to the original observations (many of which are permanently out of reach), but also a readiness to throw away large parts of the enabling narrative which help us to make sense out of our day-by-day clinical encounters. Even though it may not make sense of everything, this narrative is still better than nothing and, as a result, tends to remain in place despite any number of disconfirming observations. Even though wrong in parts, it is also true in parts; enough confirmation is provided by our daily encounters with our patients to convince us that we are on the right track. If we assume, in addition, that the correct theory is only waiting in the wings, then we may find it even less necessary to carry out a critical review of all the evidence—assuming we could somehow make it reappear.

II

In our general satisfaction with our private narrative as a predictor of behavior, supported by confirmations from our daily clinical encounters, we have tended to lose sight of the fact that everyone—you, I, and the man on the street—operates in a roughly comparable fashion. Some theories are better than others, but in every case the theory user always believes that his system is true enough and gives a sufficiently good account of the facts to justify continued use. This state of affairs comes about because of what might be called the ambiguity of everyday life, a lesson well taught by Freud. Since *any* piece of behavior can be looked at from several vantage points, we can produce any number of pattern-matches simply by choosing the piece which best fits our particular theory. To complicate matters further, this ambiguity is composed of two different types: the multiple meanings of events as they actually exist in the real world (a dream, for example, can be seen as both a source of information and a protector of sleep; a symptom as both an inconvenience and an appeal for sympathy); and second, the multiple meanings which we choose to project onto the world as we see it, meanings which are often guided by unconscious and preconscious fantasies (see Arlow, 1969). It is the second sort of ambiguity that is used to confirm the private theory of the paranoid and the mystic; the picture would be much simpler if these projected meanings could be simply set aside. But the difficulty seems to be that there is no easy way to discriminate the first set from the second—and therefore, all the more reason to be wary of private theory and subjective confirmation.

The problem is further complicated by language and the way it functions. In many situations, particularly when reality is unambiguous, it works as a simple pointer. If I say, "Look at the aardvark," I have both given you an order and, assuming you had never seen an aardvark before, a lesson in identification. But when reality becomes more ambiguous and we move from simple objects to complex relationships, then language can open the way to a great deal of mischief. Suppose I describe the case of a student who just failed an examination and say wisely, "It looks like castration anxiety." Language is pretending to be a pointer, as before, and you may hear me telling you something veridical about the student. In fact, however, I am not making an observation at all—or at least, not an observation that can be checked by a random set of other observers. On the contrary, I am invoking a piece of theory without saying so; I am making it appear as if the theory were proven rather than problematic; and by using the word *castration* in such an offhand fashion, I am giving you the feeling that *everyone* believes that castration fears have rather profound and long-lasting effects on behavior, and that this belief has been supported once again. In short,

I am mischievously using language to make it look as if we have found a confirmation of a general law—when, in fact, the notion of castration anxiety is at best a rather weak hypothesis of rather restricted scope.

How much of this mischief comes from my own projective system and how much is the sentence a valid description of the student's behavior? The answer depends on your own set of beliefs, your own theory of the world. If you are a Freudian, you will tend to hear the statement as a simple observation, a statement similar to my saying, "There is an aardvark." If you are not, you may hear it as a whimsical comment, as a metaphor, as an outrageous and unfounded accusation, or as a mixture of all these and more. If you are a Freudian, you will tend to hear my statement as an example of what Quine would call an observation sentence, defined as a sentence which does full justice to its stimulus meaning (in Quine's [1960] language, observation sentences "wear their meaning on their sleeves"). Observation sentences are the datum sentences of science; they can be described as "the bottom edge of language, where it touches experience: where speech is conditioned to stimulation" (Quine and Ullian, 1978, p. 28). Observation sentences produce agreement in all observers exposed to the same situation.

But while all observers would probably agree when I say, "There is an aardvark," a much smaller sample would agree with my statement, "It looks like castration anxiety." The nonbelievers might have been exposed to the same stimulation— the failing student—but choose to describe him in other ways. If the disagreement is large enough, we would have to call my statement something other than an observation sentence; as a result of this relabeling, it would not be used in the formation of a larger theory.

Now here is where our particular troubles begin. The bulk of putative observation sentences in our literature can never be checked because the utterances giving rise to these sentences have disappeared. As a result, their status can never be challenged, and the way is open to using them in a theory where they probably do not belong. Because of our language habits, statements which are cast in the form of observation sentences tend to be taken as valid observations; in the absence of primary data, this tendency becomes all-powerful and, as noted earlier, random comments may be elevated to the status of theory; with repetition, they are advanced to the level of eternal truths. A given proposition may be completely unfounded and yet every time it is invoked, even in the absence of any kind of confirming evidence, it carries the impression that the proposition has once more been confirmed. In the example just given, to invoke the concept of castration anxiety is to make the claim that it has once again been supported. Frequency of use breeds familiarity, and familiarity breeds persuasion. Just as a general law is strengthened with each new piece of supporting data, so a tentative proposition such as castration anxiety can be mistakenly supported simply by being invoked. Each usage may be completely without foundation, but the power of language is such that when I use words in a pointing fashion, you assume that I am being truthful and telling you something veridical about our shared world. You assume, in other words, that I am making a valid observation.

Here, then, is another way by which our theory becomes wrongly confirmed. Because it depends on incomplete data, it lends itself to pseudo-observation sentences which carry the conviction of confirmation. Because the data tend to disappear as soon as they are conceptualized, the statements about the data tend to take their place; the statements become the core of our literature and, because they are publicly accessible, they tend to function as evidence. What began as a tentative observation may be prematurely cast as a theoretical statement (see Esman, 1979) and becomes invested with authority and finality; given a certain frequency of appearance, it becomes established as tested theory. As the literature takes the place of the primary data, disputes are referred to specific papers when they should be referred to the original evidence, and concepts remain current so long as they are published and tend to drop into disuse when they are no longer cited. With attention shifted to the literature, we no longer notice the absence of primary data, the small number of recorded cases, or the gap between what can be understood from a recorded case and what was available to the treating analyst when he was treating that particular patient.

III

In one of his papers to a more general audience, Freud (1933) stressed his interest in building a general theory.

> I have told you that psycho-analysis began as a method of treatment; but I did not want to commend it to your interest as a method of treatment but on account of the truths it contains, on account of the information it gives us about what concerns human beings most of all—their own nature—and on account of the connections it discloses between the most different of their activities (p. 156).

Freud always wanted to go beyond interpretation and use the clinical material to establish general laws. He gained his insights from the individual case but hoped to avoid circularity by confirming them with other cases. His successors have tried to carry on this tradition by testing what might be called the working theory against the new circumstances of each ongoing case.

We speak and write as if this tradition was flourishing—and yet, as I have tried to make clear, on only a very few occasions is a general proposition ever confronted by the underlying evidence. The data are conspicuous mainly by their absence, and what confirmations we have are almost always incomplete and essentially private, inaccessible to the outside critic. We have no tradition which requires an assertion to be backed by *all* the evidence; on the contrary, as we have seen, Freud emphasized the right of privileged withholding, and we have followed in his footsteps. In similar fashion, we have no tradition of what might be called the loyal opposition, no forum for well-intentioned disbelievers who are not satisfied with a given set of conclusions. It may be that the lack of legitimate opposition is closely tied to the tradition of incomplete data, because so long as there is a possibility that the data are confirming but simply being withheld, the critic tends to suppress his criticism. But as in other arenas, the absence of dissent does not always indicate agreement.

I have tried to argue that narrative truth must be distinguished from theoretical truth. An interpretation may be useful because it brings together disparate pieces of a patient's life, because it reduces many pieces of behavior to one underlying cause, and because it finds a "narrative home for an anomalous happening" (Spence, 1982)—all of these satisfactions depend on the narrative and aesthetic truth of the interpretation, but they have no necessary bearing on its place in the larger body of theory. Narrative truth is useful—indeed, essential—for generating our understanding of the particular case we are treating but significantly incomplete for generating general laws. We tend to lose sight of this conclusion because we keep having experiences which seem to prove the opposite. Every day, some part of our clinical experience seems to support one or more pieces of our general theory, and in the face of these accumulating confirmations, we continue to think that the clinical happening does, after all, provide the basis for sound theory. But as we have seen, the confirmations tend to be piecemeal and can never be checked by others; and because we are working toward building up a private narrative of the theory, we tend to emphasize coherence and continuity rather than mismatch and surprise. (If there were surprises, they might never be remembered; and if they were remembered, where would they be published?)

I have argued that each of us is constantly developing his own version of the received theory—our subjective narrative. Because it is based on private data and never made public, it can never be compared with the working theory of another analyst. Nevertheless, we all believe that our own private theory is essentially the same as that of our colleagues; and furthermore, that they all correspond almost exactly to the developing general theory which will some day appear. But this assumption needs to be challenged. The working hypotheses of any particular analyst may have no necessary connection with the general theory or with any other private theory; so long as they do not violate the narrative truth of the analyst's experience, they can range over a broad landscape of ideas, some true, others not so true; and so long as the large majority of clinical happenings are never recorded, there is little likelihood that his private hypotheses will ever be tested against another set of data.

Public theory is just as much protected—because of the tradition of incomplete data. Not only does a pseudo-observation statement derive authority by simply being stated; the more often it is used, the better its credentials seem to become because it takes on the character of a general law. As I have argued above, each particular use of a proposition may be based on only soft data, but the accumulation of many soft instances builds up an air of infallibility and general truth.

Most in need of examination is our general theory. It may be necessary to recognize the unpleasant fact that Freud was being somewhat wishful in his assumption that his theory contained a body of general truths, just as he was somewhat frivolous in his approach to confirmation. Discussing the problem of corroborating an interpretation, Freud (1923) writes that

> what makes him [the analyst] certain in the end is precisely the complication of the problem before him, which is like the solution of a jig-saw puzzle. . . . If one succeeds in arranging the confused heap of fragments, each of which bears upon it an unintelligible piece of drawing, so that the picture acquires a meaning, so that there is no gap anywhere in the design and so that the whole fits into the frame—if all these conditions are fulfilled, then one knows that one has solved the puzzle and that there is no alternative solution (p. 116).

But because of the elasticity of narrative fit, there are any number of good arrangements; and as we have noted, what suits the context of discovery may not fit the context of justification. Freud was too ready to generalize from the single case—too excited, perhaps, by the rapture of discovery to realize that one swallow does not always make a summer.

We may have to reconcile ourselves to the possibility that a general theory may be a long time coming—because of the particular nature of our clinical operation which is based on narrative truth. As I have argued elsewhere, "If the analyst functions more as a pattern-maker than a pattern-finder, then we may be faced with a glaring absence of general rules. What rules there are, moreover, may pertain mainly to the more trivial aspects of our clinical material. If the impact of a particular interpretation is contingent . . . on the specific texture of time and place, the rules for it being true are just as much out of reach as the rules for any other kind of artistic masterpiece" (Spence, 1982).

Each time a particular interpretation is followed by more insight or a new set of associations, the analyst is apt to draw the mistaken conclusion that its historical truth is also being confirmed; from this, it is but a small step to conclude that something of theoretical importance has been established. But implicit in the notion that narrative truth can be distinguished from historical truth is the conclusion that narrative truth can be based on nonhistorical premises (see Viderman [1979] and his conception of an interpretation as a creative act). To the extent that interpretations work for nonfactual reasons (in the usual sense of the word), it is obviously a mistake to use clinical data as the main ingredient in a general theory. Some parts may indeed be relevant, but we are faced with the problem of never knowing, in any particular instance, which pieces of data have general relevance and which are specific to the hour and patient and analyst in question. We can imagine situations in which the persuasive power of an interpretation stemmed largely from the particular shape of the transference: the analyst, vested with all of his transference power, was more important than what he said. It would clearly be a mistake to use the content as the basis for some general theory of behavior. At other times, the content might be more relevant to the effect and could be considered as the "kernel of truth" that produced the effect. It seems clear that we have no reliable way of distinguishing the first case from the second, and the same could be said of Freud. By failing to draw the distinction, he tended to raise all significant clinical happenings to the level of theoretical propositions. By failing to distinguish narrative from historical truth, he tended to confuse the specific effects of the treatment situation with the generality of the clinical happening.

IV

What, then, are the prospects for a general theory of "what concerns human beings most of all"? I have talked about the tradition of incomplete evidence and how this has stood in the way of critical thinking and vital theory. Is there a prospect for change? The answer, it would seem, must depend on how we learn to move beyond narrative truth, or more broadly, how we move from description to explanation (see Hartmann, 1964).

Because we are working with complex patterns of form and content, it often becomes difficult to identify the relevant data. More than the wording of an interpretation needs to be known, but how much more? We would like to know something about the state of the transference, about the history of that particular interpretation, about the additional meanings suggested by the wording but not made explicit—but in every case, we need to know how much ground to search, and we have no precise guidelines. Each investigator tends to use his own standards, and as a result, what is data for one researcher may be skeletal evidence for another.

A second reason to be dubious about whether we can gain access to all the evidence bears on the problem of privileged context. The visible text of the session under study is always being heard—by patient and analyst—against the background of what each of them is thinking (see Spence, 1981). Once again, we are confronted with a complex mixture. Does conviction come from the wording of a specific interpretation or from the meshing of its lexical content with the patient's hopes and fears? In many cases, a particular interpretation gains extra force from the private meanings read into it by the patient, meanings which are invisible to the outside observer (we are back to the distinction between normative and privileged competence). The reason for giving a particular interpretation may often depend less on the demands of the analytic "conversation" than on the inner experience of the analyst who, because of some series of subjective feelings, decides that now is the time to speak; once again, this inner experience is inaccessible to the outside observer. Yet it is clearly part of the data, because without knowledge of this inner context, we can never "hear" the analytic conversation with the correct "phrasing" and "accent."

The problem of privileged context carries with it a formidable challenge. The more subjective the experience, the more difficult it is to reduce it to a set of general laws—and we might argue that any such attempt could lead only to sterile theory. We not only have the problem of how to translate a highly individual set of meanings into some kind of general formulation, but we must also find an answer to the question of how much context to include. To interpret a given session, do we need to know the detailed experience of the analyst during the preceding twenty-four hours? Forty-eight hours? Three months? Six months? The questions are endless because we have no systematic way of approaching the problem.

Thus it would appear that we will always be hampered by the tradition of incomplete data. Even with the best of intentions, there seems to be no systematic method for defining the proper size of the search space and gathering a proper context for each visible utterance. And note the irony—even with an awareness of what is missing and the knowledge that *all* the evidence must be searched, we are still helpless in formulating the next step. Perhaps Freud took his privileged stance for a reason!

As we discover that narrative truth lies at the heart of insight and therapeutic change, we are also learning that historical truth is less accessible than we are taught to believe. Toward the end of his life, Freud seemed to accept this verdict and argued for *construction* (a partly creative endeavor) over *reconstruction* (an attempt to resurrect a piece of the past); the former concerns itself with narrative truth whereas the latter is an attempt to find historical truth. In recent papers (see Shapiro [1981] in particular), we have again heard increasing doubts[2] about the possibility of ever uncovering what "really" happened during the early years of a patient's life, and a recent series of studies by Loftus (1979) has shown how easily memories can be influenced by leading questions, making us necessarily skeptical about the effect of the treatment process on the patient's associations. From every side, there seems reason to doubt the historical truth of our evidence, and we are learning to treat even fairly "hard" memories with a certain skepticism. As a result, we have tended to see more and more significance in the narrative truth of a formulation and in the central position of narrative appeal in the treatment process.

But narrative truth brings with it its own set of problems. It is first and foremost highly relative; each story is different, and what makes a particular formulation persuasive and compelling is precisely the fact that it is carefully tailored to the patient's life. (If all our interpretations were the same, word for word, they would quickly lose their power to persuade.) But if each piece of narrative truth is relative, how can we build it into a general theory? Each piece of narrative explanation tends to be somewhat ad hoc, drawing its power to persuade from an accumulation of individual details which we can never hope to replicate in any other situation. Given the explanation and given its clinical effect, how do we go about expressing it in some more general manner so that I can compare my narrative with yours and ultimately develop some general laws of what

[2] For an example of earlier doubting, see Kris (1956).

makes a good narrative? The study of literature has traditionally been concerned with what might be called the theory of the good story; we know certain things about form and content, about some of the transformations necessary to turn the chaotic details of reality into the smooth form of a persuasive story. We can also learn from the hermeneutic tradition something about how to go about finding the ingredients for our narrative—how to sift through the ambiguous material of dreams, memories, and fantasies to find the particular meanings we need. But neither story-telling nor hermeneutic discovery will teach us much about the science of man, and here is where the primary drawback of the narrative tradition comes home. If the bulk of historical "findings" are in some way biased in the telling, we have inevitably restricted the scope of our theory. We may have to recognize that the past is essentially out of reach and that our data are relevant mainly to understanding the here-and-now of a particular hour. We are in a privileged position to report on the here-and-now, but in only a weak position to report on the past. The difference may be described with the use of Russell's (1912) famous distinction between knowledge by acquaintance and knowledge by description. We are privileged observers of the data within the session and in a position to observe how a particular interpretation, let us say, is heard by the patient and how the hearing (or mishearing) can be understood in light of the transference neurosis. Experiences of this kind lead to knowledge by acquaintance. But reports of the past are a kind of hearsay with the referent permanently out of reach, and although we may make a genetic interpretation, it is always based more on knowledge by description (theoretical knowledge). An explanation rooted in the transference and reinforced by the countless details of the immediate context is always more persuasive than an explanation based on a hypothetical construction of the past.

But more than persuasion is at stake; there is also a certain respect for the evidence. By prematurely reducing a clinical observation to some earlier, hypothetical event (a primal scene, for example), we may have convinced ourselves that we have explained the observation, but once labeled in this manner, it is never looked at again. Multiply this tendency by thousands of hours across thousands of analysts and we can see the waste of data. All the time we were settling for doubtful explanation, rooted in the past, we were being exposed to thousands of clinical events which contained significant amounts of unmined clinical information about the present. But because we had less interest in what was in front of our eyes, the significant data often slipped through our fingers as we continued to confirm doubtful propositions about the past.

We can put the matter more precisely by looking again at the conflict between public and private theory. Each analyst is continuously engaged in updating his private narrative, adding the latest examples of good and bad interpretations to his accumulating store of clinical wisdom. He is always trying to *assimilate* the evidence to his working hypotheses. But it would be a mistake for the field in general to take this approach; on the contrary, it must put the emphasis on *accommodation* and find ways in which the received theory must be changed to conform to the evidence.

To this end, it might be useful to separate journal contributions into two categories: the clinical discoveries (narrative truth) and the more abstract formulations (theoretical truth). Papers in the first category might serve as the archive from which general conclusions could be drawn; formulations drawn from these cases would appear in the second category. Papers in the first category would emphasize the clinical context of a particular happening; this would include (in much more detail than is currently found) a detailed exposition of the context of the case along with an account of the privileged context of the treating analyst. If enough detail were provided, in the appropriate context, it would be possible for an outside reader (someone with only normative competence) to understand and integrate the information and be in a position to compare it with other accounts of similar events. The clinical evidence would then become publicly accessible, and theoretical discussions could be referred to one or more specific specimens, making it possible to generate public discussion and, even more important, to be able to retrace at will the path from data to construct. A new concept (e.g., "splitting") could be defined by reference to a particular sample of clinical accounts, and its evidential basis would be available for all to consider. For the first time, analytic data would become public property, publicly discussed.

If clinical detail is appropriately presented against the right kind of context, it should be possible to bring about conviction based on narrative truth alone. For almost the first time, an outside reader would be able to sense the excitement of a bona fide clinical discovery—rather than be told that such things exist, to be taken on faith, he would experience the conviction as it occurred. What has been knowledge by description would thus turn into knowledge by acquaintance. While it may be necessary to develop a mixture of literary and dramatic expertise to properly present a clinical happening in a way that can truly convince the reader, if this goal can be achieved, we will be able to capture a critical feature of narrative truth and build this into our theory.

The contents of these vignettes would be analyzed and discussed in the second category—the theoretical papers. Here the aim is to convince as well as discover; the specific reason of the particular instance would give way to the formulation of general laws (see Eagle, 1980b). Argument about formulation could thus be kept separate from argument about particulars, and a given piece of the clinical archive could be discussed by any number of authors (in contrast to the current practice of supplying new examples for each new discussion). Theoretical papers might also be judged on more general grounds; ad hoc arguments would give way to more general kinds of reasoning; and the detail of the case could be kept separate from its larger meaning. Unresolved disagreements might lead to a call for new clinical instances (rather than the formation of new institutes); new additions to the archive would generate new discussions and further clarification of theoretical issues. (One is reminded of the case system in law and the way in which new cases lead to new decisions.)

To close with a specific example of how such a scheme might work, consider a recent paper by Langs (1981) on modes of cure in psychoanalysis. He proposes the idea that *only* interpretations based on the here-and-now context of the hour are curative in any significant degree, and that other kinds of interpretations, based on manifest content or genetic formulations, may actually reinforce the resistance. *Only* interpretations which take account of the interaction between patient and analyst "can offer the patient adaptive structural change and insightful symptom resolution" (Langs, 1981, p. 212). Strong claims, one would think—where is the evidence? Unfortunately, it is largely invisible, and once again, the claims must be taken largely on faith. Whether or not the argument is true, there is no way in which it can be fairly evaluated. Think how much more convincing the argument would have been—and how much more lasting its consequences—if supporting data were available. Under those conditions, it would move from an interesting speculation to a matter of public record—from a matter of narrative truth to (if confirmed) a piece of theoretical knowledge. Very likely the original formulation would undergo several stages of modification; significant conditions might be uncovered which would increase or decrease the general effect; certain exceptions to the general rule might be discovered as it was challenged by new pieces of clinical evidence. But the end result would produce more general conviction than is possible in the absence of evidence; by embedding the rule in a context of particulars, we would move from knowledge by description (which comes cheap) to knowledge by acquaintance (which is significantly more lasting).

REFERENCES

ARLOW, J. A. (1969). Unconscious fantasy and disturbances of conscious experience. *Psychoanal. Q.*, 38:1-27.

ATKINSON, R. F. (1978). *Knowledge and Explanation in History.* Ithaca, N.Y.: Cornell Univ. Press.

EAGLE, M. (1980a). Psychoanalytic interpretation: veridicality and therapeutic effectiveness. *Nous*, 14:405-425.

———— (1980b). A critical examination of motivational explanation in psychoanalysis. *Psychoanal. Contemp. Thought*, 3:329-380.

ESMAN, A. (1979). On evidence and inference, or the Babel of tongues. *Psychoanal. Q.*, 48:628-630.

FREUD, S. (1912). Recommendations to physicians practising psycho-analysis. *S.E.*, 12.

———— (1913). On beginning the treatment (further recommendations on the technique of psycho-analysis I). *S.E.*, 12.

———— (1914). On narcissism: an introduction. *S.E.*, 14.

———— (1923). Remarks on the theory and practice of dream-interpretation. *S.E.*, 19.

———— (1933). New introductory lectures on psycho-analysis. *S.E.*, 22.

———— (1937). Constructions in analysis. *S.E.*, 23.

GUSDORF, G. (1980). Conditions and limits of autobiography. In *Autobiography*, ed. J. Olney. Princeton: Princeton Univ. Press.

HARTMANN, H. (1964). *Essays on Ego Psychology. Selected Problems in Psychoanalytic Theory.* New York: Int. Univ. Press.

KRIS, E. (1956). The recovery of childhood memories in psychoanalysis. *Psychoanal. Study Child*, 11:54-88.

LANGS, R. (1981). Modes of 'cure' in psychoanalysis and psychoanalytic psychotherapy. *Int. J. Psychoanal.*, 62:199-214.

LOFTUS, E. R. (1979). *Eyewitness Testimony.* Cambridge, Mass.: Harvard Univ. Press.

QUINE, W. V. (1960). *Word and Object.* Cambridge, Mass.: MIT Press.

———— & ULLIAN, J. S. (1978). *The Web of Belief.* New York: Random House.

REICHENBACH, H. (1951). *The Rise of Scientific Philosophy.* Berkeley: Univ. of California Press.

RICOEUR, P. (1977). The question of proof in Freud's psychoanalytic writings. *J. Amer. Psychoanal. Assn.*, 25:835-871.

RUSSELL, B. (1912). *The Problems of Philosophy.* New York: Holt.

SHAPIRO, T. (1981). On the quest for the origin of conflict. *Psychoanal. Q.*, 50:1-21.

SHERWOOD, M. (1969). *The Logic of Explanation in Psychoanalysis.* New York: Academic Press.

SPENCE, D. P. (1981). Psychoanalytic competence. *Int. J. Psychoanal.*, 62:113-124.

——— (1982). *Narrative Truth and Historical Truth*. New York: Norton. (In press.)

VIDERMAN, S. (1979). The analytic space: meaning and problems. *Psychoanal. Q.*, 48:257-291.

13

PSYCHOANALYTIC
"PROBLEMS"
AND
POSTMODERN
"SOLUTIONS"

PSYCHOANALYTIC "PROBLEMS" AND POSTMODERN "SOLUTIONS"

BY KIMBERLYN LEARY, PH.D.

A number of recent revisions of psychoanalytic theory implicitly draw on postmodern conceptualizations of human selves and human subjectivity. Though postmodern ideas have a wide currency in the humanities and in literary criticism, and are increasingly represented in critiques of science, psychoanalytic clinicians are generally less familiar with the body of writings that encompass postmodernist thought. This paper discusses the evolution of postmodernism and its emergence into psychoanalytic theory using the work of Roy Schafer and Irwin Hoffman as cases in point. I will suggest that when postmodernism is applied to psychoanalytic practice, the result is only a partial solution, at best, to the problems of metapsychology postmodernist revisions were intended to resolve.

The purpose of this paper is to evaluate critically the implications of what increasingly appears to be a "postmodernist" turn in psychoanalytic theory and practice. Psychoanalytic clinicians like Roy Schafer and Irwin Hoffman—as cases in point—have articulated new models for psychoanalysis that are implicitly informed by postmodern critiques of science, literature, and philosophy. In these accounts, psychoanalytic metapsychology is superseded by postmodern discussions of subjectivity, which

The author wishes to thank Richard Hale Shaw, Robert Hatcher, James Hansell, Steven Trierweiler, George Rosenwald, and Janice Gutfreund for their helpful comments on earlier drafts of this paper. An earlier version of this paper was presented in May 1992 at the Northwest Alliance for Psychoanalytic Study, Seattle, Washington.

emphasize that reality itself is a "social construction" and meaning jointly created by both patient and analyst. These perspectives are offered as "solutions" to the difficulties many believe are present in using a nineteenth century theory of mind to account for subjectivity on the cusp of the twenty-first century.

Despite its proliferation in academic writing and in cultural life at large, postmodernism is, for the most part, less familiar to psychoanalytic thinkers. In this paper, I will provide a description and definition of what postmodernism is meant to embrace and explore the way in which these ideas are being introduced into contemporary psychoanalysis. I will argue that relying on postmodernism offers, at best, only a partial solution to the problem of understanding human selves and human subjectivity because postmodernism is itself a problematic account of human experience. I will illuminate the considerable difficulties that arise when postmodernism is borrowed by psychoanalytic theorists to account for human agency and activity. I will also suggest that despite their limitations, postmodern reconceptualizations may still generate interdisciplinary inquiries that may come to enlarge our capacity to articulate psychoanalytic process.

Postmodernism as a Stance toward Theory

Some one hundred years ago, Freud's account of human subjectivity—the shape that human minds take in transaction with the passions of Eros, the limits of the body, and the gratifications and terrors of childhood—challenged the way in which human culture understood itself. Though the death knell of psychoanalysis has been said to sound repeatedly since then, psychoanalytic theory and practice have instead thrived, expanding into new approaches to human experience. In fact, some have argued that psychoanalysis is now experiencing something of a renaissance in contemporary culture because of the proliferation of new perspectives (e.g., relational psychoanalysis, intersubjectivity, and social constructivist models) that many suggest may more inclusively address the complexities of social and psychological life. Many of these new versions of psychoanalysis owe an often unacknowledged debt to postmodernism.

Postmodernism is emerging as the leitmotif of the latter part of the twentieth century. Like psychoanalysis, its subjects are also the relationships among selves, subjectivity, human knowledge, and reality. Though postmodernism is concerned with human experience, it is a radical critique of the traditional assumptions which undergird existing conceptions of what it means to be a human being in transaction with human society. As such, postmodernism is, in key respects, a stance that one takes toward a theory and a way of looking at theory rather than a theory itself (cf., Flax, 1990).

Most generally, postmodernism rests on the claim that what humans call "objective" knowledge is derived only by social agreements rendered through language. Accordingly, we live within realities that are constituted by the words that we use to describe them. These realities exist principally by convention and through language structures. Hence, we cannot talk about "essential meanings," "unquestionable truths," or even "unitary selves." Instead, human understanding and human identity are regarded as residing in "versions of truth." In consequence, selfhood and identity also remain transient, constantly open to revision, and in flux (Frosh, 1991). The aim of the postmodern critique is to "break the crust of convention" (Rorty, 1979; quoted in Flax, 1990), that is, to focus attention on the process of human discourse and away from any consideration of a content, reality, or product that exists outside of a language or interpretive system.

In contemporary criticism, postmodernism is considered by many to be among the most significant accounts of contemporary life where "beliefs about what may be believed" (Gergen, 1991) have been steadily eroded. The advent of a global economy, the move to flexible accumulation, and the shrinkage of space and time made possible by technological advances have

rendered constructs and conclusions that had once seemed un-
assailable open to question (Harvey, 1989). As Frosh (1991) put
it, uncertainty now remains the only enduring certainty. In order to explore the implications of postmodernism for psychoanalysis, I will discuss in detail some of the main assumptions of
the postmodernist style and the world view it implies.

*The Emergence of a Postmodern Sensibility in Literary Criticism
and Philosophy*

First encountered in discussions of utopian architectural theory (Connor, 1989), the voice of postmodern discourse is now
heard across the humanities and in literary criticism where it has
gained significant popularity. The account of postmodernism
that I will present here begins with its origins in literary theory
which took special interest in the relationship between a reader
and a text. This relationship was understood to convey something about how human beings could apprehend the world.

For most of Western history, written texts have been accepted
as containers of meanings and assumed to be repositories of
reality (Anderson, 1990). The literary canon of Western tradition achieved its status because its works were viewed as containing significant ideas that could be communicated to and
retrieved by a reader.

Under these assumptions, writing and reading were relatively
straightforward acts. The text's reality became a more or less
private possession of its author but was potentially available to a
reader. Interpreting a text meant receiving the meanings of the
text that had been intended by its author. In this account, language functioned as a vehicle of communication for ideas, emotional states, and other contents.

The literary theory of the "New Criticism," which gained as-
cendancy in American universities beginning in the 1930's,
modified this perspective. New Criticism focused attention on
the relationship between reader and author. The text now be-

longed to *both* writer and reader. As a method, New Criticism advocated that the text be read closely to explicate the meanings believed to be present in the author's words (Anderson, 1990). The authority of the text rested on the author's presented words and not on his or her authorial intention alone. The poem, for example, was understood "to mean what it meant" regardless of what the author planned to convey or the subjective feelings it aroused in the reader (Eagleton, 1983). Interpretation within New Criticism consisted of the effort to discuss how the text could illuminate as well as keep cloaked its meanings, leading to a more variegated appreciation of its complexity and reality.

Both of these accounts of language and meaning are probably familiar to psychoanalytic ears. Language is portrayed as a way to apprehend meanings that may or may not reflect what an author intended to communicate. Interpretation occurs in a dyadic context. Careful attention to the text's presentation allows the reader to develop a concept of the author's subjectivity, including that which he or she was not aware of communicating. The psychoanalytic method likewise relies on language and interpretation: talking, it is said, is a means to cure. Similarly, psychoanalytic dialogues are also dyadic and involve a search for hidden discourse which, when understood, can lead to a richer appreciation of the patient's subjectivity. So far, we remain on familiar territory.

In literary theory, however, the sanctity of the text gave way. Reader reception theory, as articulated by Stanley Fish (1980) and others, argued that text had no authority. Instead, the reader and his or her response to a text came to be viewed as the center of the text's reality. Here, the reader's response—his or her subjectivity—created what the text meant, with the words on the page representing little more than a series of "cues" or invitations to the reader (Eagleton, 1983).

Given the fact that different readers with different subjectivities respond differently to a text, the "reality" of a text must be constructed anew with each and for every reader. Therefore, the only "meaning" that a text may have is fluid, ever changing, and constantly in flux. Meaning, in this system, is but a moment in time.

Jacques Derrida (1976; Flax, 1990; Attridge, 1992), the French philosopher, and the deconstructionist school with which he was associated, expanded this conclusion in even more far-reaching ways that ultimately came to affect literary criticism. Derrida and deconstructionism de-emphasized the importance of the text in favor of its language alone. More generally, deconstructionism delinks language from the world it is purported to describe.

Derrida argued that philosophy has been led astray by the search for referents and the desire to claim the "real," what he called the "metaphysics of presence." For Derrida, the "real" could be shown to be "fictional." That is, what was accepted as real and truthful could always be shown to be a product of a particular system of meaning (Eagleton, 1983). It existed only as a belief and as a consequence of certain linguistic and philosophic practices (Flax, 1990). Any text could be undermined or "deconstructed" to show that its unity was dependent on rhetorical strategies and cultural practices that excluded certain discourses (e.g., the experience of women and of people of color) while privileging others (e.g., Eurocentric models) (Flax, 1990). The deconstructionist critic focuses attention on what has been left out and rendered invisible. In this way, the text can be shown to collapse upon itself, "embarrassed" by its own system of logic (Eagleton, 1983).

This perspective, at first glance, may remind the psychoanalytic reader of the unconscious. Yet key differences exist. In most psychoanalytic accounts, the unconscious remains a referent. *If* currently inaccessible, under the right conditions, the unconscious can be made conscious and acquire presence. But for deconstructionism, representation *per se* becomes impossible because there is nothing existing beyond the human symbolic system. In this system, there is nothing to represent outside of language. Therefore, language is the only reality and the unconscious, as a referent, may be said not to exist.

Under deconstructionism instead, it is necessary to solicit a series of interpretations from repeated readings of a text. From these interpretations, a "story" will emerge. But unlike traditional accounts of narratives, this story has not been submerged in the text, waiting to be excavated. It is instead an ever-changing product of the interpretations that create it. Meaning depends on an unfolding present and is wholly context dependent. It can, in fact, never be realized because the next interpretation applied to the text will reconfigure the story that is emerging. The story is always in process and can never be known. Given this, it follows that the only test of truth is a pragmatic one, that is, whether or not the emerging story is "plausible," generates "interesting conversation," and "pays off" within the context of the needs of a particular culture at a particular time (cf., Anderson, 1990; Flax, 1990).

Let me present an account of how deconstructionism works, using an example from popular culture. Several years ago, the singer Billy Joel recorded a popular song entitled "We Didn't Start the Fire," which consisted almost entirely of the names of celebrity figures, geographical locations, and prominent news events. It was, in effect, an exemplar of postmodern sensibility. The song had little narrative structure except for the fact that its contents were presented roughly in chronological order. For a while, the song caused something of a stir because, for most, narratives are still "about something." Letters to the editor in *Newsweek* and other national publications asked: What is this song about? Particularly meaningful events in the singer's life? Critical events that defined the decades? The general complaint from readers was that the text did not make its meaning clear. If the song spoke for itself, about what did it speak? The answer from a deconstructionist would be that the song spoke about *nothing at all*. The only meaning of this text was its ability to generate interesting speculation and a myriad of interpretations until the public tired of the song and moved on to another curiosity.

In a similar way, traditional literature can be deconstructed to show that it, too, is about nothing at all. In *King Lear*, the tale of Shakespeare's mad king is commonly accepted as one of sacrifice and tragedy. An old man, confronting his waning powers, struggles with the problem of good and evil and the doomed effort to redeem himself. With a deconstructionist reading, however, this "story" become plausible only if the reader ignores the experience of the women in Lear's orbit. A deconstructionist critic would argue that the play could also be understood as a tale of patriarchy and domination. Here the chief struggle involves the effort of women, Lear's daughters, to appropriate power and exercise independent desire (Thompson, 1988). With this, the play fragments into a multitude of texts, capable of offering a panoply of different meanings. Therefore, the text itself may be said to be about nothing at all save a particular arrangement of words on a page that can be explained in different ways (Thompson, 1988).

Postmodernism as a Consequence of Contemporary Culture

Whereas deconstructionism is concerned principally with texts, postmodernism extends its range into considerations of the subjectivity of the self, knowledge, and its relationship to power. Discussions of postmodernism typically begin by locating postmodernism in modern culture and its technologies. Here postmodernism is understood to be a reaction to the exigencies of contemporary cultural life and a response to the failed promises of modernity (Harvey, 1989; Gergen, 1991).

Cultural theorists define the modern age as beginning with an endorsement and extension of the values of the enlightenment (Harvey, 1989; Connor, 1989; Flax, 1990; Gergen, 1991). As such, modernity can be defined in terms of its foundation: the importance of rational knowledge, positivism, and the scientific method. Under the terms of modernity, the world was understood as something that could be deduced, evaluated, and known on its own terms.

Modern philosophy conceptualized the self as a distinct, stable entity, and modern literature emphasized the interior monologue and private experience (e.g., the work of Virginia Woolf and D. H. Lawrence). In keeping with its respect for empiricism, personal truths could be made accessible, publicly apprehended, and mapped out as invariant structures of knowledge as, for example, in the concepts of ego and id, systems conscious and unconscious. The so-called "grand theories" or metanarratives of science, including those of psychoanalysis and its metapsychology, were the means to understand something essential about reality and what it meant to be a human being.

Postmodern critiques, though not congruent with one another (Flax, 1990), all disavow the notion that human beings have any essential or unitary core. Postmodern accounts of human experience are united only in their opposition to the ideals of enlightenment beliefs, which are considered to be an elaborate, if also convenient, set of "fictions." Proponents of postmodernism assert that when the workings of contemporary culture are laid bare, they contradict or, at the very least, dispute the positivistic reality of a unified whole (Flax, 1990). Postmodern critics favor an assessment of self and society that is based on discursive practices and the rules of language systems.

Let me return to the contemporary conditions that set the context for the emergence of postmodernism. Postmodernists and positivistic scientists alike note that those living in the twentieth century have witnessed profound changes in the ways that human life is conducted. The contemporary world is marked by constant change and violent upheaval (Frosh, 1991). What had been taken for granted has been taken away through political, technological, and personal shifts of an unprecedented magnitude. As an example, medical technologies designed to circumvent biological limitations and to "support" life now raise discomforting questions about the boundaries between life and death. Similar tensions exist with HIV, AIDS, and the dynamics of infection where an act of love can become the vehicle of deterioration and death.

Although change and upheaval define the history of the human race, what is now revolutionary is the speed at which these changes have become commonplace occurrences and the manner in which these events have been presented, experienced, and assimilated (Harvey, 1989). Gergen (1991) writes that technological advances—the advent of the telephone, radio, television, electronic mail, and widespread global transit—make for instantaneous access and the dissolution of traditional boundaries between persons. In a similar vein, Harvey (1989) argues that modern technology has brought about a compression in the way in which space and time are experienced. Consider for a moment the perspective most of the Western world had during the recent Persian Gulf war through the telecommunications eye of CNN. Microphones set up in bomb shelters in Israel listened as air raid sirens went off. Video displays showed maps charting the trajectory of missiles to viewers worldwide before human observers could conclude that an attack had even occurred. Process was confirmed before content could be established. With this, human culture is established within the postmodern present.

Gergen (1991) further suggests that media technologies themselves transform human relationships. He asks: What other than a "relationship" develops, for example, between a person and the televised figures that regularly join him or her and which may even supersede contacts with "real" persons? In many respects, contemporary social life now takes place within imaginary worlds at a scale unmatched in previous generations.

If we cannot claim that events have some reality apart from their present-day descriptions, then it is also necessary to conclude the same about individual selves and individual identity. Postmodernist critics argue that selves are "social constructions," not private possessions, and require audiences if they are to exist and become present. The self only becomes an experience as a function of the social surround (Berger and Luckman, 1966). And, given the expanded range and varieties of technologically orchestrated contacts, one self simply will not do. Of necessity then, different selves are required to meet the demand of the different tasks and involvements of social life. Postmodern discourses argue that we routinely rely on a "multiplicity of selves" for the different stagings of self that contemporary life demands. When the world and reality are revealed as being constructions, postmodernism suggests that this can lead to a fluid and generative creativity and expanded opportunities for "play," including the opportunity to play with one's view of one's self and one's identity (Frosh, 1991).

Given the view that the world and selves are "made" aesthetic phenomena and "created stories," postmodernism asserts that the work of human life is "play." Here, play is the successor to reality (Anderson, 1990). Living a life becomes a matter of creating a life and of aesthetics (Flax, 1990). Postmodernist life, then, is always "camp," delighting in the appearance of things, especially for what they are not and with the knowledge that they are unreal (Sontag, 1966; quoted in Anderson, 1990). Postmodernism takes as its motif the celebration of this discontinuity. In the end—to paraphrase Shakespeare—the play is not just the thing, it is the only thing. Postmodernism, initially invoked as a diagnosis of the contemporary condition and offered as a means of discussing contemporary problems, is now put forth, in some of its incarnations, as a "solution," a palliative, even a cure, for the ills of contemporary society.

The Emergence of a Postmodern Sensibility in Psychoanalysis

Given that postmodernism and psychoanalysis concern themselves with developing accounts of human subjectivity, it is not surprising that these explanatory modes have been assumed to enjoy easy interpenetration. This is especially so because they often use the same terms—"self," "subjectivity," and even "constructions"—to accomplish their work of interpreting persons. It is this assumption of presumed congruence that I will now explore.

Until recently, psychoanalysis concerned itself only with the apparent discontinuities in human subjectivity (cf., Rapaport, 1944). Disruptions, inconsistencies, and "nonsense" were understood to exist temporarily until unconscious thoughts and affects could be discerned. When conscious experience was linked to its unconscious referents, continuity in mental life could be re-established. Even when Freud (1937) wrote of interpretive "constructions," it was in this same spirit: the clinical conjecture was to take the place of a content and be accorded the status of a "fact."

Increasingly, though perhaps quietly, a postmodern sensibility is beginning to find a receptive audience among a number of psychoanalytic clinicians (e.g., Benjamin, 1991; Flax, 1990; Hoffman, 1983, 1992; Schafer, 1983, 1992; Spence, 1982, 1987; Stern, 1992). Psychoanalytic theory has been recast as a postmodern discourse by Schafer (1983, 1992) and others in reconceptualizations of therapeutic process as narrative process.[1] Postmodernism has also been introduced to psychoanalysis in conceptualizations of the analytic field as a social construction (Hoffman, 1983, 1991, 1992; Stern, 1992). I shall explore the theoretical contributions made by Schafer and Hoffman as illustrative cases of a postmodernist turn in psychoanalytic thinking.

[1] Donald Spence (1982, 1987) was among the first to offer the perspective that the psychoanalytic encounter was a "narrative encounter." In my view, however, Spence settles upon narrative as an interim solution. His argument that the subject of psychoanalysis is narrative and not historical truth is based upon the proposition that analysands and analysts are unwittingly relying on accounts they take to be true but whose connection to the original, and hence whose truth value, is suspect. Spence supports this with the contention that language itself distorts its subjects, being "too rich and too poor" to represent experience adequately. For their part, analysts are biased toward coherence. Rather than listening with evenly hovering attention, the analyst instead fills in the gaps and discontinuities to make the patient intelligible. Psychoanalysis, therefore, is concerned with narrative and not historical truth. Spence (1987) goes on to suggest that psychoanalysis give up its claim to science and choose other models (e.g., legal explanations and the law) as a means for understanding what psychoanalysts actually do. Given this, Spence appears to be a reluctant postmodernist. He does not conclude that reality is not "out there," only that we cannot get "in here" because of the limits of language and discourse.

Schafer (1976, 1983, 1992) has brought a strong though largely unacknowledged postmodern sensibility to his discussions of psychoanalysis in a series of influential books and papers published over the last fifteen years. In *A New Language for Psychoanalysis* (1976), Schafer argues that psychoanalytic metapsychology relies on a mechanistic, needlessly reifying language that de-emphasizes the intentionalistic, subjectivistic, and phenomenological aspects of the psychoanalytic encounter. As a corrective for this, Schafer recommended an "action language" for psychoanalysis to replace metapsychology. Rather than turn to what he calls "hypothetical entities" (psychic structures) or "inferred forces" (drives), causal explanation is rendered in terms of *reasons*, claimed and unclaimed, for engaging in particular actions.

Later, in *The Analytic Attitude* (1983), Schafer describes the analytic encounter as representing "a species of narrative performance" (p. 186). He argues that psychoanalytic treatment involves "telling stories about ourselves to others" (p. 218) and is therefore a narrative act. Psychoanalysis, he asserts, is concerned with "language and the equivalents of language" (p. 255). When the analyst and analysand are viewed as engaged in a narrative process, then the interpretations they develop will be understood to represent only *one* of a great number of possible accounts that could have been given. To make this point clear, Schafer (1983) writes: "In the realm of the life historical narrative, there is always more than one way to tell what is the case now and so what the case must have been in the infantile past" (p. 203).

Accordingly, the analytic dialogue is not about establishing anything akin to "historical reality," and the events of the there-and-then. The analysand instead offers selective recollections of events that he or she believed to be reality but which are now retold in other terms. The therapeutic task becomes one in which analyst and analysand construct through language new, better, "non-neurotic" stories for the analysand's future. The psychoanalytic method transforms the analysand's stories into psychoanalytic stories. That is, the analysand's narrations are retold through "storylines" of incestuous desire, separation-individuation, and/or defense. As a result of a successful analysis, the analysand gives up the language of symptoms and illness, exchanging it for psychoanalytic discourse. When psychoanalysis is configured in the terms of narrative, therapeutic change means, in essential respects, becoming fluent in another tongue.

More recently, in *Retelling a Life* (1992), Schafer extends his narrational project still further. In accord with action language, subjective experience is viewed as a construction of human agency. Given the everyday observation that different people construct different experiences of the same event, Schafer concludes that human experience does not lie in wait. Instead, human beings construct, create, and build subjectivity in conjunction with reasons that may originate early in life and persist into adulthood.

> We have only versions of the true and the real. Narratively unmediated, definitive access to the truth cannot be demonstrated. In this respect, therefore, there can be no absolute foundation on which any observer or thinker stands; each must choose his/her narrative version (p. xv).

The analyst, too, relies on versions of truth operationalized in his or her commitment to various "storylines" of development. The psychoanalytic "stories" of oedipal conflict, separation/individuation, or narcissistic fragmentation cannot comfortably be taken to have some reality outside that of a narrative version. This is so because the interpretative story rendered by the analyst is always provisional, ready to admit other potential retellings. For Schafer (1983), the only "truth" to the psychoanalytic story is its ability to "withstand tough and searching questions" (p. 236).

Similarly, Schafer asserts that the self we experience as unitary and whole is, in fact, *also* a narrative construction. Schafer (1992) is quite explicit on this point: "My position on the self is anti-essentialist" (p. xvi). He writes (1983) that while he favors the storyline of the person as agent, he argues that a self can only be encountered as something told. Selves, then, are understood to be brought to life through language and in narratives which exist as a function of present-day tellings. Finally, Schafer suggests—in line with postmodern discourse—that a person may need more than one self to get along in the contemporary business of living.

To illustrate the theoretical need for multiple selves, Schafer (1992) discusses the subjective loops that one must traverse in order to apprehend what "self deception" could possibly mean. To accept the notion that a self has deceived "itself," requires an implicit narrative about two storylines and two selves. First, there must be one self about whom it is agreed that he or she "really" did something, e.g., acted in a sadistic manner. Next, there must be a second self that disavows that this was so. In order to make sense of human action, Schafer suggests that we implicitly and already rely on narratives of "multiple selves." It is, he writes, a "story that 'works' " (1992, p. 52).

Though Schafer does not fly the standard of postmodernism—nowhere, for example, does he identify himself as a postmodernist—his reconceptualizations of psychoanalysis as narrative accomplish this purpose. His psychoanalytic theory becomes postmodernist to the extent that he sets aside the claim that selves have essential capacities and contents and in his insistence that discourses create reality. Recall the rhetoric of postmodernism and compare this with the narrative language that Schafer presents. For Schafer, (1) psychoanalysis is concerned in a primary fashion with language and its equivalents; (2) subjective experience, objective reality, and selves are all constructions brought to life in language; (3) these present-day tellings could be told in other terms and do not represent real world events; (4) unitary selves are displaced by the notion that we tell useful stories about "multiple selves" in order to conduct our affairs; and (5) cure accompanies changes in discourse.

Following from this, psychoanalysis can only be concerned

with reinterpretation, and not reconstruction; presentation, and not representation; multiple selves, and not the experience of one self. Schafer's narrative view is not simply a revision of psychoanalysis but represents a very particular new vision for psychoanalysis, one located squarely within postmodernist discourse (cf., Leary, 1989).

Postmodernism has also met psychoanalysis in the writing of Irwin Hoffman (1983, 1991, 1992) and others (e.g., Stern, 1992). Hoffman offers what he refers to as a "radical critique" addressed to the positivism in psychoanalytic theory that exists across theoretical lines. Drive-structural models, self psychology, and relational psychoanalysis all come under fire to the extent that Hoffman finds in them a foundation of objectivism.

Drawing on the sociological theory of Berger and Luckman (1966), Hoffman argues for a new paradigm for psychoanalysis, that of "social constructivism." Social constructivism asserts that human knowledge and reality are not given but are instead created by people through social processes and for social ends. Given the sociological observation that what is "real" to a citizen of one culture may differ considerably from what is "real" to an individual in another culture, human reality is understood to be a "social construction." Specific notions of reality and knowledge pertain only to specific social contexts and not to the world "out there" (Berger and Luckman, 1966). In consequence, different individuals and different social groups hold different points of view that cannot be resolved by an appeal to authority alone. In this respect, social constructivism is another voice in postmodernist discourse.

Hoffman (1983, 1991) argues that psychoanalysis has, to its detriment, relied on an outdated "asocial" conception of the patient as a person in isolation and has been constrained by a limited view of the analyst as an objective observer of the patient's reality, psychic or otherwise. In line with social constructivism, Hoffman asserts that reality does not reflect a preestablished standard or absolute. Hoffman (1991) states that human beings, patients and analysts among them, all live in "innumerable, concentric worlds within worlds" (p. 95). In consequence, these "multiplicities of realities" make any social interaction highly ambiguous. He goes on to suggest that when the analytic field is viewed as a social construction, the distinction between what is intrapsychic and what is interpersonal falls away. As an example, the analytic situation will be understood to be created by and dependent on *both* the analyst and the patient, who *each* construct different understandings and experiences of each other. The theory of treatment process shifts from focusing on the manner in which the patient's experience unfolds in the consulting room to attending to the ways in which both participants create what occurs between them.

Under the terms of social constructivism, the analyst cannot stand outside of the interaction with the patient. Patient and analyst continuously and mutually influence one another, such that "whatever is explicated by the patient and the analyst about themselves or about each other, out loud or in their private thoughts, affects what happens next within and between the two people in ways that were not known before that moment" (Hoffman, 1991, p. 91). The task of the analytic dialogue then shifts from a concern with interpreting "reality" of any kind to an interest in the process by which analyst and patient create and shape an impact on the other through the play of mutual influences.

Hoffman (1991) argues that a central purpose of the social constructivist model of psychoanalysis is to deconstruct the analyst's authority. For example, when psychoanalysis is recast as social constructivism, the analyst is no longer in a position to assess with accuracy what he or she and the patient are doing and experiencing. Indeed, what meaning can "accuracy" even have when the therapeutic field is viewed as a construction?

Hoffman (1991) suggests that what follows is a paradigmatic change in the nature of the kind of information the analytic participants are thought to have of themselves and of each other. Because the analyst is viewed as incapable of standing outside the interaction with the patient, his or her participation also has a continuous effect on what the analyst understands about his or her self and about the patient in interaction. The analyst's understanding is always a function of his or her perspective of the moment and, thus, is only provisional, suspect, and prone to be modified by another point of view yet to emerge. Meaning is again but a moment in time (cf., Attridge, 1992; Derrida, 1976; Flax, 1990; Schafer, 1992).

Similarly, Hoffman (1983) suggests that the patient's transference can also be viewed in relativistic-social terms. Here, the transference would not be viewed as a distortion of the analyst's reality. Instead, in the terms of social constructivism, the transference *always* has a significant and plausible basis in the here and now.

> The perspective that the patient brings to bear in interpreting the therapist's inner attitudes is regarded as one among many perspectives that are relevant, each of which highlights different facets of the analyst's involvement (p. 394).

Hoffman (1983) argues that transference-dominated experience can be distinguished from nontransference-dominated experience but *not* on the basis of its being a distorted view of reality. Neurotic transference, Hoffman (1983) writes, represents a *selective* attention to and sensitivity only to certain facets of the analyst's ambiguous response to the patient.

Given the proposition that the analyst is, in fact, continuously involved with the patient, Hoffman argues that analytic technique needs to be reconfigured to include the analyst's subjectivity. Hoffman (1992) offers, as an ideal, the goal of displacing objectivity, thereby allowing the analyst what he calls "a special kind of authenticity," for now the analyst can be acknowledged as a co-participant.

Hoffman also discusses the technical implications that follow work within a social-constructivist paradigm. He suggests that the analyst is now freer to speak his or her mind "with the elimination of the standard of doing just the 'right' thing according to some external criterion" (1992, p. 292). This can allow the analyst the opportunity for "a spontaneous kind of expressiveness," including expressing conviction about one's point of view *as a point of view* (p. 292). The analyst's technique and interventions are now understood to have as much to do with the inner resources available to the analyst as they do with the needs of the patient. Although the analyst has lost the authoritative voice of objectivity, according to Hoffman, the analyst is now in a position to be a more credible dialogic partner.

The "Problems" of Postmodern "Solutions"

Up until this point, I have explored postmodernism uncritically in an effort to describe its assumptions and ways within the human world. Schafer's and Hoffman's reconceptualizations now make postmodernism part of the psychoanalytic world. Postmodern accounts are offered as new approaches to long-standing problems in psychoanalytic theory. These include psychoanalytic metapsychology and its "mis-placed scientism" (Schafer, 1983, 1992); the authoritarianism of the structural theory and the authority of the analyst (Hoffman, 1983, 1991, 1992); and questions about the status of psychoanalytic material (Spence, 1982, 1987). Postmodern "solutions" to these problems include a narrowing of the analytic focus to constructions of self and reality that are embedded in language and subjectivity and not in a past that can be deduced and made known.

It is clear, however, that psychoanalysis recast as postmodernism and the more familiar accounts of psychoanalytic psychology yield a clash of discourses. Postmodernism and psychoanalysis are not equivalent systems and do not employ common assumptions. Postmodern ideas simply cannot work if one holds psychoanalytic notions about prior, real world referents to conscious and unconscious mind. Similarly, psychoanalytic theories do not exist in anything approaching their usual incarnation within postmodern discourse. Instead, discussions of drive and defense, self and object, and so forth become only convenient versions of human experience with no particular validity.

Despite this, most critics of postmodernist discourse address postmodernism *as if* it were a traditional philosophy or articulated theory. These critics skillfully elucidate the inconsistencies and inadequacies of postmodern conceptualizations. Orange (1992), for example, suggests that social constructivism is "self enclosed," "self referential," and "self contradictory." She argues against the relativistic standpoint of social constructivism because it provides no basis for choosing one construction over alternate views. Flax (1990) notes that while postmodernism advocates "a multiplicity of voices," it privileges the voices of philosophy and literary criticism. She goes on to comment that, like its predecessor theories, it often excludes feminist viewpoints and is a discipline practiced by a limited few, most of whom are white and male. Flax disputes the postmodernist assertion that deep subjectivity is a fiction by noting that exactly this capacity is required, for example, for persons to appreciate their lives as aesthetic endeavors.

The difficulty with this approach is that these protests are largely irrelevant for a system of thought that easily accommodates inconsistency and contradiction and, indeed, celebrates discontinuity. In fact, it does not "matter" in any substantive sense if postmodern readings conflict with traditional ways of generating meaning and establishing truth, as these are the very systems postmodern rhetoric intends to subvert.

What I propose to do instead is to take postmodernism on its own terms, that is, to judge its "truth" on the basis of pragmatics. Do postmodern reconfigurations of psychoanalysis and the "story" it generates make for "interesting conversation" for psychoanalytic thinkers and clinicians? To what extent do postmodern discourses concerning psychoanalysis help or hinder therapeutic talk? I will respond to these questions by exploring some of the "problems" that surface when one employs postmodern "solutions." Here, I will focus on postmodern conceptions of selves, multiple realities, and the abrogation of key distinctions between fantasy and reality that are consequences of its tenets.

A central aim of the postmodern critique is, in effect, to do away with a concept of the self as a center of subjectivity. This is accomplished, in part, by relying on the perspective that everyday experience reveals that individuals have different experiential vantage points or subjectivities, and hence, "multiple selves" on which to draw (Anderson, 1990; Flax, 1990). Schafer (1992) has brought psychoanalysis into this debate with his endorsement of multiple selves as a good working "story" for the conduct of human lives. How does this story fare? Will it "do"? Where does it get us?

Reflect on the tenor of postmodern discourse as it regards selves. Given the view that selves are narrative social constructions that are encountered only as things that are told in language, selves require audiences to exist and become present (cf., Schafer, 1983, 1992). If a given self is constituted by virtue of having an audience, a different audience should readily yield a different self. Postmodernists argue that such a proliferation of selves—from one voice to a "multiplicity of voices"—brings liberation and the freedom to create and choose the self that one will be. Indeed, Gergen (1991) notes that the postmodernist is obliged to question why "one must be bound by any traditional marker of identity—profession, gender, ethnicity, nationality and so on" (p. 178).[2]

Gergen (1991) and Harvey (1989) explain the rationale for a narrative of multiple selves from another perspective as well. Modern technology permits an ever-widening web of connections and instant access that provide new opportunities for relating that did not exist before. Twentieth century relationships

[2] We are, indeed, at an interesting cultural moment. In critical theory, the postmodernist assertion that selves are not bound to "traditional markers of identity" and are free to enact any number of possibilities exists contemporaneously with multicultural perspectives emphasizing the unique contributions of race and ethnicity.

of this sort occur in sound bites, photo opportunities, and computer links with imaginary and hidden others.

The implication that follows from this is that we can, at will, assume a self that suits us if the proper audience can be assembled. The psychoanalytic clinician may now enter into this conversation by wondering what sort of "relating" occurs in transactions like these. Given the necessity of an audience for its existence, a self cannot take itself for granted. The tie that this constructed self will have to its complementary other becomes desperate. For if one "likes" the self that one is, it will be necessary to secure this audience in order to maintain one's self. Similarly, if the self-of-the-moment has little appeal, the audience is unwanted and must be discarded in favor of another.

Further, the extensions of relationships offered by technology, e.g., through computer links, that Gergen and others detail seem at least as likely to evoke disconnection and the diminution of relating as they might authentic communion. The technologies of communication may offer a shadowy and even superficial intimacy. Again, the analytic clinician may ask: To whom does one relate? For the "other" is just as often an image.

As a number of critics have pointed out, postmodern selves now seem recognizable. For the very self that postmodernists proclaim as "liberated" seems, in fact, like the familiar self of the psychoanalytic consulting room: a disjointed, decentered, and dislocated self seeking to ameliorate this very condition. A self that trumpets the absence of limits, "a multiplicity of voices," and fractional relationships, and who requires an audience to constitute him/herself is a self the analytic clinician may think of as a borderline or narcissistic self. Though beguiling, seductively and apparently full, such a self is revealed to be empty. This sort of self, for the analytic clinician, far from being liberated, is instead enslaved.

Here it is important to distinguish the aims of the practitioner from the consequence of the theory. While it is clear, for example, that Schafer intends for the construct of multiple selves to enlarge the domain of human agency, the consequences to which it leads would seem instead to shrink human possibility.

Lasch (1984) and Frosh (1991), among others, have suggested that the contemporary preoccupation with surface, presentation, and image have spawned what has come to be called "a culture of narcissism." It is my contention that when psychoanalysis is recast in the terms of postmodernism, there is the danger that the analytic dialogue and the analysand it seeks to describe are forced to adopt the discourse of narcissism. When psychoanalysis is recast in the terms of postmodernism, a diagnosis of contemporary subjective experience—for example, the fragmentation of experience—is offered as something of an ideal. In my view, a clinical diagnosis masquerades as a clinical cure.

Kernberg (1984), Kohut (1984), and many others have illuminated how the dissolution of limits is, for most people, a horrifying event. Flax (1990) has also written eloquently of the pain endured by patients with self disorders. She argues that those who call for a decentered self seem unaware of the basic cohesion within themselves that makes the fragmentation of experience something other than a terrifying slide into psychosis.

In this way, the story of multiple selves does not much "work" for psychoanalytic clinicians, for it threatens to limit the psychoanalytic dialogue to a narcissistic discourse. Rather than expand therapeutic talk, holding to a construct of multiple selves seems to constrict the analytic field. And, this does not seem "interesting."[3]

---

[3] Other problems surface with a narcissistic self at the theoretical helm: here, we can consider not only the pain and suffering of the narcissistic self, but also the pain and suffering that the narcissistic self visits upon others. In relational life, the narcissistic person treats the other as though she or he were *not* an other but a member of the narcissist's self repertory. The narcissistic person's reshaping of the other to be self represents a violation of who she or he is. Simply put, such treatment "hurts." The regular reports of countertransference irritation, anger, and defensive boredom with narcissistic patients speak to the pain that can accompany the denial of one's self.

Schafer (1992) is not unmindful of these consequences. He notes that the proliferation of selves is theoretical quicksilver and an instance of "defensively disclaimed action." The move to multiple selves, he writes, "imports into the theory the phenomenon that the theory intends to explain" (p. 31). To rectify this, he offers the storyline of the person as a narrator:

> Here, the storyline I favor is not one of one self or one mind, but of *one person* as agent. And I propose that the person be viewed as a narrator, that is, as someone who, among other noteworthy actions, narrates selves. One person narrates numerous selves both in order to develop desirable (not necessarily "happy" but at least defensively secure) versions of his or her actions and the actions of others and to act in ways that conform to these selves (p. 51).

Thus, despite his objections, Schafer retains his preference for the notion that multiple selves, in some form, expedite the business of living.

In my view, however, "housing" multiple selves within a person simply amounts to moving the party indoors. The theoretical difficulty lies with the concept of multiple selves and not with their residence. At question is the issue of why it is necessary to have a psychoanalytic theory that implicates multiple selves. It seems at least as likely that the dislocations of contemporary life that challenge human experience arise from the fact that a human being cannot escape him/herself rather than that he or she cannot manage the many selves of daily life.

I believe that the appeal of multiple selves is so because postmodernism in all of its versions, including those applied to psychoanalytic treatment, represents accounts of the "contemporary." Here, "multiple selves" are substituted in psychoanalytic theory in place of a person who exists in time and space. Such a person would be understood to act differently at different times, to be able to experience multiple desires, for example, to love *at times* and hate *at other times*, without recourse to a multitude of selves.

This illuminates another consequence of a postmodernist turn in psychoanalytic theory. The postmodern emphasis on the construction of selves and human experience biases the analytic enterprise to the present moment. This can be seen, especially, in Hoffman's (1983, 1991, 1992) social constructivist account of psychoanalysis. Hoffman's theory emphasizes the way in which patient and therapist continually and mutually create their experiences of each other, themselves, and the world they inhabit. Commentary about events outside of the interaction and language are of less importance and are afforded little status. In consequence, patient and analyst, in essential respects, are wedded to a constantly unfolding present. Given this, meaning can only be in the present tense, a moment in time, and nothing more.

In this way, postmodern reconceptualizations of psychoanalysis seem to treat both the patient and the therapist as if each were emptied of memory and the capacity to appreciate that events occur in time. The focus on the present moment obscures the fact that people behave differently at different times and can remember this. Social constructivist accounts of psychoanalysis are ahistorical: without memory, there is no history. Narrative reconceptualizations nod to historical reasons but these are then reinterpreted as present-day tellings. In key respects, postmodernism purges the analytic situation of the need to grapple with history, with things that once were and had an effect.

Postmodernist discourse may now sound like a foreign tongue to psychoanalytic ears. The emphasis on the present and the unfolding moment diverts attention from that which *endures* in persons, in social transactions, and in the world in which they occur. Again, while this is clearly not the intent of either Schafer or Hoffman, it is one consequence of their social constructivist and narrative theories.

Postmodernism is, perhaps, most starkly limiting when it fails to take into account that selves and their subjectivities reside in bodies. Consider again the postmodernist argument that selves are in flux, dependent on context for significance, and the assertion that human beings live with versions of reality, and not with reality itself (cf., Schafer, 1983). This is indeed a way of talking about human experience but it does not exempt the postmodernist from participating in the corporeal world. A postmodern self has weight and mass like any other self. For example, however one might *think* or *talk* about gendered experience, some events (e.g., pregnancy or the urgency of impending ejaculation) remain the province of only one sex. What it *means* to be male and female in a given life span, culture, or epoch may change and be in flux, but on most occasions, maleness and femaleness *also* remain invariant, unchanging, and the difference important. To say otherwise—for example, that biological sex differences are "trivial" (cf., Hare-Mustin and Marecek, 1988)—is akin to arguing that because medical technology can render the boundary between life and death less certain, the difference between life and death is unimportant.

Clinical experience with those who have endured traumatic events provides another venue to appreciate that the notion of a self and the implacable reality of the body, as a representative of the corporeal world, are more than heuristics. Catastrophic illness and maltreatment are traumatic because they are a violation; they breach boundaries and force confrontation with that which is beyond the self and beyond personal control (cf., Herman, 1992; Krystal, 1988; Shengold, 1989; Terr, 1990). Outside of the consulting room, Terry Anderson—the freed Middle East hostage—gave voice to this claim when he said that one of the most difficult to discuss horrors of his confinement was the limitations his captors placed on when he could use the toilet.

Benjamin (1990) makes a similar point from the perspective of developmental theory. She writes that developmental theory must recognize that, in the interaction between a mother and her infant, the mother remains an other who is also another subject. By this, she means that the mother must be understood to have a separate center of independent subjectivity "whose responses [to the infant] are not entirely predictable and assimilable to fantasy" (p. 36). Quoting Winnicott (1964)—that "fantasy and fact, both important, are nevertheless different from each other"—Benjamin (1990, p. 41) argues that authentic recognition of the other means appreciating that people have separate minds. These minds can share similar feelings but can also disagree. The father whom the child angrily abandons in fantasy continues to persist in the world, sometimes maddeningly so. Human development, she writes, proceeds with the increasing ability to tolerate the fact that the other has an "externality" and occupies a referential place from which he or she cannot be moved by an act of mind. Furthermore, in Benjamin's version of intersubjectivity, she argues that "the clash of wills" is an inherent part of human relations and that "no perfect environment can take the sting from the encounter with otherness" (p. 44).

Hoffman (1991) struggles with this distinction. On first approach, his theory is consonant with the need to account for externality. Echoing Berger and Luckman (1966), he notes that the analytic situation involves a dialectic between the individual and the social, the personal and the technical: ". . . whichever aspect is in the foreground can be understood only in the context of its complement in the background" (Hoffman, 1991, p. 102). Yet at many points in his social constructivist account of psychoanalysis, this distinction begins to fade. This can be seen, for example, when Hoffman (1983) argues that the transference always has a significant basis in the here-and-now that can be distinguished as a "selective reading" of the analyst. Such a perspective obscures the fact that, in actuality, not all of the patient's (or the analyst's) readings *are* credible and tenable. For example, a patient's repeated expectation of his or her analyst's rageful attack can no longer be plausible in the here-and-now if the shared therapeutic history between patient and analyst includes the experience that the analyst does not ragefully attack. The expectation of rageful attack is not plausible in the here-and-now, although it remains a credible reading of some past or even of some other present.

To the extent that Hoffman adopts the goal of displacing objectivity, the analyst must accept that all accounts are plausible, if selective, as he or she has no authoritative approach to make any other decision. In this way, postmodern accounts of "multiple realities" of this sort make indistinguishable the contrast between the way things "seem" and the way things "are."

In my view, what gets lost is the difference between *appreciating* the patient's point of view and *agreeing* that it is so. Appreciation of the patient's perspective can allow for its elaboration. This may result in the development of a shared perspective or the absence of agreement which can then pave the way for discovering something more. In Hoffman's account, the analyst's ability to disagree is constrained. In this way, although the analyst is permitted a point of view, social constructivist accounts of psychoanalysis render the analyst less able to use it. With the insistence of the plausibility of all transference reactions, the analyst's externality slips away. Whatever else he or she is, the analyst is also a separate center of his or her *own* subjectivity (cf., Benjamin, 1990), whether perceived as a "new object" by the patient or as disappointingly recapitulating the past. When Hoffman argues for a social constructivist rereading of psychoanalysis in order to make the analyst a full dialogic partner, the analyst oddly loses his/her voice.

For the analytic clinician, the story that postmodernism generates has proved to be much less interesting at the conclusion than at the outset. However, despite a number of problems, the reconceptualizations offered by Schafer and Hoffman are also quite useful and may prove to be roadmarkers directing psychoanalysis to new paradigms yet to come or to elaborations of current paradigms (cf., Hartman, 1993). First, these accounts remind the psychoanalytic clinician that treatment does indeed involve two people in the same room who interact with one another. Hoffman, in particular, emphasizes that the analyst has a point of view in the interaction that must be acknowledged as such. New perspectives—among them, intersubjectivity, relational models, interpersonal psychoanalysis—all stress this fact, which has been neglected. Recognition of the importance of interaction, countertransference, and enactments underscores the fact that the analytic situation is profoundly relational and corrects deficits in theory.

Second, Schafer and Hoffman also remind the analytic clinician to cultivate skepticism and to question, rather than take for granted, what he or she accepts as so. Narrative and social constructivist renderings of psychoanalysis invite the therapist to be a friendly critic. In this way, these models widen the analytic field by calling for a new look at what the analyst may believe, erroneously, to have already been revealed.

Third, these models direct analytic attention to the process of relating and communicating rather than to the contents of relationships and communications alone. By focusing in a more fine-grained way on process, these models offer the possibility of building an even more complexly articulated three-dimensional rendering of the analytic situation.

Although Schafer and Hoffman implicitly and explicitly argue that a dialectical interchange between the individual and the world in which he or she lives is "interesting," the terms of their theories make this dialectic difficult to sustain because of their postmodern commitments to multiple selves and multiple realities. Experience outside of the self or person has an inconstant reality in their conceptualizations.

Despite this, in these "conversations" a dialectic emerges between positivistic psychoanalytic theories and postmodern revisions that is compelling and may direct theoreticians to a new model. For example, if change is endemic to human selves, what does it mean to talk of therapeutic change? "What" changes?

The analytic clinician, like the postmodernist, holds fast to the belief that selves are indeed malleable. Development, trauma, and new experience are understood to occasion changes in the self. The whole notion of a psychoanalytic treatment rests on the foundation that change is possible. As a result of an analysis, symptoms can recede, character soften, inhibitions ease, and psychic life be lived differently. Human beings are indeed flexible and may think of themselves in innumerable ways. Change, however, is circumscribed. Change, when it occurs, may reflect more of a dimensional rather than an absolute transformation (Leary and Shulman, 1987). For example, the flat image of mother as cruel and abusive may be seen, upon being unpacked, to hold a missing dimension—that she was also, at other times, a person to turn to for comfort, and was seen as cruel to preserve the idea of one's own perfect nonagressiveness. After a successful analysis, however, the analysand is still recognizably the same *even* as she or he is different.

A new and perhaps more "interesting" dialectic for psychoanalysis would involve appreciating how human beings can interact and influence each other even as they are constrained by history, constitution, and biology. The clinical and empirical endeavor would shift to specifying what is "fixed" in human beings and human encounters *and* what remains "flexible." Such a move would go beyond the acknowledgment that human beings must also consort with reality to discussing how they specifically do so.

The ability to discuss events of this sort—flexible change around fixed referents—may result in new methods and, from them, to theories that provide new accounts of psychoanalytic interaction. A number of promising models are emerging across the social sciences that attempt to attend to what is fixed and what is flexible in human transactions. In cognitive science, "reality monitoring" (Schooler, et al., 1986) refers to an empirical protocol in which subjects provide descriptions of perceived and imagined events. Research has shown that judges can distinguish perceived and imagined narratives on the basis of their qualitative features. Reality monitoring leads to the proposition that fantasy and reality are encoded differently and in ways that are reflected in language. Here, distinctions between the way things "seem" and the way they "are" find a home.

Similarly, Kenny (1987) advocates the use of a methodological procedure he calls a "nested design" to study dyadic interactions. This technique allows researchers to specify how a participant behaves in relationships in *general* and how she or he behaves *uniquely* in a given interchange.

Finally, negotiation has been offered as a new model for understanding the treatment process (e.g., Goldberg, 1987; Hatcher, 1992; Shor, 1992). When a psychotherapeutic process is viewed as a negotiation process, the analytic encounter becomes a joint venture in which participants with different interests and strategies accommodate to each other to advance their individual goals *and* to further the work of the treatment in which they jointly participate.

These models, and numerous others, have the potential to meet both positivistic and postmodern agendas. They may offer a way to discuss the dislocations of self that arise in contemporary life, which psychoanalysis and postmodernism describe so well, while *simultaneously* referencing that self in a history and a world that exists beyond the imagination and that cannot be altered by an act of mind alone. It is in this explicit tension between what is fixed and what is flexible that postmodernist and psychoanalytic critics may have the most interesting conversation of all.

REFERENCES

ANDERSON, W. (1990). *Reality Isn't What It Used To Be: Theatrical Politics, Ready-to-Wear Religion, Global Myths, Primitive Chic, and Other Wonders of the Postmodern World.* San Francisco: Harper & Row.

ATTRIDGE, D. (1992). *Derrida: Acts of Literature.* New York: Routledge.

BENJAMIN, J. (1990). An outline of subjectivity: the development of recognition. *Psychoanal. Psychol.*, Suppl., 7:33-46.

───── (1991). Commentary on Irwin Z. Hoffman's discussion: towards a social constructivist view of the psychoanalytic situation. *Psychoanal. Dialogues*, 1:525-533.

BERGER, R. & LUCKMAN, T. (1966). *The Social Construction of Reality.* New York: Doubleday/Anchor Books.

CONNOR, S. (1989). *Postmodern Culture: An Introduction to Theories of the Contemporary.* Cambridge/New York: Basil Blackwell.

DERRIDA, J. (1976). *Of Grammatology.* Translated by G. C. Spivak. Baltimore/London: Johns Hopkins Univ. Press.

EAGLETON, T. (1983). *Literary Theory: An Introduction.* Minneapolis: Univ. of Minnesota Press.

FISH, S. (1980). *Is There a Text in This Class?* Cambridge: Harvard Univ. Press.

FLAX, J. (1990). *Thinking Fragments: Psychoanalysis, Feminism & Postmodernism in the Contemporary West.* Berkeley: Univ. of California Press.

FREUD, S. (1937). Constructions in analysis. *S.E.*, 23.

FROSH, S. (1991). *Identity Crisis: Modernity, Psychoanalysis and the Self.* New York: Routledge.

GERGEN, K. (1991). *The Saturated Self: Dilemmas of Identity in Contemporary Life.* New York: Basic Books.

GOLDBERG, A. (1987). Psychoanalysis and negotiation. *Psychoanal. Q.*, 56:109-129.

HARE-MUSTIN, R. & MARECEK, R. (1988). The meaning of difference: gender theory, postmodernism and psychology. *Amer. Psychologist*, 43:455-464.

HARTMAN, J. (1993). Intrapsychic and interpersonal frames of reference in the psychoanalytic situation. Presented at the Michigan Psychoanalytic Institute, Southfield.

HARVEY, D. (1989). *The Condition of Postmodernity.* Cambridge: Basil Blackwell.

HATCHER, R. (1992). Negotiation between the patient and therapist in the psychotherapy hour. Presented as part of a panel, Psychotherapy as Negotiation (J. Hansell, Moderator), at the Spring Meeting of the American Psychological Association's Division of Psychoanalysis (39), Philadelphia.

HERMAN, J. L. (1992). *Trauma and Recovery.* New York: Basic Books.

HOFFMAN, I. (1983). The patient as interpreter of the analyst's experience. *Contemp. Psychoanal.*, 19:389-422.

—— (1991). Discussion. Towards a social-constructivist view of the psychoanalytic situation. *Psychoanal. Dialogues*, 1:74-105.

—— (1992). Some practical implications of a social-constructivist view of the psychoanalytic situation. *Psychoanal. Dialogues*: 2:287-304.

KENNY, D. (1987). Accuracy in interpersonal perception: a social relations analysis. *Psychol. Bull.*, 102:390-402.

KERNBERG, O. (1984). *Severe Personality Disorders: Psycho-therapeutic Strategies.* New Haven/London: Yale Univ. Press.

KOHUT, H. (1984). *How Does Analysis Cure?* Chicago/London: Univ. of Chicago Press.

KRYSTAL, H. (1988). *Integration and Self Healing. Affect—Trauma—Alexithymia.* Hillsdale, NJ: Analytic Press.

LASCH, C. (1984). *The Minimal Self.* New York: Norton.

LEARY, K. R. (1989). Psychoanalytic process and narrative process: a critical consideration of Schafer's 'narrational project.' *Int. Rev. Psychoanal.*, 16:179-190.

—— & SHULMAN, M. (1987). The reality of psychic reality. Presented at the Michigan Society for Psychoanalytic Psychology, Traverse City.

ORANGE, D. (1992). Commentary on Irwin Hoffman's discussion: towards a social-constructivist view of the psychoanalytic situation. *Psychoanal. Dialogues*, 2:561-566.

RAPAPORT, D. (1944). The scientific methodology of psychoanalysis. In *The Collected Papers of David Rapaport*, ed. M. M. Gill. New York: Basic Books, 1967, pp. 165-220.

RORTY, R. (1979). *Philosophy and the Mirror of Nature.* Princeton: Princeton Univ. Press.

SCHAFER, R. (1976). *A New Language for Psychoanalysis.* New Haven: Yale Univ. Press.

—— (1983). *The Analytic Attitude.* New York: Basic Books.

—— (1992). *Retelling a Life. Narration and Dialogue in Psychoanalysis.* New York: Basic Books.

SCHOOLER, J., et al. (1986). Qualities of the unreal. *J. Experimental Psychol.*, 12:171-181.

SHENGOLD, L. (1989). *Soul Murder. The Effects of Childhood Abuse and Deprivation.* New Haven/London: Yale Univ. Press.

SHOR, M. (1992). *Work, Love and Play: Self Repair in the Psychoanalytic Dialogue.* New York: Brunner/Mazel.

SONTAG, S. (1966). *Against Interpretation.* New York: Farrar, Straus & Giroux.

SPENCE, D. P. (1982). *Narrative Truth and Historical Truth. Meaning and Interpretation in Psychoanalysis.* New York: Norton.

——— (1987). *The Freudian Metaphor. Toward Paradigm Change in Psychoanalysis.* New York: Norton.

STERN, D. (1992). Commentary on constructivism in clinical psychoanalysis. *Psychoanal. Dialogues*, 2:331-364.

TERR, L. (1990). *Too Scared to Cry.* New York: Harper & Row.

THOMPSON, A. (1988). *King Lear: An Introduction to the Variety of Criticism.* Atlantic Highlands, NJ: Humanities Press Int.

WINNICOTT, D. W. (1964). *The Child, the Family and the Outside World.* Harmondsworth, UK: Penguin.

14

A Confusion of Tongues or Whose Reality Is It?

A CONFUSION OF TONGUES OR WHOSE REALITY IS IT?

BY ARNOLD H. MODELL, M.D.

In a 1933 paper Ferenczi implied that conflict between the adult's and the child's construction of reality is traumatic for the child. As all individuals construct their own view of reality, it is inevitable that there will be conflicting constructions between child and adult—and between analyst and analysand. This may be biologically rooted; recent ethological studies suggest that parent-child conflict is ubiquitous because of a divergence of needs. When a child perceives a marked divergence between his or her construction of reality and that of the caretaker, the child may tend to reject the information proffered by the caretaker. This may appear later as a resistance to learning from the analyst. The divergence of needs between child and caretaker may have a profound influence on the child's cognitive development. The capacity to share other constructions of reality is a developmental achievement which may be facilitated by the psychoanalytic process.

In this presentation I shall develop certain issues raised by Ferenczi (1933) in his historically important but largely neglected paper, "Confusion of Tongues between Adults and the Child." That paper, presented at the International Psycho-Analytical Congress in Wiesbaden in 1932, reflected Ferenczi's growing estrangement from Freud, in that he revived the theory of the traumatic etiology of the neuroses which Freud had abandoned (see Dupont, 1985). Before presenting the paper, he read it to Freud, who expressed the opinion to his colleague, Eitingon, that it was harmless, but stupid and inadequate. Freud attempted to persuade Ferenczi not to present it (Gay, 1988, p. 583).

The confusion of tongues refers to the child who is sexually seduced by an adult and is confused by the conflict and contradiction between his or her own language of tenderness and the adult's language of passion, lust, and hypocrisy. Ferenczi sensed a principle that goes beyond the specific issue of sexual seduction. I would restate "the confusion of tongues" as the conflict between the adult's construction of reality and that of the child. It is a conflict that represents their different desires and needs. My focus in this paper will therefore not be on the specific problem of the adult's sexual seduction of the child, but on the traumatic effects that ensue when there is a marked divergence between the child's construction of reality and the construction of reality that is communicated to the child by the caretakers.

Ferenczi described one such typical reaction to trauma: children compliantly identify with the adult construction of reality, which results in a loss of trust in their own judgment of reality. This compliance does not reflect a true internalization, as it is frequently accompanied by the very opposite attitude: a permanent distrust of knowledge that is obtained from others. I recall, for example, a patient, who would repeat exactly what I said to her, never altering my choice of words. This puzzled me until we discovered that she never accepted anything that I said to her: her compliant, parroting repetition masked the opposite attitude of absolute defiance and rejection. Some individuals become quite adept at compliant learning of this sort. Divining what the situation requires may lead to successful social adaptation, but it does not represent knowledge that becomes part of the self.

Ferenczi described how the seduced child identifies with the aggressor's hypocritical and false interpretation of reality—that nothing, in fact, had really happened. As a consequence, the child's confidence in the testimony of her or his senses is broken. Ferenczi (1933) noted that he understood why his patients refused so obstinately to follow his advice (p. 163). This inability to assimilate what is presented from without may be accompanied by a paradoxically overly credulous gullibility. Calef and Weinshel (1981) described a syndrome that they called "gaslighting," a term they borrowed from the movie, *Gaslight*, which was based on the play, *Angel Street*. In the story, a newly married young woman is convinced by her husband that she is going crazy. This syndrome, in which one partner uncritically assimilates the other partner's wildly divergent interpretation of reality is more common, I believe, than has been acknowledged. From the foregoing discussion it is clear that when there is a marked divergence between the caretaker's and the child's construction of reality, the child will have good reasons for not accepting the parent's instruction and guidance. This impairment in the capacity to learn from others will undoubtedly extend to the psychoanalytic situation as well.

Whether to believe in the environmental or in the intrapsychic origin of the neuroses, which in part formed the content of Freud's controversy with Ferenczi, has been a continuing dialectic since the beginning of psychoanalysis. Currently, the balance is tipping in the direction of a traumatic etiology. This is not only due to the recognition that sexual abuse of children by adults is widespread and not a fantasy; we have also learned to recognize the far-reaching traumatic effects of the caretaker's affective unresponsiveness or affective hypocrisy. That is to say, we have learned to recognize the traumatic effects not of a single event, but of the chronic influence upon the child of certain elements within the caretaker's personality.

Ferenczi's paper was several generations ahead of its time, in that it proposed a constructionist view of reality. Such ideas were not systematically recognized in psychology until the monumental researches of Piaget. As important as Piaget's contribution to cognitive science is, its application to psychoanalysis has been somewhat limited by the fact that Piaget observed the child's cognitive development in an average expectable environ-

ment. The influence of the child's caretakers was not a subject
that he investigated. Although Winnicott did not use the term
construction of reality, this is essentially what he described under
the heading of creativity. Winnicott, unlike Piaget, was not interested in the development of cognitive structures, but was fascinated by the problem of the border between subjective and
objective reality. In contrast to Piaget, Winnicott believed that
the child's creative construction of reality could not be separated from the facilitating maternal environment.

Before I discuss Winnicott's contribution, I hope to demonstrate that the question—whose reality is it?—is not just a question for philosophers but one that has direct clinical relevance.
The question has been implicit since the beginning of psychoanalysis. When Freud transformed himself from a hypnotist
into a psychoanalyst, he was confronted with the difference between the analyst's interpretation and the hypnotist's suggestion. The hypnotic suggestion, the authoritarian hypnotic command, is a product of the hypnotist's mind that is then "suggested" or placed into the mind of the subject, whereas an
analytic interpretation, Freud believed, is based upon what the
analyst observes in the analysand's mind by means of the process of free association. Freud believed that through the method
of free association, as applied especially to the dream and to the
transference, the analyst has access to the patient's unconscious
mind and reflects this insight back to the patient in the form of
an interpretation. Although Freud never doubted that the analyst interpreted what was in the patient's mind, he acknowledged that the patient's acceptance of the analyst's interpretation depended on some measure of suggestion. He stated:

> Thus our therapeutic work falls into two phases. In the first,
> all the libido is forced from the symptoms into the transfer-
> ence and concentrated there; in the second, the struggle is
> waged around this new object and the libido is liberated from
> it. The change which is decisive for favourable outcome is the
> elimination of repression in the renewed conflict, so that the

libido cannot withdraw once more from the ego by a flight into the unconscious. This is made possible by the alteration of the ego which is accomplished under the influence of the doctor's suggestion (1917, p. 455).

Although we do not exactly know what Freud meant by the term *suggestion*, it does connote a compliant, uncritical submission to a reality external to the self.

Freud's unquestioned assumption that the analyst interprets what is in the patient's mind has been challenged by Schafer (1983) and Spence (1982). They have asserted that an interpretation is merely the analyst's narrative construction. Psychoanalytic interpretations, according to these authors, are analogous to the interpretation of a text: they both speak of the interpretation as achieving a certain "narrative fit." Schafer calls it the "analyst's story line," and Spence asserts that interpretations depend more on their power to persuade, on their linguistic characteristics, than on their "truthfulness." Schafer believes, a priori, that the analysand "can never have direct access to [past] events" and that his or her "experience of these events is always subjective" (Panel, 1983, p. 240) and therefore open to further, interminable, interpretation. The analyst's interpretations are "acts of retelling or narrative revision" (pp. 239-240). An "accurate" interpretation is an impossibility, for the analyst is only offering the patient an alternative "story line"; the analyst is merely substituting *his or her* narrative for that of the patient.

Freud did not deal with the question, whose reality is it?, head on, but he did make an important distinction between the analyst's insight and the patient's insight. The analyst's insight is a step ahead of the patient's insight, but the analysand only becomes convinced of the truth of the analyst's interpretation after it has been demonstrated directly through the experience of transference. Freud implied that in the act of interpretation, there is an interplay between the analyst's and the analysand's construction of reality.

The Interplay between the Child's and the Mother's Construction
  of Reality

When there has been a persistent divergence between the
child's reality and the adult's, the individual will, as Ferenczi
observed, either develop a cynical distrust of the knowledge
proffered by others or a naïve and uncritical acceptance in
which the individual abdicates his or her own critical judgment.
It is not uncommon to find both attitudes co-existing in the
same person. Infants and children construct their own realities,
but at the same time they are totally dependent upon their
caretaker's construction of reality for their safety in the world.
There comes a time when children begin to discover discrepancies between their construction of reality and that of their caretakers. Winnicott suggests how this conflict might be normally
resolved.

Winnicott, as mentioned before, did not speak of the child's
construction of reality, but referred instead to creativity, which
he believed begins at birth: "At the first feed the baby is ready to
create, and the mother makes it possible for the baby to have
the illusion that the breast has been created by impulse out of
need" (1988, p. 101). This illusion is made possible if the
mother responds synchronously to the baby's desire. A "good
enough mother," with a sensitivity based upon her identification with the baby, will reinforce the baby's illusion of omnipotent magical control of the breast. Winnicott asserted that the
importance of the mother's sensitive adaptation to the baby's
needs can hardly be overestimated, in that it provides a core
that remains the foundation for a continuing positive attitude
toward external reality. The infant needs the mother, yet the
infant has the illusion of creating the breast out of need. There
is a paradox here: the mother provides the necessary environment so that the baby can have the illusion of self-creation, but
it is the mother's perception of the world that will insure the
baby's safety. We know that for the young child the mother is an
alternative environment interposed between the child and the
dangers of the real world. The child's safety in the world de-

pends upon the caretakers who provide the child with those signals of danger that are the instinctive endowment of other species. In a certain sense the mother *is* reality, in that she is the source of vital information concerning the real world. As Freud (1926) observed, "Man seems not to have been endowed, or to have been endowed to only a very small degree, with an instinctive recognition of the dangers that threaten him from without. Small children are constantly doing things which endanger their lives, and that is precisely why they cannot afford to be without a protecting object" (p. 168).

I have often referred to the observations that Anna Freud and Dorothy Burlingham (1943) made regarding young children during the bombing of London in World War II. These children remained calm during a raid if their mothers were not unduly anxious. In this way the mother functions as a transcendent reality interposed between the child and a dangerous world. When the mothers or other caretakers provide what has been called a background of safety, children are allowed to live within a self-created world of fantasy and magical action which neither mothers nor children question. In the absence of such parental protection, the self-created world may take on a very different function, a function essential for children's psychic survival, for then children must construct a substitute world in which they are their own caretakers. In those instances the self-created world is likely to have at its center fantasies of omnipotent self-sufficiency.

Winnicott's theory of the transitional object indicates how, in health, these two constructions of reality, that of the child and that of the mother, might interact with each other. It is a theory of shared constructed realities. It is here that Winnicott posited the formation of a third area of reality that he called a *potential space* between the child and the mother. It is an illusory world that belongs neither to the subject nor to the object; it is neither inner reality nor external fact.

As is characteristic for Winnicott (1971), the center of his thought rests on a paradox:

Of the transitional object it can be said that it is a matter of
agreement between us and the baby that we will never ask the
question "Did you conceive of this or was it presented to you
from without?" The important point is that no decision on this
point is expected. The question is not to be formulated (p.
100).

Within the illusion of the potential space the mother accepts
and does not challenge the child's construction of reality: the
question, whose reality is it?, does not arise. Winnicott general-
ized from the observation of infants to suggest that this potential space characterizes the mental process that underlies the
shared illusions of aesthetic and cultural experiences. From the
standpoint of an outside observer, this potential space is a space
that belongs neither entirely to the subject's inner world nor to
objective external reality; it represents the subject's creative
transformation of the external world. From the standpoint of
the subject, this potential space symbolizes the interplay of separateness and union. Playful merging requires a sense of sure-
ness regarding the self, which means that the autonomy of the
self is preserved. This is in contrast to those who fear being
merged or swallowed up by the object.

Winnicott further suggested that this creative apperception
should be distinguished from compliant learning that is characteristic of a false self. For when the self enters into the object,
one can in this way make learning truly one's own. This interplay of separateness and union with the other person permits
one to learn from others while maintaining the autonomy of the
self. The most effective interpretations are those made when we
do not know whose construction it is, ours or the patient's. The
importance of this process can be observed in the negative, that
is, by its absence, which results in a relative inability to learn
from others.

We all know of some patients who cannot take in anything
that they have not already thought of themselves. I described
elsewhere (Modell, 1985) a case of a professional man, who, in-

stead of taking something in and making it his own, learned in a fashion that was quick, superficial, and shallow. He picked up information from the air, so to speak; he was *au courant* with all the latest stylish professional jargon, catchwords that he picked up from conversations and from skimming professional journals. He achieved his professional credentials by cramming for examinations and was very skillful at multiple choice ques-- tions. But he rightly felt himself to be an impostor, for nothing stuck to him. Early in the analysis he informed me that he never read a book that was not required as a school assignment; I dismissed this at first as an exaggeration but later learned that it was literally true. Confrontation with other constructions of reality produced anxiety. Such individuals may act as if they are learning from the analysis, but one discovers that one has been writing in the sand, that nothing has been truly taken in. As far as it could be determined, in this particular case there was a major failure of the early holding environment: his mother had left him at the age of two in the care of an elderly, nearly blind grandfather who spoke only Yiddish, which the patient did not understand.

Winnicott believed that primary creativity is supported by the mother's intuitive response to the infant's desire—a response that arises out of identification with the infant based upon the mother's love; but he also believed that the child's acceptance of the externality, the separateness, of the object is supported by the mother's acceptance of the baby's *hatred*. Extrapolating from his experience with adult patients in psychoanalysis, Winnicott claimed that in order to accept both the limitation of personal omnipotence and the separateness of others, the child must also have experienced both intense hatred toward the mother and the mother's acceptance of that hatred. To know that they have both survived hatred, Winnicott (1971, p. 92) thought, was essential for the capacity to playfully merge. Looked at from this point of view, the sharing of constructed realities may require this developmental step. There is some support for this theory: in some analyses the capacity to learn from the analyst begins only after both analyst and analysand have survived a point of maximum destructiveness in the transference.

Divergence in the Constructed Realities of Children and Their Caretakers

The divergence of constructed realities must also reflect the enormous variability of our central nervous systems. Recent advances in neuroscience (Edelman, 1987) indicate that the nervous system is not as genetically hard-wired as had been previously supposed; that even within the constraints of genetic instruction, the embryological development of the nervous system shows a remarkable degree of variability from the level of the cell to the level of global functioning. This variability results from a dynamic interaction with the environment. Not only do significant variations in morphology arise in this manner, but the functional organization of the central nervous system is also dynamically responsive to the environment at every level of organization. This means that genetically identical twins, even at birth, do not perceive the world identically; each person perceives the world uniquely, that is to say, all individuals construct their own reality. Modern science has confirmed what William Blake apprehended intuitively: "A fool sees not the same tree that a wise man sees."

We must assume, as I noted earlier, that at a certain point in development, children will begin to observe the differences between their own construction of the world and that of their parents. I suspect that children perceive a great deal more about their caretaker's construction of reality than they are able to articulate. Growing children may find their parent's judgment of the real world eccentric and, in a sense, crazy. Not infrequently, intelligent children correctly judge that a parent's view of reality is off. For example, one patient who was, in fact, intellectually precocious perceived at the age of two or three that his mother was mad, although the extent of her madness was hidden and not acknowledged by her family or by her neighbors. This child knew that his mother's judgment was unreliable and could not assure his safety in the world. Another patient, during latency, correctly observed that his mother was flighty, childish, and fatuous. This is not to say that children articulate their observations as I am doing now, but these perceptions are taken in, whether consciously or not, and have profound consequences for further development. Such a recognition will result in the child's turning away from the caretaker as a source of information and knowledge and may lead to a distrust of the judgment of others.

Something analogous but less serious may occur with extremely intelligent children or with those who are brighter than their parents. It can also be found in immigrants' children who have a greater mastery of the language and local culture than their parents. These children learn that their world view is apt to be more dependable than that of their parents. The loss of their parents as protective objects induces a precocious yet fragile maturation supported by grandiose illusions regarding the self, illusions that prove to be necessary for the child's psychic survival. In addition to the need to retain omnipotent and grandiose illusions regarding the self, such individuals, whose parents' construction of reality is markedly divergent, may suffer from a subtle cognitive impairment. Although in some cases they may appear to be competent students, they recognize that their knowledge is facile and shallow, and they fear that they will be discovered to be impostors. They doubt whether they know anything.

Kinship Theory and the Divergent Construction of Reality

I noted earlier that divergent constructions of reality between parent and offspring may be attributed simply to differences in their nervous systems, a biological given. Another "biological given" that may contribute to this divergence is the ubiquity of parent-offspring conflict (Trivers, 1985). Ethologists and evolutionary behaviorists have recently observed what appears to them to be the nearly ubiquitous occurrence of parent-offspring conflict in a variety of mammals and birds. They understand this conflict to be the consequence of the divergent needs of parents and their offspring. Such observations are seen to support the belief that the altruistic behavior observed in many species is correlated with the degree of kinship—the extent to which there is shared genetic material. From this point of view, altruism may be a disguised form of self-interest, as one could argue teleologically that from an evolutionary point of view, the ultimate self-interest is the preservation of one's own genetic material. Altruism is greatest toward offspring, but offspring share in only one-half of each parent's genetic material and in terms of evolutionary forces are competing with yet unborn siblings. Some evolutionary biologists believe that parent-child conflict follows from these genetic differences.

Older ethological studies have focused upon the mutuality of need between parent and offspring, such as seen in nursing behavior. These studies contributed to Bowlby's (1969) theory of attachment behavior. Kinship theory, on the other hand, has resulted in the positing of a nearly universal existence of parent-offspring conflict based on the divergence of needs between the two. The foremost exponent of this point of view is the evolutionary biologist, Trivers (1985). He describes a cost/benefit ratio in the weaning behavior of many species. Consider the example of a newborn caribou and its mother. For the mother, the benefits of nursing the calf compared to the cost, the danger to the calf from predators, decreases rapidly with the increase in size of the calf. Continued nursing may be beneficial for the calf's survival, but it places the mother's survival at greater risk. There is therefore an inevitable divergence of self-interest. For the evolutionary biologist, self-interest is equated with reproductive success expressed as *inclusive fitness*. Trivers says that "conflict results from an underlying difference in the way each party maximizes its inclusive fitness" (p. 149). For other species as well as humans, this divergence of self-interest affects the capacity of the offspring to learn from its parents. Trivers states: "Although [the offspring] is expected to learn useful information . . . [it] cannot rely on its parents for disinterested guidance. . . . Thus from the offspring's standpoint, an important distinction ought to be made between reinforcement schedules that are imposed by a disinterested environment and ones that are imposed by other organisms, which may be attempting to manipulate it against its own best interests" (p. 159).

Malcolm Slavin (1985) was the first to note the relevance of Trivers's work for psychoanalytic theory. He states that "overlapping yet distinct interests in parent and offspring [have] the following major implication: that on virtually every crucial psychological issue in the course of development . . . the parent as a functioning biological organism will tend to hold a view of reality which is consistent with its own interests, derived from its own experience and biased toward those individuals . . . to whom it is most closely, reciprocally tied" (p. 418).

The Parent's Self-Interest

In cases of the sexual seduction of the child by an adult, the divergence between the needs of the adult and those of the child is all too painfully obvious. But if we assume that even in the best regulated and happiest of families, there is an inevitable conflict between the needs of parent and child, which the child recognizes, how do we distinguish normative from pathologic development? A commonsense answer is that under the best of circumstances the parents will see to it that the child's needs take precedence over their own.

The subject of parental self-interest may be hidden within the too inclusive term *narcissism*. What is usually meant is that the parent is unable to perceive the child's separateness and accordingly treats the child as an extension of the self; the child then becomes the recipient of the parent's self-love and self-hatred. A banal example is seen in parents who have an explicit agenda for the child based on their own needs and not their child's needs. We are all familiar with those patients who believe that they were not loved for themselves but felt that their parents' love was contingent on their living up to certain expectations. When such individuals first encounter an analyst, they may need to test the analyst in order to discover whether he or she is committed to them or to his or her own hidden agenda. This is especially true when the analyst or therapist does, in fact, have another tacit agenda for the patient's treatment.

For example, I treated a patient in psychotherapy behind a one-way mirror in a teaching exercise. This clinic patient was informed about the project and agreed to this intrusive arrangement as a trade-off so that he could obtain the services of an experienced therapist for a possibly long-term treatment. As therapy proceeded, it became apparent that the patient felt he had not been loved for himself as a child, that he had been loved only when he performed in a manner that provided pleasure to his parents. Predictably, this man did everything in his power to demonstrate to the class that he was a "bad" patient and that I was an ineffectual therapist. It was essential for him to discover whether I was committed to him and to his treatment or whether my primary intent was to demonstrate to the class my therapeutic prowess. It was crucial for him to learn the extent to which I was motivated by my own self-interest. I recall another instance when a prospective analysand, in the initial interview, peremptorily demanded that I refrain from smoking during *her* analysis. At that time I smoked small cigars, and although I did not know the meaning of this woman's demand, I assented to her request. Later, during the course of the analysis, I learned that it was absolutely necessary that this patient discover whether I could forgo my own pleasures in favor of her needs. She had experienced both parents as self-indulgent, selfish people who were incapable of giving up anything for their children. Both of these patients were understandably distrustful of my formulations.

Therapeutic Implications

This quasi-philosophical excursion into questions concerning divergent constructions of reality does have some practical consequences for the therapist, inasmuch as it enables us to approach the subject of resistance from a different perspective. For example, if a patient rejects our interpretation, in addition to the familiar motives for such a rejection—that the interpretation is inaccurate, that the patient is prematurely confronted with unacceptable warded-off ideas, and so forth—our interpretation may be rejected simply for the reason that it is *our* interpretation. The capacity to incorporate divergent realities is another way of considering the capacity to learn from others; our understanding of this process may provide a rationale for and the possibility of codifying some aspects of our technique. For example, we have learned by trial and error of the untoward consequences of premature intrusions of our own constructions as a substitute for the patient's construction. Psychotherapists of many different persuasions agree on this point, and it has become the basis of certain techniques. Recall the technique of Carl Rogers (1942) of simply repeating the patient's utterances. This has become the subject of ridicule and caricature, but it may be based on a recognition that the therapist should be careful not to go beyond what the patient communicates. Balint (1968), in his book *The Basic Fault*, included a chapter entitled "The Non-Intrusive Analyst." And Winnicott (1971, p. 57) learned that correct interpretations could prove to be traumatic if they are experienced as evidence of the analyst's cleverness. The use of empathy as a therapeutic technique, which has been so much emphasized recently, is not unlike the Rogerian technique, in that an empathic comment does not go beyond what the patient is already aware of. I do not wish to be misunderstood as suggesting that we foreswear the use of interpretations. But Freud, as well as subsequent generations of psychoanalysts, knew that interpretations should be only a short step beyond what the patient was already aware of. We also know how complex and variegated the act of interpretation is. There are interpretations that reverberate with the patient's experience, and there are others that are more the product of the therapist's mind and are therefore experienced as something imposed, as it were, from the outside.[1]

Those patients whom we refer to as schizoid are attached to their inner world defensively and in many instances the retreat to this inner world has proven to be a life-preserving alternative to the constructed world of their caretakers. For them, there is a danger in learning from others. I have described (Modell, 1984) schizoid patients as encased in a cocoon which nothing leaves and into which nothing enters. It can be a veritable fortress. This life-sustaining inner core of constructed reality may be felt to be at risk if such patients accept the therapist's ideas; any ideas that the patients have not already considered themselves may be viewed as an alien reality. I recall an extreme instance of this problem in the analysis of a patient whose parents were, in fact, both psychotic; for obvious reasons, the patient literally could not accept anything that I said. Even if I paraphrased what she had just told me and in the process introduced something of myself by using my own language, this would provoke a violent rejection.

But how is it possible to avoid intruding one's own construction of reality? The patient is, after all, paying you because of the assumption that you are the one who knows. Of course, the analyst betrays his or her own construction of the world in every possible way, in addition to the act of interpretation. The patient learns from the analyst not only as result of the analyst's interpretations; the analysand is also exposed to what has been

---

[1] I have discussed this subject in greater detail elsewhere (Modell, 1990).

described as the *analytic attitude* (Schafer, 1983)—an attitude toward life and living that can be described as an analytic *Weltanschauung*. The psychoanalytic *Weltanschauung* includes certain tacit assumptions regarding the virtues of an examined life. More specifically, it includes a search for unconscious meaning behind all thoughts and actions. In this search there is also an ethical position that states that only behaviors and not thoughts have ethical consequences and that empathic examination of all experience can be carried out while maintaining moral neutrality or objectivity.

The divergent constructions of reality of child and caretaker which reflect a divergence of need are repeated in the psychoanalytic situation when there is a divergence between the therapist's agenda for the patient and what the patient desires for him/herself. We all know that we try not to impose our moral values on our patients, but nevertheless we retain certain convictions regarding the aims of treatment which exist as an explicit or implicit agenda. I am not saying that it is wrong to have such agendas, as we all have some ideas of what we wish to accomplish in our treatment of patients. But we must be very clear in recognizing that these are our ideas and tacit assumptions and are not necessarily our patient's assumptions. Such beliefs, whatever they may be, are incorporated into the goals and aims that we have for our patients. Such goals may include the belief that treatment will enable the patient to establish a more "mature" object relationship;[2] that treatment will lead to a greater emotional spontaneity and authenticity; that treatment will lead to greater self-knowledge, and so forth. We all have such implicit agendas for our patients which are necessary and not unreasonable. The ideal treatment situation may be one in which we do not ask the question: "Whose reality is it?" Accordingly, from this point of view, one aim of psychoanalytic treatment might be described as enabling the patient, through the

---

[2] Kohut (1984) has emphasized the untoward effects of analysts' imposition of *their* definition of mental health.

play of merging and separateness, to share in other constructed realities.

REFERENCES

BALINT, M. (1968). *The Basic Fault. Therapeutic Aspects of Regression.* London: Tavistock.

BOWLBY, J. (1969). *Attachment and Loss. Vol. 1, Attachment.* New York: Basic Books.

CALEF, V. & WEINSHEL, E. M. (1981). Some clinical consequences of introjection: gaslighting. *Psychoanal. Q.*, 50:44-66.

DUPONT, J., EDITOR (1985). *The Clinical Diary of Sándor Ferenczi.* Translated by M. Balint & N. Z. Jackson. Cambridge, MA/London: Harvard Univ. Press, 1988.

EDELMAN, G. (1987). *Neural Darwinism.* New York: Basic Books.

FERENCZI, S. (1933). Confusion of tongues between adults and the child. In *Final Contributions to the Problems and Methods of Psycho-Analysis.* New York: Brunner/Mazel, 1955, pp. 156-167.

FREUD, A. & BURLINGHAM, D. T. (1943). *War and Children.* New York: Int. Univ. Press, 1944.

FREUD, S. (1917). Introductory lectures on psycho-analysis. Part 3. General theory of the neuroses. *S.E.*, 16.

———— (1926). Inhibitions, symptoms and anxiety. *S.E.*, 20.

GAY, P. (1988). *Freud. A Life for Our Time.* New York/London: Norton.

KOHUT, H. (1984). *How Does Analysis Cure?* Chicago/London: Univ. of Chicago Press.

MODELL, A. H. (1984). *Psychoanalysis in a New Context.* New York: Int. Univ. Press.

———— (1985). Object Relations theory. In *Models of the Mind*, ed. A. Rothstein. New York: Int. Univ. Press, pp. 85-100.

———— (1990). *Other Times, Other Realities. Toward a Theory of Psychoanalytic Treatment.* Cambridge, MA/London. Harvard Univ. Press.

PANEL (1983). Interpretation: toward a contemporary understanding of the term. A. Rothstein, Reporter. *J. Amer. Psychoanal. Assn.*, 31:237-245.

ROGERS, C. R. (1942). *Counseling and Psychotherapy.* Boston: Houghton Mifflin.

SCHAFER, R. (1983). *The Analytic Attitude.* New York: Basic Books.

SLAVIN, M. O. (1985). The origins of psychic conflict and the adaptive function of repression. An evolutionary biological view. *Psychoanal. Contemp. Thought*, 8:407-440.

SPENCE, D. P. (1982). *Narrative Truth and Historical Truth. Meaning and Interpretation in Psychoanalysis.* New York: Norton.

TRIVERS, R. (1985). *Social Evolution.* Menlo Park, CA: Benjamin/Cummings.

WINNICOTT, D. W. (1971). *Playing and Reality.* New York: Basic Books.

———— (1988). *Human Nature.* New York: Schocken.

15

ANALYTIC INTERACTION: CONCEPTUALIZING TECHNIQUE IN LIGHT OF THE ANALYST'S IRREDUCIBLE SUBJECTIVITY

ANALYTIC INTERACTION: CONCEPTUALIZING TECHNIQUE IN LIGHT OF THE ANALYST'S IRREDUCIBLE SUBJECTIVITY

BY OWEN RENIK, M.D.

Every aspect of an analyst's clinical activity is determined in part by his or her personal psychology. The implications for our theory of technique of taking the analyst's subjectivity fully into account—which we have tended not to do—are discussed.

Contemporary analysts acknowledge that every psychoanalysis inevitably consists of an interaction between the patient, with all his or her values, assumptions, and psychological idiosyncracies, and the analyst, with all his or hers. When we refer to a psychoanalytic interaction, we mean an interaction between two complete psyches, and the realization that this is so has been exerting an increasing influence on the way we think about what actually takes place in treatment: various basic psychoanalytic concepts are currently coming up for reconsideration in light of the understanding that an analyst is a *participant*-observer. For example, Boesky (1990) recently proposed that each analytic couple negotiates its own unique forms of resistance—a valid and useful formulation, in my opinion, and one that shows just how far we have come from the image of the analyst as detached psychic surgeon, dissecting the patient's mental operations in an antiseptic field.

Yet, having said this, I would add that even our most up-to-date conceptions of the psychoanalytic process (the sequence of events that characterizes a successful clinical analysis) tend not to acknowledge fully the fact that clinical analysis is an interaction, in the sense just described. I think that despite our new understanding in principle, we retain an implicit obsolete theory of technique, evident in the model that most of us strive toward as we make moment-to-moment choices about whether and how to intervene with patients.

Let's consider the *action* that is involved in psychoanalytic *interaction*. A patient's expressions of his or her personal motivations in action during analytic sessions are expected and welcomed: speech is a form of action, and the things a patient says that proceed from his or her most intimate wishes, fears, and concerns, rational and irrational, make up the desired text that allows analysis of transference to take place.

What about actions on an analyst's part during sessions that proceed from his or her personal motivations? What role in the psychoanalytic process is played by the things an analyst says that proceed from his or her most intimate wishes, fears, and concerns, rational and irrational? Our conception of the analytic couple is clearly not symmetrical in this regard. According to the prevailing view, while an analyst's *awareness* of his or her personal motivations is certainly seen as useful, expression of them *in action* is not. Countertransference[1] fantasies are considered a rich source of information, but countertransference enactment is generally understood to be, in principle, a hindrance to analytic work.

An analyst is supposed to try to become aware of his or her emotionally determined urges *before* they get translated into speech or any other form of behavior. The goal is for the analyst to *imagine* how he or she might wish to act on an impulse before acting on it. Of course, recognizing human fallibility, an analyst expects to fail significantly in this endeavor; but concern about failure is ameliorated by the analyst's further expectation of being able to learn from his or her lapses and the patient's reaction to them. Our literature contains many accounts of how a countertransference enactment, once it occurs, can be put to

---

[1] To use the conveniently familiar term without, for the moment, discussing its disadvantages.

use. It is important to note that such a turn of events, common-place enough, is conceptualized as the productive exploitation *post facto* of a departure from model technique—the skillful re-covery of an error. This is the conceptualization that is implicit, for example, even in Jacobs's (1986) beautifully evocative por-trayals of the ubiquity and subtlety of countertransference en-actment, the ways countertransference enactment can coincide with appropriate and generally accepted psychoanalytic proce-dure, and the yield of analytic work when the analyst becomes aware of countertransference enactments and their determi-nants.

According to the current consensual theory of psychoanalytic technique, as I understand it, countertransference awareness ideally takes the place of countertransference enactment, and it is toward the ideal of self-analysis forestalling personally moti-vated actions that an analyst continually strives. The principle of *awareness instead of action* guides analytic technique, though that principle is never, in practice, realized.

Thus, the fundamental conception we hold is of psychoanal-ysis as an interaction between two complete psyches, *but regret-tably so*: our theory of technique directs the analyst to eliminate personally motivated action as much as he or she can. The cur-rent state of affairs is therefore a bit confusing: on one hand, tolerance for and interest in the intensely personal nature of an analyst's participation in clinical work has gained an increasing place in our thinking about psychoanalytic process and tech-nique; but on the other hand, the theory we retain still concep-tualizes the patient's psyche as a specimen to be held apart for examination in a field as free as possible from contamination by elements of the analyst's personal psychology.

Today's analysts readily acknowledge that dispassionate ana-lytic technique is only an ideal, a goal approached but never perfectly achieved. However, this acknowledgment has the ef-fect of helping us accommodate and perpetuate what is really a significant problem with our theory: we admit the fact that an analyst's individual psychology constantly determines his or her activity in analysis without taking systematic account of that fact in our conception of technique.

Everything I know about my own work and that of my colleagues leads me to the conclusion that an analyst's awareness of his or her emotional responses as they arise in the course of an analysis *necessarily* follows translation of those responses into action—i.e., awareness of countertransference is always retrospective, preceded by countertransference enactment. It is my impression that those instances in which we find ourselves able to profit from subsequent exploration of technical errors committed on the basis of the analyst's emotional involvement simply show us with unusual vividness what in fact is *invariably* the case; these "errors" differ from the rest of our preliminary countertransference enactments only in that circumstances conspire to bring them explicitly and dramatically to our attention.

Here is an everyday clinical sequence. A patient is describing her joyless marriage. As I listen, I am aware of a sense of immobility—I am sitting absolutely motionless in my chair, and my limbs feel heavy. Possible interventions come to mind, but I decide against them, one after the other; I have the feeling each time that what I might say just would not lead to anything useful. I note that the remarks I keep thinking of making all aim at a rather active investigation of my patient's situation—questions about her attitudes toward her husband and the future of their relationship, how she regards her options. I realize I have an urge to rescue her from her marriage and end her distress. The feeling is a familiar one to me, reminiscent of, among other things, my childhood wish to be my mother's savior.

We could summarize this vignette by saying that a piece of self-analysis led me to become aware of an omnipotent rescue fantasy generated by my own psychology, a fantasy that was not appropriate to my actual task as an analyst and my responsibilities toward my patient. The insight I gained was quite useful: keeping it in mind allowed me to avoid embarking on a mission of my own I might otherwise have pursued at my patient's expense. Thus, in this instance it was true that self-analysis forestalled analytically unproductive, personally motivated behavior on my part; awareness of a countertransference urge took the place of enactment of it, with beneficial results.

However, it was also true that before I became aware of it, the countertransference urge in question had already been determining my activity, my technique. The posture and the physical sensations I observed in myself were manifestations of an inhibition I was employing to guard against anxieties generated by my impulse to rescue my patient, and this driven passivity on my part was exerting a very significant influence on how I was listening to what my patient said, as well as on my interpretive efforts. The possible interventions that were coming to mind I rejected one after another, not because I had thought through the issue of their analytic utility, but because they carried a forbidden meaning for me. In fact, once I became more fully aware of my state of mind and some of its personal historical determinants, I allowed myself to facilitate more actively my patient's exploration of how she was dealing with her husband. The outcome of this line of investigation was analytically quite fruitful, too. Eventually, as you might expect, we even came to look into my patient's need to elicit rescue by me and her difficulty initiating her own efforts to extricate herself from her marital problems.

It seems to me that when we can look closely enough, we always see that an analyst's awareness of a personal motivation in the clinical situation has its origins in self-observation of a behavioral manifestation, in some form or other, of that motivation. Sometimes what the analyst notices about himself or herself can be an activity on the very finest scale of magnitude—a subtle kinesthetic tension, for example. It is tempting to believe that such microactivity remains essentially private and has no significant impact on the treatment relationship, so that, for all practical purposes, countertransference awareness can precede countertransference enactment. However, experience indicates otherwise. Even the slightest nuance of disposition influences how an analyst hears material, influences whether the analyst decides to remain silent or to intervene, influences how the analyst chooses his or her words and in what tone they are spoken if the analyst does make a comment, etc., all of which is of the greatest importance, as we know.

I would say that the data of introspection favor Darwin's (1872) conclusion that a motor behavior lies at the core of every affect. In the same vein, William James (1890) proposed that our awareness of emotion arises from observation of our actions—which was the case for me in the clinical experience I just recounted. I think James was right, and I believe the only reason that psychoanalysts look at things differently is that we have perpetuated, without realizing it, what is really an unsubstantiated and incorrect theory Freud put forward early in his thinking, as part of his beginning effort to account for dreams and hallucinations.

In *The Interpretation of Dreams* (1900), Freud developed a model of mental function based on the spinal reflex-arc (as the reflex-arc was understood by late nineteenth century neurology). According to that model, motivations are conceptualized as impulses that can take either one of two quite separate paths: the efferent, leading to motor activity, or the afferent, leading to fantasy formation via stimulation of the sensory apparatus from within. From this conceptualization, it follows that thought and motor behavior are mutually exclusive alternatives: to the extent that one acts, one will not think, and vice versa. Hence the notion that a patient's "acting out" should be blocked, so that his or her motivations will be made available for analysis in the form of fantasy; and hence the notion that an analyst should become aware of countertransference by *imagining* how he or she might behave in the clinical situation, not by *observing* how he or she actually has been behaving.

So far as I know, there has never been any empirical corroboration of this early protoneurological conceptualization of Freud's. Certainly, if one becomes aware of an unrealistic fantasy and of the irrational motivations that produce it, awareness often puts an end to enactment of the fantasy; and, if one remains determinedly unaware of an unrealistic fantasy and of the irrational motivations that produce it, enactment of the fantasy is more likely to continue. However, these observations, which every clinical analyst has had the opportunity to confirm, in no way support the premise that thought and motor action are mutually exclusive alternatives. Rather, there is every reason to believe that thought is a trial form of behavior involving highly attenuated motor activity. Freud in effect superseded his early reflex-arc model of mental function when he began to develop a sophisticated ego psychology (in *Inhibitions, Symptoms and Anxiety* [1926], Freud agreed with Darwin's view of emotion), though Freud never specifically reviewed and discarded his early model. In practice, we have increasingly gotten away from the assumption that a patient needs to frustrate his or her urges in order to think about them, but we have not gone as far in considering how an analyst's self-analysis takes place.

If we accept that an analyst's activity—including how an analyst listens and all the various moment-to-moment technical decisions an analyst makes—is constantly determined by his or her individual psychology in ways of which the analyst can become aware only after the fact, then we acknowledge the necessary subjectivity of even ideal analytic technique. Many authors have pointed to the participation of an analyst's individual psychology in analytic work. Atwood and Stolorow (1984), for example, define psychoanalysis as the "science of the intersubjective," stating: "Patient and analyst together form an indissoluble psychological system, and it is this system that constitutes the domain of psychoanalytic inquiry" (p. 64). Any number of analysts have written similarly.

Our difficulty has been in moving from broad epistemological assertions to a practical theory of analytic technique that takes account of the inherent subjectivity of every aspect of an analyst's activity. Just the fact that we still use the term *interpretation* would seem to indicate the extent to which we retain a conception of analytic technique as potentially objective, rather than inherently subjective—the extent to which we implicitly see the analyst trying to transcend his or her own psychology in order to deal with the patient's psyche "out there." The term *interpretation* dates from a conception of the psychoanalytic process that is now generally criticized, a conception in which the analyst decodes the patient's thoughts to reveal the unconscious, decides what hidden meanings lie beneath the manifest content of the patient's verbalizations—like the well-traveled railway conductor of Freud's famous analogy who tells the ignorant passenger where he is. In ordinary speech, *interpretation* refers to translation from one language to another, to exegesis of a religious text, to giving meaning to a work of art, etc. (see Dimon, 1992). The interpreter is always better informed than the recipient of the interpretation. In psychoanalysis, if we speak of an analyst making interpretations, our implication is that the analyst is better informed—despite the fact that the patient's psychic reality is the subject of investigation.

Schwaber (1992) has directly engaged the problem of the analyst's subjectivity in her extensive study of modes of analytic listening. Here is a clear statement by Schwaber of the way she sees the dilemma: "As analysts, we may agree with certain basic tenets: we should not impose our truths, whether or not theory-laden; we should maintain our focus on the ·patient's inner reality. . . . But again and again, we fail to adhere to these precepts. *Despite our best intentions, we seem to have a fundamental disinclination to maintaining these positions*" (pp. 359-360).

I think that Schwaber articulates here, as she says, the generally agreed-upon basic conception of analytic technique. My own conclusion about subjectivity and analytic technique goes a bit farther, as will have been obvious from what I have already presented. Instead of saying that is it *difficult* for an analyst to *maintain* a position in which his or her analytic activity objectively focuses on a patient's inner reality, I would say that it is *impossible* for an analyst to be in that position *even for an instant*: since we are constantly acting in the analytic situation on the basis of personal motivations of which we cannot be aware until after the fact, our technique, listening included, is *inescapably* subjective.

Although I very much agree with the intent of Schwaber's recommendations, it seems to me pointless to ask an analyst to set aside personal values and views of reality when listening or interpreting. Everything an analyst does in the analytic situation is based upon his or her personal psychology. This limitation cannot be reduced, let alone done away with; we have only the choice of admitting it or denying it. I think we tend to give lip service to the important truth that an analyst cannot, ultimately, know a patient's point of view; an analyst can only know his or her own point of view. Thus, Schwaber has entitled her latest paper "Countertransference as a Retreat from the Patient's Vantage Point," and in it she urges the analyst, through attentiveness and humility, to reverse the retreat. If we are to take seriously the fact of an analyst's subjectivity, we need to question the concept of countertransference used as Schwaber has, the assumption that an analyst's personal responses can be isolated and subtracted from the rest of his or her analytic activity. It has been said, justifiably, that one person's countertransference is another person's empathy; I think we could equally add that one person's countertransference enactment is another person's good interpretation.

It is commonly asserted nowadays that an analyst is not and should not think of himself or herself as simply a reflecting mirror. Yet our usual underlying conception of technique asks the analyst to aspire to be a reflecting mirror, inasmuch as we encourage the analyst to be maximally objective by minimizing the influence of his or her individual psychology. This pursuit of a technical ideal that departs entirely from the true nature of clinical events, like the related effort to be aware of personal motivations before acting on them, can never be a successful strategy.

The unavoidable fact of the analyst's subjectivity is the psychoanalytic version of a universal and familiar scientific problem: the influence of the observing instrument on the thing observed. Consider an analogy from physics. Let us say that we want to ascertain the exact temperature of a glass of water. As soon as we introduce a thermometer into the water, we alter the temperature we want to measure. The change may be tiny, but it is certain. There is no way to eliminate this effect; but neither is there any need to. We only have to study it and take account of it. We establish the temperature, volume, and specific heat of the thermometer, use it to take the temperature of the water, the volume and specific heat of which are known, and calculate what the heat transfer must have been. We then use this information to obtain from our reading the true temperature of the water prior to introduction of the thermometer.

Analogously, in the analytic situation an analyst cannot eliminate, or even diminish, his or her subjectivity. However, an analyst can acknowledge his or her irreducible subjectivity and study its effects. Objectivity, in the Einsteinian rather than the Newtonian sense, requires that we do so. Our inclination is to think that the subjectivity of technique is a quantitative matter: that we become more or less emotionally involved at various moments, and that we can try to detect the extent to which we are acting on the basis of subjective considerations by noting our deviations from established baselines. It seems to me that, on the contrary, we are always completely personally involved in our judgments and decisions, and it is precisely at those moments when we believe that we are able to be objective-as-opposed-to-subjective that we are in the greatest danger of self-deception and departure from sound methodology.

What are the practical implications of a conception of analytic technique that accepts the analyst's constant subjectivity? For one thing, it means we discard a widely accepted principle of technique which holds that countertransference enactment, so called, is to be avoided. While emotional satisfaction for the analyst is clearly not an objective to be pursued, in and of itself, in making technical decisions, neither does recognition that a given course of action will serve the analyst's personal purposes constitute a contraindication to going forward. What distinguishes good technique from bad technique is not whether the analyst is gratified or reassured, consciously or unconsciously, by what he or she does; good technique can be gratifying or reassuring to the analyst, and bad technique frustrating or anxiety-provoking for the analyst, or vice versa.

Actually, analysts by and large tend to be quite conscientious, in my experience, so that interferences with optimal technique arise from constraining inhibitions and reaction formations designed to prevent satisfaction of some urge or another at least as often as from the direct pursuit of satisfaction per se. This was so for me with respect to my wish to rescue my patient in the vignette I presented. Elsewhere (Renik, 1993), I described how acting unself-consciously on a wish to compete with and punish a patient was the basis for a very effective analytic intervention. I find, all in all, that the technique of beginning analysts tends to suffer more from stiffness than from an excess of spontaneity; and it seems to me that veteran analysts become more effective and comfortable not because they reduce the extent to which they act out of personal motivation, but because they become less defensive about it and more confident about being able to explore their patients' reactions to expressions of the analyst's personality.

An analyst can aim for maximum awareness of the personal motivations that determine his or her analytic activity without assuming that acting in a way that satisfies personal motivations will necessarily oppose the analytic process. Sometimes it is useful for an analyst to accept the need to act under the influence of personal motivations of which he or she has become aware before those motivations can be thoroughly investigated. I think this is the conclusion we reach if we follow, for example, Sandler's (1976) concept of "free-floating behavioral responsiveness" to its ultimate implications.

In this same vein, Jacobs (1991) makes the following assertion: "Reacting spontaneously with responses that inevitably include a mix of some personal as well as objective elements, the analyst uses his intuitive understanding of the patient's state of mind and character to make unconscious adjustments in his technique" (p. 12). Now, we may ask, why are these adjustments *unconscious?* Freud's (1915, p. 194) often-quoted comment, "It is a very remarkable thing that the *Ucs.* of one human being can react upon that of another, without passing through the *Cs.*," tends to mystify and glamorize the phenomenon a bit, I think, and distract us from considering that if the analyst's responses and technical "adjustments" are made unconsciously, it is likely because the analyst is *motivated* to remain unconscious of them— not a remarkable situation at all, but a very common and familiar one.

This brings us to a second implication of a theory of technique that accepts the analyst's constant subjectivity, namely, that *unconscious* personal motivations expressed in action by the analyst are not only unavoidable, but *necessary to the analytic process.* Here we enter into a crucial subject that deserves more extensive discussion than I can give it without departing from the immediate purposes of my presentation (for a fuller discussion, see Renik, 1993). For the moment, I will only suggest that it is precisely because of the analyst's capacity for self-deception, the analyst's *willingness to be self-deceived,* that he or she is able to enter spontaneously and sincerely into corrective emotional experiences with the patient without the presumption and hypocrisy of deliberate role-playing. These interactions provide a crucial series of gratifications and frustrations to the analysand that form the basis for a successful analytic process. Continuous examination of them as they occur, and the retrospective understanding continuously reached and refined, is what we usually refer to as the analysis of the transference. We can emphatically agree with Boesky (1990) when he observes, "If the analyst does not get emotionally involved sooner or later in a manner that he had not intended, the analysis will not proceed to a successful conclusion" (p. 573).

We come to a problematic third implication of a theory of technique that accepts the analyst's constant subjectivity. Since an analyst acting on his or her personal motivations is inherent in productive technique, how are we to say where analytic work leaves off and exploitation of the analytic situation by the analyst begins? There is no avoiding this very disconcerting question. In struggling to answer it, we cannot afford to deny the fact of an analyst's personal involvement.

What we have been used to calling countertransference, in the widest sense of the term, is the ever-present raw material of technique. We need to learn more about what combines with it in order to distinguish helpful analytic treatment from exploitation. We do not profit, ultimately, from the comforting but misconceived ideal of what is essentially an impersonal use of the self of the analyst in clinical analysis.

Instead of the analyst as surgeon or reflecting mirror, our guiding metaphor might be the analyst as skier or surfer—someone who allows himself or herself to be acted upon by powerful forces, knowing that they are to be managed and harnessed, rather than completely controlled. Of course, the forces with which an analyst contends in his or her work are internal ones. In this sense, perhaps we should think of effective clinical psychoanalytic practice as not unlike good sex, in that it is impossible to arrive at the desired outcome without, in some measure, relinquishing self-control as a goal. In making this analogy, of course, I am suggesting that interferences in both arenas may arise from the same causes.

By granting that the analyst's personally motivated behavior plays a constructive role in the analytic process, it might seem that we are opening the way for an "anything goes" attitude in analysis; but this is not really the case. Our traditional ideals of abstinence and transcendent objectivity provide no real protection at all against exploitation of the analytic situation by the analyst (as we have ample reason to know) because they advocate pursuit of an illusion. The notion that an analyst can minimize the personal involvement and subjectivity of his or her participation in clinical work offers only a false and dangerous complacency. An analyst's use of the clinical setting for personal gain is in fact more easily rationalized, and effective self-analysis impeded, by maintenance of the belief that countertransference is separate from technique.

We have no reason to believe that our prevailing theories
about the analyst's personal motivations in relation to technique
have helped us avoid exploiting our patients. Every effective
clinician learns that appropriate gratifications for analyst and
analysand are an essential feature of the successful analytic process; thus, the principle of abstinence is obviously flawed and
does not provide an effective safeguard. In practice we struggle
to determine which gratifications are effective and appropriate
and which are counterproductive and exploitative, and in this
context abuse can easily be excused as therapeutic. Actually, it is
the ethical norms we establish and maintain in our analytic com-
munities, rather than our theories, that prevent us from taking
advantage of our patients. We do not have sex with our patients
or borrow money from them for the same reasons that internists
and surgeons refrain from doing these things with their patients
(because responsible caregivers do not want to trade on the
hopes and fears of people who rely upon them), not because we
conceptualize that enactment of fantasies interferes with the
analysis of transference.

Another implication of a conception of technique that accepts
the analyst's subjectivity is that communication to the patient of
even an implicit pretense of objectivity on the analyst's part is to
be avoided. In this regard, perhaps we can look upon our continued use of the term *interpretation* as helpful in a way, since it
constitutes an admission, really, that the analyst is always imposing his or her truth.

Hoffman (1983), in his paper "The Patient as Interpreter of
the Analyst's Experience," cautions against the error of responding to a patient's speculations about the analyst's psychology as if their possible accuracy were not relevant. In issuing his
warning, Hoffman joins those who emphasize that the analyst's
interpretation of reality is not authoritative. I definitely agree,
and I think it is also most important to add and to emphasize
that neither is the patient's interpretation of reality authoritative. Surely there can be *no* privileged interpreter of reality
within the analytic couple. Analyst and patient each develop

their own interpretations of reality and operate on the basis of them. Progress in analysis occurs through the interaction between two individual interpretations; and though I think we generally find the interaction to be dialectical, it is by no means necessary for consensus to be achieved between patient and analyst on every point. In fact, I have the impression that when analytic work goes well, there are usually some matters about which analyst and patient agree to disagree, or to consider impossible to determine.

I would therefore take some issue with Schwaber's (1992) suggestion that the analyst focus on the patient's vantage point instead of the analyst's own. Certainly, the patient's exploration of his or her psychic reality is the objective of clinical analysis. However, sometimes the best way to facilitate a patient's self-exploration can be for an analyst to present his or her own, different interpretation of reality for the patient's consideration—even to present it as persuasively as possible, in order to be sure that the patient has taken full account of it. When an analyst feels constrained against doing this, an important tool is lost. Lipton (1977), for example, has discussed times when it is necessary for an analyst to introduce perspectives to which the patient will not come of his or her own accord, and I have suggested that the analyst communicating his or her own construction of reality is central to the analysis of certain fetishistic transference phenomena (Renik, 1992). I very much concur with Hoffman's (1992) view that if "analysts embrace the uncertainty that derives from knowing that their subjectivity can never be fully transcended . . . analysts can . . . 'speak their minds,' including expressing conviction about their points of view, even sometimes when they clash with those of their patients" (p. 287).

It seems to me a fundamental principle of analytic collaboration that an analyst's aim in offering an interpretation is not to have it accepted by the patient, but rather to have the patient consider it in making up his or her own mind. If the analyst is clear about this, then respect for the patient's autonomy—we might even say insistence on the patient's autonomy—comes through, and it can be useful for the analyst to communicate a definite point of view, even a sense of conviction about his or her own inferences. If, on the contrary, an analyst is not clear about the patient's autonomy, if an analyst holds persuading the patient to the analyst's own view as the goal of interpretation, then no amount of ostensible focus on the patient's vantage point will help—it can even act to keep the analyst's subjectivity covert, and therefore all the more insidious. An analyst is much more disposed to being inadvertently coercive toward agreement with his or her underlying assumptions when the analyst believes that he or she has been successful in putting aside subjectivity and allowing the patient's inner reality to determine the investigation.

To look at it from a slightly different angle, the problem with an analyst believing that he or she can transcend subjectivity and focus on the patient's inner reality is that it can promote idealization of the analyst. If an analyst communicates a feeling of being able to offer interpretations concerning the patient's psychic reality *not as that reality appears to the analyst through the lens of his or her own constructions, but from the patient's vantage point*, then the patient and analyst together become susceptible to colluding in a disavowal of the distinction between developing one's own meanings and accepting the meanings implicitly communicated by another. The analytic work relationship may be experienced like the relationship between mother and infant, in which giving meaning encourages development. So the analyst, like the good mother of early infancy, "understands" perfectly. While this is perhaps a necessary and useful illusion for a time in some treatments, if it persists the patient's autonomy is coopted in the name of empathy or analytic humility.

Psychoanalysis has frequently been criticized from without for being a clinical method that cultivates the patient's reliance on an idealized analyst, and analysts themselves have recognized this difficulty as a limiting factor, for example, in training analyses. I think we have much to learn on this score, in particular from French analysts, who are especially sensitive to the issue of subjectivity and its implications for technique. The French do not speak of analytic "training" (*éducation*, in French) because training means subordination of the trainee to the purposes of the trainer, e.g., what one does with a horse; they refer instead to the "formation" (*formation*) of the student analyst.

Although he may not have been successful himself in overcoming the problem, Lacan (1975) did repeatedly call attention to the ease with which an analyst is cast in the clinical situation as *le sujet supposé savoir*, the one who is supposed to know; and, partly as a result of contending with Lacan's assertion, French analysts tend to operate with a particular mindfulness of the epistemological privacy of the patient's psychic reality. Interpretations are considered more as stimuli to the patient's self-investigation than as truths about the patient's mental life to be communicated to him or her. I have the impression that this helpful perspective on interpretation is one we too easily lose track of in the United States. *It seems to me that the most effective way to avoid danger of an analyst imposing his or her own subjective constructions upon a patient is not for the analyst to try to abandon those constructions, but rather for the analyst to acknowledge them and to make every effort to identify and question ways in which the analyst is idealized and his or her constructions given undeserved authority by the patient.*

When we accept the subjectivity of analytic technique, we admit the role of suggestion in a successful analytic process, inasmuch as suggestion consists of the imposition by an analyst, wittingly or unwittingly, of his or her own views upon a patient. Many papers have been written about the fate of suggestion in clinical analysis. Since earliest days psychoanalysts have been at pains to distinguish psychoanalysis from other therapeutic modalities explicitly based on suggestion—at first from hypnotism and faith healing, then from the technical innovations recommended by Alexander and French, and more recently from systematic desensitization, cognitive therapy, and various other psychotherapies. It seems to me that this concern to preserve a psychoanalytic identity, so to speak, has occasioned a certain defensiveness. Analysts have often felt the need to deny the role of suggestion in analytic technique, whereas the truly scientific approach is to study the role of suggestion in effective analytic technique (see also Gill, 1991; Stolorow, 1990).

In our clinical lore, we have a group of maxims designed to counteract suggestion by reducing the analyst's subjective biases. We are cautioned to be modest, to remain open to surprise, to see ourselves as students who learn from our patients, to focus on the patient's inner psychic reality. I think all of these recommendations are well intended, and useful, as far as they go; but I also think it is very important that we realize that they are all double-edged swords—as I have already tried to point out with regard to some of Schwaber's suggestions—principles that can be inhibiting instead of liberating, if they are followed categorically. The reason that this is so, in my opinion, is that these recommendations substitute for a systematic, comprehensive theoretical conception of analytic technique that takes into account the unavoidable, pervasive subjectivity of the analyst. The more a theory of technique places the analyst in a position of authority as the privileged interpreter of reality, the greater the need to compensate by exhorting the analyst to humility. The more the theory of technique denies the inevitable subjectivity of technique, the stronger the call for objectivity on the part of the analyst. It has been my purpose to propose that we aim toward a revision in our basic theory of technique that will make it unnecessary for us to ask ourselves, in vain, not to be passionately and irrationally involved in our everyday clinical work.

REFERENCES

ATWOOD, G. E. & STOLOROW, R. D. (1984). *Structures of Subjectivity: Explorations in Psychoanalytic Phenomenology.* Hillsdale, NJ: Analytic Press.
BOESKY, D. (1990). The psychoanalytic process and its components. *Psychoanal. Q.,* 59:550-584.
DARWIN, C. (1872). *The Expression of the Emotions in Man and Animals.* Edited by F. Darwin. Chicago: Univ. of Chicago Press, 1965.

DIMON, J. (1992). A review of the literature. *Psychoanal. Inquiry*, 12:182-195.

FREUD, S. (1900). The interpretation of dreams. *S.E.*, 4/5.

—— (1915). The unconscious. *S.E.*, 14.

—— (1926). Inhibitions, symptoms and anxiety. *S.E.*, 20.

GILL, M. M. (1991). Indirect suggestion. In *Interpretation and Interaction. Psychoanalysis or Psychotherapy?* By J. D. Oremland. Hillsdale, NJ/London: Analytic Press.

HOFFMAN, I. Z. (1983). The patient as interpreter of the analyst's experience. *Contemp. Psychoanal.*, 19:389-422.

—— (1992). Some practical implications of a social-constructivist view of the psychoanalytic situation. *Psychoanal. Dialogues*, 2:287-304.

JACOBS, T. J. (1986). On countertransference enactments. *J. Amer. Psychoanal. Assn.*, 34:289-307.

—— (1991). *The Use of the Self. Countertransference and Communication in the Analytic Situation.* Madison, CT: Int. Univ. Press.

JAMES, W. (1890). *The Principles of Psychology.* New York: Dover, 1950.

LACAN, J. (1975). *Les écrits techniques de Freud.* Paris: Éditions du Seuil.

LIPTON, S. D. (1977). Clinical observations on resistance to the transference. *Int. J. Psychoanal.*, 58:463-472.

RENIK, O. (1992). Use of the analyst as a fetish. *Psychoanal. Q.*, 61:542-563.

—— (1993). Countertransference enactment and the psychoanalytic process. In *Psychic Structure and Psychic Change. Essays in Honor of Robert S. Wallerstein, M.D.*, ed. M. J. Horowitz, O. F. Kernberg & E. M. Weinshel. Madison, CT: Int. Univ. Press, pp. 135-158.

SANDLER, J. (1976). Countertransference and role-responsiveness. *Int. Rev. Psychoanal.*, 3:43-48.

SCHWABER, E. A. (1992). Countertransference: the analyst's retreat from the patient's vantage point. *Int. J. Psychoanal.*, 73:349-362.

STOLOROW, R. D. (1990). Converting psychotherapy to psychoanalysis: a critique of the underlying assumptions. *Psychoanal. Inq.*, 10:119-129.

CREDITS

ABOUT THE EDITORS

Sander M. Abend, M.D., is a former Editor-in-Chief of *The Psychoanalytic Quarterly* and is currently an Associate Editor. He is a Training and Supervising Analyst on the faculty of the New York Psychoanalytic Institute. He is a past President of the New York Psychoanalytic Institute, and has also served as Secretary of the American Psychoanalytic Association.

Jacob Arlow, M.D., is past President of the American Psychoanalytic Association, former Editor-in-Chief of *The Psychoanalytic Quarterly*, and Clinical Professor of Psychiatry, New York University College of Medicine. He is also a faculty member at the New York University Psychoanalytic Institute, the Columbia University Center for Psychoanalytic Training and Research, and the New York Psychoanalytic Institute.

Dale Boesky, M.D., is Training and Supervising Analyst at the Michigan Psychoanalytic Institute and Clinical Associate Professor of Psychiatry at Wayne State University School of Medicine. He is a past Editor-in-Chief and currently an Associate Editor of *The Psychoanalytic Quarterly*.

Owen Renik, M.D., is Training and Supervising Analyst at the San Francisco Psychoanalytic Institute. He is currently Editor-in-Chief of *The Psychoanalytic Quarterly*, Chair of the Program Committee of the American Psychoanalytic Association, and former Secretary of the Board on Professional Standards of the American Psychoanalytic Association.

INDEX